A CATALOGUE OF THE
PRINTED MUSIC AND
BOOKS ON MUSIC
IN DURHAM CATHEDRAL
LIBRARY

A CATALOGUE OF THE
PRINTED MUSIC AND BOOKS ON MUSIC
IN DURHAM CATHEDRAL LIBRARY

BY

R. ALEC HARMAN

LONDON
OXFORD UNIVERSITY PRESS
NEW YORK   TORONTO
1968

Oxford University Press, Ely House, London W. 1
GLASGOW NEW YORK TORONTO MELBOURNE WELLINGTON
CAPE TOWN SALISBURY IBADAN NAIROBI LUSAKA ADDIS ABABA
BOMBAY CALCUTTA MADRAS KARACHI LAHORE DACCA
KUALA LUMPUR HONG KONG TOKYO

© *The Dean and Chapter of Durham Cathedral 1968*

PRINTED IN GREAT BRITAIN
AT THE UNIVERSITY PRESS, OXFORD
BY VIVIAN RIDLER
PRINTER TO THE UNIVERSITY

CONTENTS

ABBREVIATIONS	*page* vii
INTRODUCTION	ix
VOCAL WORKS	1
INSTRUMENTAL WORKS	61
THEORETICAL WORKS	108
INDEX I	120
INDEX II	127
INDEX III	130
INDEX IV	132
INDEX V	135

ABBREVIATIONS

A.	alto
Acc.	accompaniment
Arr.	arrangement
B.	bass (vocal)
BC.	basso continuo
Bk.	book
BM.	British Museum
Bsn.	bassoon
BUCEM	British United Catalogue of Early Music
Coll.	collection
Conc.	concertino
Ded.	dedicated, dedication
Ed.	edition
Fig.	figured
Fl.	flute
Ger.	German
Hpsi.	harpsichord
Imp.	imperfect
Instr.	instrument
Kb.	keyboard
Mvt.	movement
Ob.	oboe
Pf.	pianoforte
Pt.	part
Pt-bk.	part-book
Pub.	publication
Q-L	Eitner's *Quellen-Lexicon*
Recit.	recitative
Rip.	ripieno
S.	soprano
S.sh.	single sheet
T.	tenor
T-p.	title-page
Vc.	violoncello
Vl.	violin

INTRODUCTION

THE printed music and books on music that are housed in Durham Cathedral Library are mostly made up of two private collections. The earlier and larger of the two belonged to Philip Falle, who was born in Jersey in 1656, and who died at Shenley, near Barnet, Hertfordshire in 1742. Falle was educated in England, and having graduated M.A. from Exeter College, Oxford, in 1676, was ordained into the Anglican ministry three years later. After some years as rector in two parishes in Jersey, and one year as tutor to Lord Jermyn's son, he was chosen, in 1693, as one of two delegates from the island to petition the British Government concerning the dangers of Jersey falling into French hands. To strengthen his case he wrote an *Account of Jersey*, which was published in 1694, and it was probably this, together with the impression he made on various members of the Government, that led, in the same year, to his appointment as chaplain to William III. In 1699 he was made prebendary of Durham Cathedral, and in 1722 bequeathed the music section of his library to the Dean and Chapter,[1] presenting the remainder to his native island. (The *Dictionary of National Biography* states incorrectly that Falle gave his entire library to Jersey.)

Although Falle's bequest was made in 1722 it is reasonable to assume that he continued to collect music after this date, and that these later acquisitions were presented to Durham Cathedral at his death. On this assumption his collection comprised 212 volumes (counting a set of part-books as one volume), or 266 items, to which were subsequently added (I cannot trace by whom) 40 volumes of Arnold's edition of Handel's works, and a further 59 volumes (97 items), making a total of 311 volumes or 403 items (counting each volume of Arnold's edition as one item, though many of them contain two or more works).

During his chaplaincy Falle undoubtedly accompanied the

[1] See *A History of Durham Cathedral Library*, by H. D. Hughes, 1925.

King on his frequent visits to Holland, and this is reflected in the number of items in his collection that were issued by publishing houses in Amsterdam and Antwerp (presumably the port of entry), notably Estienne Roger in the former and Pierre Phalèse in the latter; only Walsh, and his associates Hare and P. Randall, are more generously represented than Roger, and only Henry Playford and Walsh than Phalèse.

The second private collection formed part of the library at Bamburgh Castle, Northumberland, which consisted almost entirely of printed books (including music) acquired by three generations of the Sharp family, beginning with John I (1644–1714), Archbishop of York from 1691, and ending with his two grandsons, John III (1723–92) and Thomas II (1725–72). In 1704 Bamburgh Castle was purchased by Nathaniel, Lord Crewe, Bishop of Durham from 1674 until his death in 1721, and it eventually became the responsibility of the charitable trust that he founded. In 1779 John III, who, like his father, was a Trustee of Lord Crewe's Charity, and who had inherited the libraries of his grandfather, father, and uncle, purchased his brother's books to form the nucleus of a permanent library at the Castle, to which was added the family collection, bequeathed by John at his death.[1] It was the two grandsons of Archbishop Sharp who collected by far the greater part of the music section of the Bamburgh Library, to be precise 114 volumes (counting a set of part-books as one volume) or 384 items, over 150 of these latter being single-sheet copies of songs and arias. These numbers include a few duplications and also the forty-four volumes of Arnold's edition of Handel's works which John probably began to purchase before his death; they exclude seven volumes published after John's death. As in Falle's collection there are comparatively few manuscripts.

The Trustees of Lord Crewe's Charity controlled the Bamburgh Library until 1958, in which year the music section was transferred to Durham Cathedral Library on indefinite loan. The Bamburgh Library as a whole consists of some 8,000 items, and

[1] See 'Unfamiliar Libraries. IV. The Bamburgh Library' by I. A. Doyle in *The Book Collector*, 1959, p. 14.

INTRODUCTION

had been regarded by the Crewe Trustees as sufficiently important to merit two printed catalogues, neither of which, however, incorporates any of the music or books on music.[1] Moreover, the existence of the music section of the Bamburgh Library seems to have been completely unknown until its transference to Durham, and hence none of its contents are included in *BUCEM*.

Falle's collection (designated by the shelf-marks 'A' to 'E' followed by a number) is very well preserved. The Bamburgh collection, on the other hand (designated by the shelf-mark 'M' followed by a number), has suffered much from what I suspect were servants in search of fire-lighting materials. Whatever the cause the sad fact remains that nearly a quarter of the surviving items are mutilated to a greater or lesser degree by having pages partly or wholly torn out; indeed, so great is the damage in some cases that identification has proved impossible. Moreover, apart from the evidence of page fragments, some of which represent single-sheet songs, some much larger works, it is clear from a small manuscript catalogue made by John Sharp of his own collection that a number of volumes have disappeared altogether; precisely how many one cannot say, because, of the original 62 pages in the catalogue, pp. 1–12, 14, 15, 24–27, 34–37, 41, 42, 57, and 58 are either wholly or largely missing, but the following five items, included in the catalogue, are no longer in the collection: 'A Cantata and 6 English Songs' by 'Fireman' (Henry Firmin? No composer of this name, or like it, in *BUCEM*); 'Somervile chase set to musick—in score. other songs' (i.e. *The Chace . . . with several other songs in score. . . .* Walsh [1743]) by William Flackton; '12 Duetti a due Traverse 2 parts, 2 Books' by 'Francisco Gizziello' (composer not in *BUCEM*, but in Q–L without Christian name, and merely as a contributor to John Simpson's *Companion*—1740); '24 Duets for two German Flutes—Opera terza—in score' (i.e. *XXIV Duets for German flutes . . . Opera terza . . .* Simpson [1747]) by Lewis Christian Austin Granom; *Douze duos Italiens. . . .* 2 bks.[2] [*c.* 1750] by Leonardo Pescatore.

[1] *A Catalogue of the Library at Bamburgh Castle*, Durham [1799?]. *Catalogue of the Library at Bamburgh Castle*, 2 vols., London, 1859. [By J. Stevenson.]
[2] *BUCEM* lists only one copy of this work in the British Museum.

It is, perhaps, worth mentioning at this point the more obscure composers noted in what remains of Sharp's catalogue who were represented solely in manuscript copies: 'Francesca Barbella'— 3 Concertos for violins etc.—7 parts—7 books' (these not listed in Q–L); 'Bennegar' (Antonio Benegger?)—'Concerto for the Clarinet' (not listed in Q–L); 'Carlo Cailo'—'1 Trio duo Violini con basso—parts' (composer not in Q–L); 'Nicolà Fiorenza'— '1 Concerto for Violins etc.—7 parts—7 books. Original Ital: copy'; '1 Trio for two violins con basso 3 parts—3 books' (works not listed in Q–L); 'Gravina'—'1 Trio Violini duo con basso in parts'; 'Pietro Marchitelli'—'2 Trios Violini duo con basso—in parts' (composer in Q–L but without Christian name); 'Claudio Roiero'—'1 Trio Violini duo con basso—in parts'.

This is not the place to give a detailed analysis of the contents of this catalogue but a few comments of a general nature may be of interest. The mutilation of Sharp's catalogue and of the Bamburgh music collection almost certainly took place during the nineteenth century, for the missing volumes of printed music enumerated above are not included in another manuscript catalogue made in 1916 by E. V. Stocks, Librarian of Durham University. Nevertheless, what remains is of considerable value, for apart from increasing the number of known copies of music that were printed before 1800, nearly one sixth of the items are unique, so far as British libraries are concerned. This proportion is remarkable enough, but it is exceeded in Falle's collection, where well over one-quarter of the items are unique.

The two collections are largely complementary to each other, there being gratifyingly few duplications. This is somewhat surprising when we consider that Falle and the Sharps, especially the latter, tended to buy contemporary publications, that the Sharps were collecting independently for well over thirty years before Thomas's death (though it is possible that John rejected duplicates when he bought his brother's library), and that for about the first twenty years of this period Falle was probably collecting also, quite apart from the fact that there are a fair number of items in the Bamburgh collection dating from the early decades of the

INTRODUCTION xiii

eighteenth century, when Falle was assembling the bulk of his collection.

The Sharps, like Falle, were Anglican priests, and the contents of the two collections reflect the secularism of the eighteenth century, a secularism that grew as the century progressed and which affected ecclesiastics and laymen alike. Thus, while in Falle's collection secular vocal music, sacred vocal music, and musical writings—some of these last concerned with the 'efficacy' or 'lawfulness' of church music—each occupy slightly over one sixth of the collection, the remainder (nearly half) consisting of instrumental works, in the Bamburgh collection almost half of the items are secular vocal, and nearly one-third are instrumental, the remainder being sacred, apart from five theoretical works.

The additions made to Falle's music library at Durham after his death show a pronounced bias towards sacred music, $35\frac{1}{2}$ volumes (47 items) as opposed to $6\frac{1}{2}$ volumes (29 items) of secular music (20 items being single-sheet songs in one volume), 14 volumes (18 items) of instrumental music, and 3 theoretical works. It can be argued that this preponderance of sacred music, probably acquired by some of the Cathedral's organists, reflected the difference between a priest's private collection, designed to entertain as well as edify, and that of an ecclesiastical institution, where practical considerations tended to be of paramount importance, for in fact only 5 of the 47 items noted above were not intended for use in the Anglican Service.

In order to include all the more interesting items in the music section of the Durham Cathedral Library I have chosen 1825 as the upper limiting date, i.e. twenty-five years later than that adopted by the BM.'s Reading Room 'Catalogue of Old Music' and *BUCEM*. The catalogue is divided into three main sections: vocal music (which includes libretti and texts of anthems), instrumental music, and theoretical works (including writings on music and one catalogue). In each section the items are arranged alphabetically by composer for single-composer works, or by title for works by more than one composer, except for Psalms, which are grouped together in chronological order. Each item is represented by a catalogue number, composer or title, shelf-mark,[1] a transcript from the title-page, and beneath this a description of the item in italic type, including format (part-books, score, etc.) where this is likely to be unclear, number of pages (unnumbered pages in round brackets), contents (unless adequately described in the title-page transcript), and, if in the original, names of composers and performers (original spelling; where there are variants the first spelling is adopted), dedicator (if other than the composer or author), dedicatee, and a note of lists of works by composers, authors, or publishers, list of subscribers, and index; Roman type implies a quotation, except in the title-page transcript; square brackets indicate an editorial insertion. An asterisk before the shelf-mark means that an item is unique, and under this term I include: (*a*) music which, if complete, exists nowhere else, or only in imperfect copies, or if imperfect, is the only copy, using *BUCEM* as the reference source for items published in or before 1800, and the BM. 'Catalogue of Modern Music' for later items; (*b*) theoretical works, etc., which are not in any of the general or music catalogues in the Reading Room of the British Museum. A dagger before the shelf-mark indicates that the item is either omitted from or imperfectly entered in Sartori's *Bibliografia della musicale strumentale*. . . . Unique items receive a fuller treatment than other items, particularly as regards description. Five indexes have been added: I—names, excluding publishers; II—publishers, music-sellers, engravers; III—Stage works; IV—song titles and first lines; V—subject, including instruments. In each index reference is to catalogue number, unless the entry occurs in this Introduction, and the spelling has been modernized except in Index IV.

My original purpose in making this catalogue was to satisfy my own interest in the Cathedral music library, and to provide the librarian with a complete and accurate list of the printed material contained in it, so far as I was able. Some three years ago, however, the Dean and Chapter decided that the contents merited a

[1] The items by Burney and Hawkins are in the Cathedral's main library, and have different shelf-marks from the Falle and Bamburgh collections.

printed catalogue. I should like to thank the Chapter Librarian, Canon A. H. Couratin, for his enthusiasm and patience, and also Miss Margot Johnson, the former Assistant Librarian, and the library staff for their help in a variety of ways, and finally Mr. A. Hyatt King of the British Museum, whose expert advice I sought on a number of matters.

R. ALEC HARMAN

Durham, 1966

I. VOCAL WORKS

1. ABELL, JOHN. D37. A Collection of Songs, in Several Languages. Compos'd by Mr. John Abell. London. Printed by William Pearson . . . for the Author. 1701. fol.
    Pp. (1), 24. Ded. to William III.

2. ACHILLE ET POLIXENE. B19. Achille et Polixene, Tragedie Dont le Prologue & les quatre derniers Actes ont esté mis en Musique Par P. Collasse, . . . Et le premier Acte par feu Mre. J. B. de Lully. . . . A Paris, Par Christophe Ballard. . . . MDCLXXXVII. fol.
    Pp. (2), xxxviii, 316. Full Score. Includes Ded. to Louis XIV by Colasse.

3. ADDISON, JOSEPH. A39. Rosamond. An Opera. . . . The Third Edition. London: Printed for J. Tonson. . . . MDCCXIII. 8⁰
    Pp. 25–76, (4). Libretto. Preceded by Addison's poem The Campaign. Includes verses to Addison by Tickell, and 4 pp. of Tonson's pubs. Ded. to Duchess of Marlborough.

4. ALCOCK, JOHN. E45. Six and Twenty Select Anthems in Score: . . . To which are added A Burial Service . . . by John Alcock. . . . 1771. . . . fol.
    Pp. vii, 210. Includes Ded. to Frederick, Archbishop of Canterbury, List of subscribers, Contents. Engraved by Thomas Baker. 5 copies.

5. ALMAHIDE. D39. Songs in the New Opera Call'd Almahide. . . . Sold by I. Walsh . . . & P. Randall . . . & I. Hare. . . . [1710] fol.
    Pp. (1), 64. Preceded by full page engraving which gives Walsh only as the publisher. The singers are: Signora Margherita, Signor Nicolini, Signor Valentini, Mrs. Isabella Girardeau, Mr. Dogget, Mrs. Lindley, Mrs. Cross, Signor Cassani. Includes list of operas printed for Walsh.

6. ALOYSIUS, JOANNES BAPTISTA. *D29 (iii). Celeste Palco in cui vaghi affetti, espressi con Musicali accenti. . . . Gio. Battista

VOCAL WORKS

Alovisi. . . . Opera Seconda. Stampa del Gardano. In Venetia MDCXXVIII. Appresso Bartolomeo Magni. fol.

Pp. (*1*), *39*, (*1*). *Ded. to the* Signore Sonatrici & Cantatrici *of the Monastery of* Cittelle Gasparine di Padova. *Solo voice with fig. bass in score. Index. Music consists of motets:* Repeleatur os meum. Dominator Domine. Quis Deus Magnus. Sacramento Caelesti. Sacrificemus Reginae Coeli. Stabat Virgo Maria. Exultavit cor meum. Nolite timere. Ingredere anima mea. O Iesu mi Dulcissime. O nimis cara Deo. Anima mea cessa. Exaltabo te Deus. Quemadmodum desiderat. Omnia quae fecisti nobis. Inimici mei. *Antiphons:* Alma Redemptoris Mater. Ave Regina Caelorum. Regina Caeli Laetare. Salve Regina. *For S., A., T., or B.*

7. ANTIOCO. *M98 (lxxxv). Antiochus Sung by Signr. Nicolini in the Opera of Antiochus. [Music by F. Gasparini.] [London, *c.* 1712] fol.

    Pp. (*2*). *Imp., lacking most of p.* (*2*). *Begins* Questo conforto.

8. ARNE, THOMAS AUGUSTINE. M78 (i). Vocal Melody. An Entire New Collection of English Songs and a Cantata Compos'd by Mr. Arne. . . . London. Printed for I. Walsh. . . . [1746] fol.

    Pp. (*1*), *42*. *Licence for printing dated 29. i. 1740.* (*See below.*)

9. —— M78 (ii). Vocal Melody. Book II. An Entire [etc., as above]. [1748?] fol.

    Pp. (*1*), *21-42*. *Licence as above. Imp., lacking Vols. I, III, and IV.*

10. ASK. *M77 (xvi). A new favourite Song Sung by Mr. Lowe at Vaux Hall [London, *c.* 1745] fol.

    S.sh. Begins Ask me not how calmly I. *Includes arr. for Ger. Fl.*

11. ATTWOOD, THOMAS. D17 (xvi). Reflections of Marie Antoinette. . . . The Music by Thos. Attwood, and sung by Mrs. Crouch at the Theatre Royal. London, Printed & Sold by Preston & Son. . . . [1793] fol.

    Pp. 4. With acc. for Kb. and Ger. Fl. Begins To bid the World along Farewell.

12. BAILDON, JOSEPH. M158 (vi). The Laurel. A New Collection of English Songs Sung by Mr. Lowe and Miss Falkner. . . .

VOCAL WORKS

Compos'd by Mr. Joseph Baildon. London. Printed for I. Walsh. . . . [1750] fol.

Pp. 10. Imp., Bk. I only and pp. 9, 10 defective. Includes list of Walsh's pubs.

13. BALIN. M77 (xxviii). Balin a mone Sung by Mr. Barington in the double Disappointment. [London, 1747?] fol.

    S.sh. Begins Where ever I'm going and all the Day long. *Includes arr. for Ger. Fl.*

14. BARRETT, JOHN. *M77 (xii). Love and Folly A New Song Sung by Miss Stephenson at Vaux-Hall. [London, 1711?] fol.

    Pp. (2). Begins Love and Folly were at Play. *Includes arr. for Ger. Fl.*

15. —— M98 (xlvi). A Song Sett by Mr Barrett, Sung by Mr Hughes at the Theatre. [London, *c.* 1710] fol.

    Pp. (2). Imp., p. (2) defective. Begins Love and Folly were at Play.

16. —— M98 (xii). Liberia. A Song Set to Musick by Mr. John Barrett. [London, *c.* 1715] fol.

    S.sh. Begins Liberia's all my Thought.

17. BASSANI, GIOVANNI BATTISTA. †B21. Canto Primo Messe Concertate a 4. e 5. voci, con Violini, e Ripieni. Del Signor Gio. Battista Bassani. . . . Opera Decima Octava Et Messa Per Li Defonti Concertata a quatro voci, con Viole, e Ripieni Opera Vigesima. In Bologna, Per Marino Silvani. E se vendono a Amsterdam, apresso Estienne Roger. . . . [1698] fol.

    In 14 pt-bks. There are 3 Masses in Op. 18. The Vc. pt-bk. contains 1 p. of Roger's pubs. Canto Primo, *pp. 24;* Canto Primo Ripieno, *pp. 22;* Canto secundo, *pp. 16;* Canto Secundo Ripieno, *pp. 8;* Alto, *pp. 24;* Alto Ripieno, *pp. 14;* Tenore, *pp. 20;* Tenore Ripieno, *pp. 14;* Basso, *pp. 18;* Basso Ripieno, *pp. 14;* Violino Primo, *pp. 20;* Violino Secundo, *pp. 20;* Violoncello, *pp. 28;* Organo, *pp. 28.*

19. BILLINGTON, THOMAS. D17 (xx). The Soldier's Farewell On the Eve of a Battle. . . . set to music by Mr. Billington. . . . London Printed by G. Goulding. . . . [*c.* 1787] fol.

Pp. 17. Song preceded by Overture and March for Pf. and Fl. Includes List of Billington's pubs. Begins Night expecting the dread morrow.

20. BLOW, JOHN. M85. Amphion Anglicus. A Work of many Compositions, For One, Two, Three, and Four Voices: and A Thorow-Bass to each Song. . . . By Dr. John Blow. London. Printed by William Pearson, for the Author. . . . MDCC. fol.

Pp. (6), viii, (2), 216. Includes Ded. to Princess Ann of Denmark, Verses, Index, List of H. Playford's pubs.

21. —— B2 (ii). An Ode on the Death of Mr. Henry Purcell. . . . The Words by Mr. Dryden, and Sett to Musick by Dr. Blow. London, Printed by J. Heptinstall, for Henry Playford. . . . 1696. fol.

Pp. (1), 30. Includes text of the Ode and List of Playford's pubs. Inserted into Orpheus Britannicus *(see No. 303) immediately before p. 1.*

22. BOWMAN, THOMAS. M77 (vii). Two Cantatas and Eight English Songs Set to Musick by Mr. Thos. Bowman. . . . London Printed and Sold by Iohn Tyther. . . . [c. 1750] fol.

Pp. 19. Imp., 3 pp. defective.

23. BOYCE, WILLIAM. M78 (v). The Chaplet. A Musical Entertainment. . . . Compos'd by Dr. Boyce. London. Printed for I. Walsh. . . . [1750] fol.

Imp., all pp. missing after t-p.

24. —— M77 (i–iii). Lyra Britannica: Being A collection of Songs, Duets, and Cantatas. . . . Compos'd by Mr. Boyce. London. Printed for and sold by I. Walsh. [c. 1745–c. 1755] fol.

Pp. 47. Before p. 22 comes 2nd t-p.: Lyra Britannica: Book II. *[etc., as above]. Before p. 35 comes 3rd t-p.:* Lyra Britannica Book 3d. A Cantata and English Songs Set to Musick by Mr. Boyce. *[etc., as above.] Imp., lacking bks. IV–VI. Includes Licence and advertisement of Boyce's sonatas for 2 Vls.*

25. —— M78 (iii). *Another copy of Bk. I, with the original pagination altered in MS.*

26. —— M78 (iv). *Another copy of Bk. III, with the original pagination altered in MS.*

27. —— B6. An Ode Perform'd in the Senate House at Cambridge, ... At the Installation of his Grace The Duke of Newcastle, Chancellor of the University. ... To which is added an Anthem. ... The Musick by Dr. William Boyce. [1749] fol.
 Pp. (1), 70. *Ded. to Thomas Holles, Duke of Newcastle.*

28. —— M77 (xxii). A new favourite Song sung by Mr. Lowe at Ruckholt House. ... Printed with the Permission of Mr. Boyce for J. Simpson. ... [London, *c.* 1745] fol.
 S.sh. Begins Come all ye young Lovers.

29. —— M77 (xxiii). The Constant Lover A new Song, Set by Mr. Boyce. [London, *c.* 1740] fol.
 S.sh. Begins If you my wandring Heart wou'd find. *Includes arr. for Fl.*

30. —— *M78 (xviii). The Ravish'd Lover. Set for the German Flute. Printed for J. Simpson. ... [London, *c.* 1736] fol.
 S.sh. Begins When Fanny Blooming fair. *Includes arr. for Fl. Printer's colophon occurs at foot of page; missing on other copies in BUCEM.*

31. BRITISH ORPHEUS. M101 (i–iv). The British Orpheus A Collection of Favourite English Songs Never Before Publish'd Compos'd By Different Authors London. Printed for I. Walsh. ... [1741–3] fol.
 Pp. 48. In 4 pts., each with separate t-p., viz.: No. 11. The British Orpheus [etc., as above], *pp. 13–24; similarly for Pt. 3, pp. 25–36; Pt. 4:*—The British Orpheus [etc., as above]. ... Compos'd by Mr. Howard &c. Book IV. London [etc., as above], *pp. 37–48. Imp., pp. 46–48 defective. Composers are:* Arne, Barberini, Boyce, Carey, Froude, Gladwin, Handel, Holcombe, Howard, Lampe, Leveridge, John Randall, Russel, Stanley, Travers, Thomas Vincent. *Includes list of Walsh's pubs.*

32. CALYPSO AND TELEMACHUS.* M98 (lxxxvii). [Calypso. Sung by Signra Margaritta in the Opera of Calypso] fol.
 Pp. (2). *Begins* Pleasing visions shall attend thee. *Page heading half cut off. P.* (2) *paginated* (9). *From* Songs in the Opera of Calypso & Telemachus as they are Perform'd at the Queens Theatre. Compos'd by Mr Galliard. ... London Printed for J:Walsh. ... & J: Hare. ... [1712] (*see No. 151*).

6 VOCAL WORKS

33. —— *M98 (lxxxviii). Telemachus Sung by Mrs. Barbier in the Opera of Calypso. fol.

   Pp. (2). Begins O Cupid, gentle Boy. From same Coll. as No. 32.

34. —— *M98 (lxxxix). Proteus. Sung by Mr. Leveridge in Calypso. fol.

   Pp. (2). Begins Pursue ye flying Fair. Paginated 12, 13. From same Coll. as No. 32.

35. CAMILLA. M98 (xxxii). Sung by the Barrns. in the Opera call'd Camilla, at the Theatre Royall. fol.

   S.sh. Begins Fair Dorinda happy may'st thou Ever be. Includes arr. for Fl. Paginated 11. From Songs In The New Opera, Call'd Camilla as they are perform'd at the Theatre Royall Sold by I: Walsh. . . . [Music by M. A. Bononcini] [London, c. 1709]

36. —— M98 (xxxiii). Sung by Mrs. Lindsey, in the Opera call'd Camilla, at the Theatre Royall. fol.

   S.sh. Begins These Eyes are made so killing. Includes arr. for Fl. Paginated 37. From same Coll. as No. 35.

37. —— *M98 (xxxiv). Sung by the Boy, in the Opera call'd Camilla, at the Theatre Royall. fol.

   S.sh. Begins O Nymph of Race divine. Includes arr. for Fl. Paginated 2. From same Coll. as No. 35.

38. —— *M98 (xxxv). Sung by the Boy, in the Opera call'd Camilla, at the Theatre Royall. fol.

   S.sh. Begins Ungrateful you Fly me. Includes arr. for Fl. Paginated 29. From same Coll. as No. 35.

39. —— *M98 (xxxvi). Sung by the Boy in the Opera call'd Camilla, at the Theatre Royall. fol.

   S.sh. Begins In vain I Fly from sorrow. Includes arr. for Fl. Paginated 19. From same Coll. as No. 35.

40. —— *M98 (xxxvii). Sung by Mrs Toft, in the Opera call'd Camilla, at the Theatre Royall. fol.

   S.sh. Begins Fortune Ever known to vary. Includes arr. for Fl. Paginated 5. From same Coll. as No. 35.

VOCAL WORKS

41. —— *M98 (xxxviii). Turnus. Sung by Mr. Hughs in the Opera of Camilla. fol.

    S.sh. Begins A Round her see Cupid flying. Includes arr. for Fl. From Songs In The New Opera, Call'd Camilla as they are perform'd at the Theatre Royall. Sold by I. Walsh . . . and I. Hare. . . . [Music by M. A. Bononcini] [London, 1706]

42. —— *M98 (xxxix). Turnus. Sung by Mr. Hughs in ye Opera of Camilla. fol.

    S.sh. Begins Cease cruell tyrannising. Includes arr. for Fl. Paginated 44. From same Coll. as No. 41.

43. —— *M98 (xl). Sung by the Boy in the Opera call'd Camilla, at the Theatre Royall. fol.

    S.sh. Begins Cupid O at lenght (sic) reward me. Includes arr. for Fl. Paginated 39. From same Coll. as No. 41.

44. —— *M98 (xli). [Prenesto. Sung by M: D'lapine in ye Opera of Camilla.] fol.

    S.sh. Begins Charming fair for thee I languish. Page heading cut off. Includes arr. for Fl. Paginated 12. From same Coll. as No. 41.

45. —— *M98 (xlii). [Turnus. Sung by Mr. Hughs in ye Opera of Camilla.] fol.

    S.sh. Begins The Flood shall quit ye Ocean. Page heading cut off. Includes arr. for Fl. Paginated 39. From same Coll. as No. 41.

46. CANTICA SACRA. B25 (ii). Cantus Cantica Sacra: Containing Hymns and Anthems for Two Voices to the Organ, both Latine and English. Composed by Mr. Richard Dering. Dr. Benjamin Rogers. Dr. Christoph: Gibbons. Mr. Matth. Locke, and Others. The Second Sett. London, Printed by W. Godbid, for John Playford. 1674. fol.

    In 3 pt-bks. Cantus, pp. (2), 45, (1), includes Ded. to Charles II by Playford, Address by Playford, Index; Bassus, pp. (2), 45, (1), includes as above; Basso Continuo, pp. 33, (1), includes Index. Bound in with Cantus Primus, Bassus, and Bassus Continuus of No. 95. Composers, other than above: Isaac Blackwell, John Jackson, George Jeffries, Henry Lawes, John Playford, Michael Wise.

VOCAL WORKS

47. CASATI, GASPARO. *B22. Gasparis Casati Domus Novariensis Capellae Magistri, Operis Primi Pars, prior, Continens Moteta Una et Duabus Vocibus ad Organum Concertata. Vox Prima. Antuerpiae, Apud Haeredes Petri Phalesii Typographi Musices ad insigne Davidis Regis. MDCLIV. 4⁰

In 3 pt-bks. Vox Prima, *pp. 59, (1), includes Index;* Vox Secunda, *pp. 55, (1), includes Index;* Organum, *pp. 63, (1), includes Index, and motets for 1 voice in score, for 2 voices just fig. bass. Voices range from S. to B. 6 motets for 1 voice, 20 for 2 voices.*

48. CASSON, MARGARET. D17 (xviii). Noon. . . . Composed by Miss Margaret Casson. . . . The words by Mrs. Cobbold. London [*c.* 1800] fol.

Pp. 4. Acc. for Kb. and Guitar. Begins 'Tis fervid Noon.

49. CATCHES. B45 (iv). A Second Collection of Catches Canons and Glees For Three, Four, Five and Eight Voices Most humbly inscrib'd to the Noblemen and Gentlemen of the Catch-Club at St. Alban's Tavern By . . . Thos. Warren. London Printed for Peter Welcker. . . . [*c.* 1764] obl. fol.

Pp. 51. Includes Index. Composers: [Anon.], Dr. Arne, Mr. J. Baildon, Mr. G. Berg, Monsr. L'Clerc, Sigr. Cocchi, Dr. Hayes, Mr. Howard, Sigr. Lidarti, J. B. Marella, H. Purcel, Sigr. Trajetta, Mr. Warren.

50. CATHEDRAL MUSIC. E66. Cathedral Music: Being A Collection in Score of . . . Compositions. . . . By the Several English Masters Of the last Two Hundred Years. The Whole Selected and Carefully Revis'd by Dr. William Boyce. . . . Volume the First. London: Printed for the Editor. MDCCLX. fol.

Pp. xii, 290. Includes Preface, List of subscribers, Short accounts of some of the composers, Index. Composers are: Aldrich, Bevin, Blow, Child, Farrant, Gibbons, Morley, Rogers, Tallis.

51. —— E67. Cathedral Music: [etc., as above]. . . . Volume the Second. . . . MDCCLXVIII. fol.

Pp. (xii), 306. Includes Ded. to Charles II, List of subscribers, Continuation of accounts of composers, Index. Composers are: Aldrich, Batten, Bird, Blow, Child, Clark, Creyghton, Croft, Farrant, Gibbons, Goldwin, Humphrys, W. Lawes, Lock, Purcell, Rogers, Tallis, Tye, Weldon, Wise.

VOCAL WORKS 9

52. —— E68. *Another copy. Imp., lacking t-p.*

53. —— E69. Cathedral Music: [etc., as above]. . . . Volume the Third. . . . MDCCLXXIII.

> *Pp. xii, 300. Includes Ded. to Charles II, Preface (different from Vol. I), List of subscribers, Continuation of accounts of composers, Index. Composers are:* Bird, Blow, Bull, Child, J. Clark, Humphrys, Purcell, Turner, Wise.

54. —— E64. Cathedral Music: Organ Part Selected & Revised By Dr. Samuel Arnold. . . . Printed for the Editor. [1790] fol.

> *Pp. 305. Includes Ded. to George III, Index. Imp., lacking Vols. I–III. Composers are:* Aldrich, Ayrton, Boyce, Bryan, Child, Clark, Croft, Dupuis, Goldwin, Greene, Hall & Hine, Kent, King, Nares, Patrick, Purcell, Tallis, Travers, Tudway, Weldon.

55. —— E65. *Another copy. Imp., lacking t-p.*

56. CAZZATI, MAURITIO. *B 24. Canto. Motetti a Due, Tre, e Quattro Voci, con Instrumenti. Di Mauritio Cazzatti, Maestro di Cappella dell' Illustrissima Academia, della Morte in Ferrara Opera Duodecima. En Anversa, Presso i Heredi di Pietro Phalesio, Ale Re David. MDCLXII. Sm. 4⁰

> *In 5 pt-bks.* Canto (*S., S. 1, Vl. 1*), *pp. 41,* (*1*); Alto (*S. 2, A., Vl. 2*), *pp. 57,* (*1*); Tenore (*S. 2, S. 3, A., A. 2, T., T. 1*), *pp. 54,* (*1*); Basso (*T., T. 2, B.*), *pp. 46,* (*1*); Organo (*fig. bass*), *pp. 49,* (*1*). *Each pt. includes Index. Music consists of motets: a2*—Victoria. Ecce Ignis. Quis est hic. Alma Redemptoris. Puer Natus. Gaudent omnes. Ave dulce lignum. *a3*—Benedic anima mea. Surgite. Regina Caeli. Peccantem. O quam Pulcra. O Dulcissime Iesu. O Gloriosa Virginum. Salve Regina. O quam dulce. Puer qui natus. O Vos populi. O Bona Crux. O Dulcissima Maria. Bone Sancte. Regina Caeli. *a4*—Canite spiritus. O Sacro-Sancta. Salve Regina. Gaude. *a2, Vls. 1 and 2*—Alma Redemptoris.

57. CELIA. *M158 (iii). Celia a favourite Cantata [n.d.] fol.

> *Pp. (2). The above is taken from the heading on p. (1). Begins with ritornello for Kb., then recit.* O 'tis Eliziam all *and aria* To my Lips than Nectar sweeter.

VOCAL WORKS

58. CHILCOT, THOMAS. M67 (ii). Twelve English Songs With their Symphonies. The Words by Shakespeare and other Celebrated Poets Set to Musick by Mr. Thomas Chilcot. ... London Printed and sold by John Johnson. ... [1744] fol.

> *Imp., containing pp. (4), 30, and 9 songs only. Includes Ded. to Samuel Strode, List of subscribers.*

59. CLARKE, JOHN. D14 (i). A Miscellaneous Volume of Morning and Evening Services in Score ... by John Clarke. ... Vol. 2. ... London Printed for the Author by Broderip & Wilkinson. ... [1805] fol.

> *Pp. (4), 109. Ded. to Masters and Fellows of Trinity and St. John's Colleges, Cambridge. 2 copies.*

60. ―― D14 (ii). Twelve Anthems, in Score ... by John Clarke. ... Vol. 3. ... London [etc., as above] [1805] fol.

> *Pp. (1), 104. Ded. as above. 2 copies.*

61. CLAYTON, THOMAS. D40. Songs in the New Opera, Call'd Arsinoe Queen of Cyprus Compos'd by Mr. Tho. Clayton Sold by I. Walsh ... & P. Randall ... and I. Hare. ... [London, 1706] fol.

> *Pp. (1), 49. Preceded by full page engraving which gives Walsh and Hare as publishers, with Hare's imprint added in different typography. Singers are:* Mr. Hughs, Mrs. Tofts, Mr. Ramondon, Mr. Leveridge, Mrs. Cross, Mrs. Lynsey, Mr. Good.

62. ―― M98 (xxx). The first Song in the Opera of Arsino'e, Sung by Mr Hughs. [London, c. 1708] fol.
> *S.sh. Begins* Queen of Darkness Sable night. *Includes arr. for Fl.*

63. ―― M98 (xxxi). A Song in the Opera of Arsino'e Queen of Ciprus. Sung by Mr Hughes. Looking on Arsinoe's Picture. ... fol.
> *S.sh. Begins* Charming Creature, every Feature. Within the Compass of the Flute *placed within the first stave. P. 21 of Coll. No. 61.*

64. ―― D41. Songs in the New Opera Call'd Rosamond ... by Mr. Tho Clayton London Printed for I. Walsh ... and P. Randall. ... [1707] fol.

> *Pp. (1), 47. Preceded by full page engraving. The singer sare:* Mrs·

VOCAL WORKS

Tofts, Mr. Holcombe, Mr. Leveridge, Mrs. Lindsey, Mrs. or Signora Maria Gallia, Mr. Hughs, Mr. Lawrence, Mrs. Reding or Miss Redding.

65. CLOTILDA. *M98 (lxxvi). Sung by Mr. Laurance in the Opera call'd Clotilda. fol.
  S.sh. Begins Still I follow, still she Fly's me. Includes arr. for Fl. P. 9 from Songs in the Opera Call'd Clotilda London Printed for & Sold by Iohn Walsh. . . . [Music by F. Conti] [c. 1710]

66. —— *M98 (lxxviii). Sung by Mr Laurance in the Opera call'd Clotilda. fol.
  S.sh. Begins When Loves inciting and Pow'r inviteing. Includes arr. for Fl. P. 23 from above Coll.

67. COLLECTION. A6 (i). A Collection of Anthems, As the same are now perform'd in the Cathedral Church of Durham. Durham: Printed by Isaac Lane, MDCCXLIX. 8°
  Pp. 205, (13). Words only. Index.

68. —— A5 (i). Another copy. Imp., lacking t-p., p. 205, (13).

69. —— A40. Another copy printed on slightly larger sheets.

70. —— A6 (ii). A Collection of Anthems [etc., as above]. . . . Durham: Printed by L. Pennington, Bookseller. MDCCXCV. 8°
  Pp. 85, (6). Words only. Imp., lacking pp. 65, 66, replaced by page stitched in with incipits of texts in MS. Includes Messiah, an Oratorio, in three parts. Composed by Mr. Handel. Durham. Printed by L. Pennington. . . . MDCCXCV. Pp. 73–85. (See No. 190.)

71. —— A6 (iii). A Collection of Anthems [etc., as above]. . . . Durham: Printed by L. Pennington, Bookseller. MDCCXCVI. 8°
  Pp. (1), 52. Words only. Includes Advertisement, Index.

72. —— A5 (iii). Imp., being the Advertisement only. Preceded by pp. 15, 16 of unidentified Coll.

73. —— A5 (v). Another copy of A6 (iii). Imp., lacking second t-p. for Full Anthems and Advertisement.

VOCAL WORKS

74. —— A6 (iv). A Collection of Anthems [etc., as above]. . . .
MDCCCI. 8°
Pp. viii, 86. Words only. Index.

75. —— A5 (vii). *Pp. 12. Imp., lacking t-p. Unidentified.*

76. —— A6 (v). *Another copy of A5 (vii). Imp., lacking pp. 9–12.*

77. —— A5 (iv). *Pp. (5). Imp., lacking t-p. Unidentified.*

78. —— A5 (vi). *Pp. (7). Imp., lacking t-p. Unidentified.*

79. —— *M78 (xxii). *Pp. (8). Imp., lacking t-p. and the remaining pages of a Coll. of two-part songs (?). Original pagination replaced by MS. nos. to follow No. 222. Contains:*

   (a) *P. (1).* A Dialogue to the famous Cebell of Signr Baptist Lully. *Begins* Pray now John let Jug prevail. *Includes arr. for Fl.*

   (b) *Pp. (2–3).* A Dialogue Sung by Mr Doggett and Mrs Bracegirdle Set by Mr John Eccles. *Begins* By those Pigs neyes.

   (c) *Pp. (4–5).* A two Part Song Set by Mr Henry Purcell. *Begins* Fair Cloe my Breast so alarms.

   (d) *Pp. (6–7).* A two Part Song set by Dr Blow. *Begins* Go, go, go, go, Perjur'd Maid.

   (e) *Pp. (8).* The Caution Set by Mr Travers. *Begins* When India's waves are known to freeze. *Duet. Includes arr. for Fl.*
   [London, 1711?] fol.

80. COMPOSITIONI SACRE. *B44. Compositioni Sacre de Diversi Excellenti Autori Moderni a Une, Due, Trè è Quattro Voci, parte con Instromenti è parte senza instromenti. . . . Prima Parte. In Anversa, Presso i Heredi di Pietro Phalesio, . . . MDCLXV. 4°

   In 5 pt-bks. Pt. I (Canto, Canto Primo, Alto, Tenor, Tenor Primo), *pp. 47; Pt. II* (Canto, Canto Secondo, Alto, Tenore, Tenor Sec.), *pp. 37; Pt. III* (Alto, *Vl. 1, Vl. 2 on opposite pages*), *pp. 23; Pt. IV* (Basso, Viola), *pp. 29; Pt. V* (B. Continuo), *pp. 38. Composers are:* Sig. Giuseppe Allevi, Sig. Francesco Lucio, Padre Fr. Ant. Accorona. *Music consists of motets: a2*—O Admirabile Convivium. Omnes gentes (*Allevi*). In odorem unguentorum (*Accorona*). *a3*—Conciniunt Superi. O Iucunda dies. Lauda

Ierusalem (*Lucio*). Ad Aepulas Caeli. Ah Anima infaelix (*Accorona*). *a4*—Ad laudes (*Allevi*). Voice, 2 *Vls.*—O Anima mea. Caelestes Angeli (*Allevi*). *a2*, 2 *Vls.*, Viola—Exurgat psalterium (*Accorona*). *a3*, 2 *Vls.*—Erumpe in gaudia (*Allevi*). All with BC.

81. CORFE, JAMES. M100 (iii). Six English Songs for two & three voices set to Musick by Mr. James Corfe London Printed for John Johnson.... [*c.* 1740] fol.

    Pp. 10.

82. —— *M100 (iv). Twelve English Songs with their Symphonies The Words by Several Authors Set to Musick by Mr. James Corfe London Printed for, and sold by John Johnson.... [*c.* 1745] fol.

    Pp. 62. Most of the songs include an arr. for Fl.:—The Power of Music (*Fl.*); The Lady of the May; The Coquette, or Complaining Shepherd (*Fl.*); The Honey Moon (*Fl.*); The Swain in Extasy (*Fl.*); The Shy Decoyer (*Fl.*); The British Phoenix (*Fl.*); The Charms of Belinda (*Fl.*); The Female Rake (*from* Unburied Dead, *a farce by Bickerstaff. Fl.*); The Enchantress (*Fl.*); The Impertinent Poet (*Fl.*); The Generous Protestation (*Fl.*). *No. 9 mentions a singer*, Mrs. Dunstall.

83. CORFE, JOSEPH. E48. Church Music Consisting of a Te Deum, Jubilate, Cantate Domino ... by Joseph Corfe.... London. Printed for the Author, by Preston.... [1815?] fol.

    Pp. 125, (1). Includes Ded. to the Bishop and Dean and Chapter of Salisbury, Index.

84. —— E58–61. *Four copies.*

85. CORRI, DOMENICO. D17 (xix). A New & Complete Collection of the Most Favourite Scots Songs Including a few English & Irish with proper Graces and Ornaments peculiar to their Character.... By Sig. Corri Edinburgh printed for & Sold by Corrie & Sutherland.... [1788] fol.

    Pp. 31. Imp., lacking arr. of each song for Fl., pp. (3), and Index, p. (1), at end of Coll. Sigr. Giordani composed 1 of the songs. Singers are: Mr. Du Bellamy, Miss Wheeler, Mr. Suett.

86. COURTEVILLE, RAPHAEL. M98 (i). A Song Set by Mr.

Courteville, and exactly engraved by Tho. Cross. [London, c. 1700] fol.

>Pp. (2). Begins Fly fly ye winged Cupids. This is the first surviving song in what was originally a much larger miscellaneous coll., paginated in MS, this song being pp. 116, 117.

87. —— M98 (x). A Song. . . . Sung by Mr. Hughs at the Theater in Drury-Lane. [London, c. 1700] fol.

>Pp. (2), with No. 239 sandwiched between. Begins To touch your Heart. Includes arr. for Fl.

88. CROFT, WILLIAM. D31. Musicus Apparatus Academicus, Being a Composition of Two Odes. . . . Perform'd . . . at Oxford on July 13th. 1713. The Words by the Reverend Mr. Ioseph Trapp . . . set to Musick by William Croft. . . . London Printed for the Author and are to be had at his House. . . . At Mrs. Turners . . . And at Richd. Mears. . . . [1720] fol.

>Pp. (1), 64. Place of publication, etc. occurs on a preceding full page engraving. Includes Preface. Followed by 2nd identical engraving before 2nd Ode, p. 27.

89. —— *M98 (xix). A Song Set by Mr W. Croft Sung by Mrs Hodgson. [London, c. 1720] fol.

>S.sh. Begins In Cloes sparkling, sparkling Eyes.

90. —— M106 (i). [Musica Sacra: or Select Anthems in Score. . . . Compos'd by Dr. William Croft. . . . Vol. I. London Printed for . . . John Walsh . . . and Joseph Hare. . . .] [1724] fol.

>Pp. (1), 4, (4), 184. Imp., with frontispiece, t-p. defective and pp. 183–4 missing (supplied by 2 MS. pages). Includes Ded. to George I, Licence, Preface, List of subscribers, Index.

91. —— M106 (ii). Musica Sacra [etc., as above]. . . . Vol. II. [etc., as above] [1725] fol.

>Pp. (2), 155. Includes Ded. to George, Prince of Wales, Index.

92. DAPHNE AND AMINTOR. B45 (ii). Daphne and Amintor a Comic Opera in One Act. . . . for the Voice and Harpsichord By the Author of The Maid of the Mill. London. Printed for and sold by Robert Bremner. . . . [1765] obl. fol.

>Pp. 30. A pastiche arr. by Samuel Arnold, the music by: [Anon—

VOCAL WORKS

Arnold?], Sigr. Cocchi, Sigr. Galluppi, Monsignier, Sigr. Picini, Mr. Shalon, Sigr. Vento. *The singers are:* Miss Young, Miss Wright, Mr. Vernon.

93. DEFESCH, WILLEM. M78 (vii). VI English Songs With Violins, and German Flutes, and a Through Bass for the Harpsicord. Sung by Miss Falkner. . . . Set to Music by W. Defesch London Printed for and Sold by the Author. . . . [*c.* 1748] fol.
    Pp. 9, altered in MS. to follow No. 137.

94. —— M77 (xxi). Polly . . . sung by Miss Falkner at Marybone Gardens. [London, *c.* 1750] fol.
    S.sh. Begins Spring renewing all things gay.

95. DERING, RICHARD. B25 (i). Cantus Primus. Cantica Sacra. Ad Duas & Tres Voces Composita, cum Basso continuo ad Organum. Authore Ricardo Deringo . . . Londini, Typis Guil. Godbid pro Joh. Playford. . . . MDCLXII. fol.
    In 4 pt-bks. Cantus Primus, *pp.* (2), 24; Cantus Secundus, *pp.* (2), 11; Bassus, *pp.* (2), 24; Bassus Continuus, *pp.* (2), 16. *Includes 1 piece by* Alex Grande. *Includes Ded. to Henrietta Maria, Dowager Queen by Playford, Index.* (*See No. 46.*)

96. DIBDIN, CHARLES. *D17 (ii). The Soldiers Life. a favorite Song Composed by Mr. Dibdin, . . . London, Printed & Sold by Preston. . . . [*c.* 1785] fol.
    Pp. (3). Begins This this my lad's a Soldiers life. *Includes arr. for Ger. Fl.*

97. —— *D17 (iii). When faintly gleams the doubtful Day. a favorite Hunting Song Composed by Mr. Dibdin, & Sung by him . . . & by Mr. Bannister in Liberty Hall. London, Printed & Sold by Preston. . . . [*c.* 1785] fol.
    Pp. 4. Includes arr. for Ger. Fl.

98. —— *D17 (iv). The Tinker. a favorite Comic Song Composed by Mr. Dibdin, . . . London, Printed & Sold by Preston. . . . [*c.* 1785] fol.
    Pp. 4. Begins A Tinker I am, my name's natty Sam. *Includes arr. for Ger. Fl. or Guitar.*

99. —— *D17 (v). Bright Gems that twinkle from afar. a favorite Song Composed by Mr. Dibdin, & Sung by him . . . & by Miss Romanzini in The Land of Enchantment. London, Printed & Sold by Preston. . . . [c. 1785] fol.

Pp. (3). Includes arr. for Ger. Fl.

100. —— *D17 (vi). Ere raging Seas between us roll. Sung by Mr. Incledon . . . at Vauxhall Gardens; written by a Lady of Distinction The Music by Mr. Dibdin. London, Printed & Sold by Preston. . . . [c. 1785] fol.

Pp. 3. Acc. for Kb. and Fl. in score.

101. —— D17 (vii). The Fox Chase. Hunting Song Sung . . . by Mr. Incledon, at Vauxhall Gardens: Composed by Mr. Dibdin. London, Printed & Sold by Preston. . . . [c. 1785] fol.

Pp. 4. Begins At the sound of the horn we rise in the morn. Includes arr. for Ger. Fl. or Guitar. Mentions 2nd Coll. of Songs by Mr. Hook. Acc. for Kb. and Fl. in score.

102. —— *D17 (viii). What argufies Pride & Ambition. a favorite Drinking Song, Composed by Mr. Dibdin, . . . London, Printed & Sold by Preston. . . . [c. 1785] fol.

Pp. 6, 7, (8). Includes arr. for Ger. Fl.

103. —— *D17 (ix). When Fairies are lighted by Nights Silver Queen. a favorite Song Composed by Mr. Dibdin & Sung by him . . . & by Mrs. Crouch in Liberty Hall. London, Printed & Sold by Preston. . . . [c. 1785] fol.

Pp. 4. Includes arr. for Ger. Fl.

104. —— *D17 (x). Who to my wounds a balm advises. a favorite Song Composed by Mr. Dibdin, & Sung by him . . . & by Mrs. Crouch in Liberty Hall. London, Printed & Sold by Preston. . . . [c. 1785] fol.

Pp. 4. Includes arr. for Ger. Fl.

105. *—— D17 (xi). Nothing Like Grog. a favorite Drinking Song Composed by Mr. Dibdin, . . . London, Printed & Sold by Preston. . . . [c. 1785] fol.

Pp. 10, 11, (12). Begins A plague of those musty old lubbers. Includes arr. for Ger. Fl.

VOCAL WORKS

106. —— *D17 (xii). Jack Ratlin a favorite Song Sung by Mr. Bannister in Liberty Hall, Composed by C. Dibdin. London, Printed & Sold by Preston. ... [c. 1785] fol.

> Pp. (3). Begins Jack Ratlin was the ablest Seaman. Includes arr. for Guitar or Ger. Fl. 3 other songs by Dibdin advertised.

107. —— *D17 (xiii). Lawyers Pay You With Words a favorite Song Composed by Mr. Dibdin. ... London, Printed & Sold by Preston. ... [c. 1785] fol.

> Pp. 4. Includes arr. for Ger. Fl. or Guitar.

108. —— *D17 (xiv). 'Oh Men what silly things you are' A Favorite Rondo Sung by Miss Romanzini in the Graces, Composed by C. Dibdin. London, Printed & Sold by T. Preston. ... [c. 1782] fol.

> Pp. 4. Includes arr. for Ger. Fl.

109. —— *D17 (xv). The Race Horse a Celebrated Song Sung by Mr. Bannister in Liberty Hall and Mr. Dignum. ... Composed by C. Dibdin. London, Printed & Sold by T. Preston. ... [c. 1785] fol.

> Pp. 4. Begins See the Course throng'd with gazers. Includes arr. for Ger. Fl.

110. DIVINE COMPANION. A8 (ii). The Divine Companion: Being A Collection Of New And Easie Hymns and Anthems, For one, two and three Voices Compos'd by the best Masters. ... London, Printed by William Pearson ... for Henry Playford. ... 1701. 8°

> Pp. 96. Composers are: Mr. Samuel Akeroyde, Dr. John Blow, Mr. Jeremy Clarke, Mr. Tho. Clark, Mr. John Church, Mr. William Croft, Mr. Robert King, Dr. Turner, Mr. Weldon. Includes list of Playford's pubs., Ded. to John, Archbishop of York by Playford, Preface, Verses.

111. A11. Another copy.

112. DIVINE HARMONY. A7. Divine Harmony; or a new Collection of select Anthems, Us'd at Her Majesty's Chappels Royal, Westminster Abbey. ... London, Printed and Sold

by S. Keble ... C. King ... and J. Hazard.... 1712. [London] 8⁰

Pp. (*5*), *104*, (*8*). *Words only. Includes 'To the Reader', Errata, Index, List of composers.*

113. DUNI, EGIDIO ROMUALDO. D97. Arie Composte per Il Regio Teatro, Cantate dal Signor Carlo Broschi Farinello; ... Egidio Duni. Londra nel MDCCXXXVII. obl. fol.

Pp. 22. In score. 6 arias from Duni's 'Demofoonte', performed King's Theatre 1732. Ded. to Signora Madamigella Caterina Edwin.

114. DUPUIS, THOMAS SANDERS. E50. Cathedral Music in Score. ... By the Late T. S. Dupuis. ... Carefully Revised by John Spencer Esqr. Volume I London. Published for the Benefit of the New Musical Fund at Smart's Music Warehouse ... [1797] fol.

Pp. 2, (*2*), *130. Includes Address by Spencer, Index.*

115. —— E51. Cathedral Music [etc., as above]. ... Volume [2]. London. [etc., as above] fol.

Pp. (*1*), *132. The vol. no. has been formed in pencil from 'I'. Includes Index.*

116. —— E52. Organ Part to the Cathedral Music. ... By the Late T. S. Dupuis. Adapted by John Spencer Esqr. [etc., as above] fol.

Pp. (*1*), *139. Includes Index.*

117. DURAND, CASPAR CHRYSOSTOMUS. *B26. Exultans Halleluja, h.e. Novum & excellens Opus Musicum, Cantatis, Jubilatis, Laudatis, & Exultatis, refertum, cum plerumq; adjecto Alleluja, duar: trium & quatuor vocum: publici juris factum per Casparum Chrysostomum Durandum. Vox Prima. Dresdae, Stanno Seyffertino, 1667. 4⁰

In 4 pt-bks. Vox Prima (Canto, Canto primo), *pp. 92*, (*1*); Vox Secunda (Canto 2do, Alto), *pp. 90*, (*2*) (*includes 1 p. of errata for all 4 pts.*); Vox Tertia & Quarta (Basso, *T. and B. on opposite pages*), *pp. 37*, (*2*); Bassus Continuus (Continovo, Basso Continovo, Organo), *pp. 54. Each pt. includes Index and Address to* Vir Clarissime *except BC, which has Ded. to* Lectorem and Philomusum. *Music consists of motets: a2*—Omnes gentes plaudite manibus. Jubilate Deo omnis terra. Cantate Domino, Psalmum dicite. Cantate Domino Canticum novum. Cantate Domino . . . Jubilate. Jubilate Deo, omnis Terra. Laudate Dominum omnes gentes. Laudate Nomen Domini. Laudate Dominum. . . . Laudate. Laudate Dominum de Coelis. Cantate Domino Canticum novum. Laudate Dominum in Sanctis. *a3*—Exultate Deo. Laudate Pueri Dominum. Lauda Anima mea Dominum. Laude Jerusalem. *a4*—Exultate Justi. Laudate Dominum Te Terra. *All with BC.*

118. EBDON, THOMAS. D15. Sacred Music, Composed for the Use of the Choir of Durham by Thomas Ebdon. . . . London. Printed for the Author, and Sold by Preston & Son. . . . [*c.* 1790] fol.

Pp. 5, (1), 108. Includes Ded. to Queen Charlotte Sophia, List of Subscribers. 2 copies, 1 imp.

119. —— E33 a. *Another copy. Imp., lacking Ded.*

120. —— M107 (i). *Another copy. Imp., t-p. only.*

121. —— D16. A Second Volume, of Sacred Music in Score . . . by Thomas Ebdon. . . . London, Published for the Author, by Goulding D'Almaine, Potter & Co. . . . [1811] fol.

Pp. 6, 122. Ded. to Dean and Chapter of Durham. 9 copies, some lacking t-p.

122. —— M107 (ii). *Another copy. Imp., lacking pp. 103–22.*

123. —— *D17 (i). Six Favorite Songs for the Voice with an Accompaniment for the Piano-Forte, Composed by Thomas Ebden of Durham. Op. 4th. Printed by G. Goulding. . . . London. [*c.* 1797] fol.

Pp. 18. In score. Acc. for 2 Vls. and Kb., with arr. for Ger. Fl. for Nos. 2 and 5. Titles are: Fancy;[1] The Sympathizing Tear;[2] Content;[3] Lapland Song;[4] Away to the Woodlands away;[5] O what had my Youth with Ambition to do.[6]

[1] *Begins* Fancy leads the fetter'd senses.
[2] *Begins* Let all your boast of wealth and Love.
[3] *Begins* O'er Moorlands and Mountains, rude, barren & bare.
[4] *Begins* Snows are dissolving on Torne's rude side.
[5] *Begins* When Phebus begins Just to peep o'er the Hills.
[6] *Begins* MY Sheep I've forsaken and left my Sheep hook.

VOCAL WORKS

124. ECCLES, JOHN. M98 (iv). I Gently touch'd her Hand A Song Set by Mr. Iohn Eccles. [London, *c.* 1710] fol.

   Pp. (2). *Include sarr. for Fl. Followed by p.* (2) *of unidentified 2-page song* Sung by Mrs Campion of the Theater Royall.

125. —— M98 (ix). A Song in the Fair Penitant Sung by Mrs Hudson Set by Mr Eccles. [London, *c.* 1704] fol.

   S.sh. Begins Stay, ah stay, ah turn. *Includes arr. for Fl.*

126. —— *M98 (xiii). A Song in the Villain Sung by Mrs. Hodgson. [London, *c.* 1704] fol.

   S.sh. Begins Find me a lonely Cave. *Paginated* 33.

127. —— M98 (xiv). A Song in the Farce call'd Women will have their Wills Sung by Mr. Gouge. [London, *c.* 1700] fol.

   S.sh. Begins Belinda's pretty, pretty pleasing Form. *Includes arr. for Fl. Paginated* 120.

128. —— *M98 (xxiv). A Song Set by Mr. John Eccles [London, 1699?] fol.

   Pp. (2). *Begins* Ye gentle gales that fan the Air. *Includes arr. for Fl.*

129. —— *M98 (xxiii). A Song in the Chances Set to Musick by Mr Iohn Eccles Sung by Mr Wiltshire and exactly engrav'd by Tho: Cross. [London, *c.* 1700] fol.

   Pp. (2). *Begins* Wasted with Sighs. *Words by* Sr. Robt. Howard.

130. —— *M98 (xxv). A Song in the Mad Lover Sung by Mrs Bracegirdle. [London, *c.* 1661] fol.

   Pp. (2). *Begins* Must then a faithful Lover go. *Includes arr. for Fl. Paginated* 86 *on p.* (1).

131. —— *M98 (xliv). A Song in the Opera call'd the British Enchanters Set by Mr I. Eccles. [London, *c.* 1706] fol.

   S.sh. Begins Plague us not with Idle storys. *Includes arr. for Fl.*

132. —— *M98 (xlv). A Song in the Opera call'd the British Enchanters Set by Mr I. Eccles. [London, *c.* 1706] fol.

   S.sh. Begins Help th' unpractis'd Conqu'ror.

VOCAL WORKS

133. —— *M98 (i). The Rich Rivall, the Words out of Cowleys Mistress, a Cantata Set by Mr. John Eccles,... [London, 1700?] fol.

> Pp. (3). *Begins recit.* They say you're Angry.

134. EMINENT MASTER. *M78 (xvi). A Song Set by an Eminent Master. Printed for J. Simpson.... [London, 1750?] fol.

> S.sh. *Begins* The Charms which blooming Beauty shews. *Includes arr. for Fl. Printer's colophon at foot of page.*

135. —— *M98 (xlvii). A Song Set by an Eminent Master. [London, 1750?] fol.

> S.sh. *Begins* Were Celia kind as she is Fair. *Includes arr. for Fl.*

136. FESTING, MICHAEL CHRISTIAN. M77 (v). Milton's May-Morning And several other English Songs Set to Musick by Michael Christian Festing.... London Printed & sold for the Author by J. Simpson.... [c. 1748] fol.

> Pp. 13. *In score. Includes Licence.*

137. —— M78 (vi). *Another copy. Imp., lacking t-p., pp. 1–4, 13.*

138. —— M100 (ii). An English Cantata Call'd Sylvia And two English Songs Set to Musick by Michael Christian Festing, London Printed by William Smith.... [1744] fol.

> Pp. 8. *Includes Licence, List of other published works by Festing.*

139. —— M68 (iii). *Another copy. Imp., pp. 6–8 defective.*

140. —— *M77 (iv). An Ode Upon the Return of His Royal Highness the Duke of Cumberland from Scotland. Set to Musick b[y] Michael Chr[istian Festing.] ... London Printed & sold for the A[uthor by J. Simpson].... [1745?] fol.

> Pp. 16. *Imp., t-p., pp. 1, 2 defective, pp. 9–12 missing. In score. Includes Licence.*

141. FINGER, GOTTFRIED. M98 (iii). I'o Victoria A Song Sett by Mr. Finger. [London, c. 1710] fol.

> S.sh. *Begins* I'o Victoria round my Temples bind. *Includes arr. for Fl.*

142. FISCHER, JOHANN CHRISTIAN. M77 (xxv). A Song Set to Musick by Mr. Fischer. [London, c. 1770] fol.
>
> S.sh. Begins How wellcome my Shepherd. In score.

143. FISHER, WILLIAM. M78 (xi). A New Song Set to Musick by Mr Fisher. [London, c. 1740] fol.
>
> S.sh. Begins Why has not love reflections Eyes? In score. For Fl., Vl., Voice, BC.

144. —— M77 (xxiv). Another copy.

145. FOETUS. *B23. Gasparis Casati et Pauli Cornetti Praecellentissimorum Ingeniorum Primi Partus Foetus Alter Trium IV. V. et VI Vocum vel Instrumentor. . . . Pars I. Antuerpiae. Apud Haeredes Petri Phalesii Typographi Musices ad Insigne Davidis Regis. MDCLVIII. 4°
>
> In 6 pt-bks. Pt. I (S. 1, A., T. 1, Vl. 1), pp. 47, (1); Pt. II (S. 2, A., T. 2, B.), pp. 43, (1); Pt. III (S. 2, T., T. 2, B., Vl. 2), pp. 46, (1); Pt. IV (B., Vls. 1 & 2, Bsn.), pp. 30, (1); Pt. V (T. 2, Quintus, Sesto, Vl. 2, Bsn.), pp. 15, (1); Pt. VI (BC), pp. 38, (1). Music consists of motets: Voice, 2 Vls.—Flores flores quantes. O dulcissima Maria. a3—Laetentur caeli. Quantum tibi debes. Beatus vir qui inventus. Salve Regina mater. Alma Redemptoris mater (Casati). Audi amantissime Iesu. Eja laudemus Magdadalenam (Cornetti). a2, 2 Vls.—Venite Reges gentium. O quam speciosa facta. a4—O suavis aura caeli. Missa concertata (Casati). Egredimini omnes. Voice, 2 Vls., Bsn.—Ab occidente suscitant. Quam pulchra est castagen. a2, Vl., Chitarone— Exulta, jubila & laetare. a5—Quo progrediar amantissime. O vos omnes qui caeli. a3, 2 Vls., Bsn.—Resonate coeli. a6— Litaniae Lauretanae (Cornetti). All with BC. Each pt. includes Index.

146. FOGGIA, FRANCESCO. *B27. Concentus Ecclesiastici Binis, Ternis, Quaternis, Quinisque Vocibus ad Organum concinandi. Auctore Francisco Foggia Romano. Sacrosanctae Basilicae Lateranensis Musical Praefecto. Cantus. Antuerpiae, Typis Haeredium Petri Phalesii. MDCLVIII. 4°
>
> In 5 pt-bks. Cantus (S. 1), pp. 35, (1); Altus (S. 2, A., T. 2), pp. 15, (1); Tenor (S. 2, T., B.), pp. 36; Bassus (T., B.), pp. 17, (1); B. Continuus (BC), pp. 38, (1). Music consists of motets: a2—

Iubilate exultate. Laetentur caeli. Laetentur omnes. O bone Iesu. Solemniis Mariae. *a3*—Cibavit nos Dominus. Ego sum panis. Iubilate cantate. Quare suspiras. Venite ad Cantus. Alma Redemptoris. *a4*—Beatus ille servus. Salve Iesu. *a5*—Salve Regina. *All with BC. Each pt. includes Index.*

147. FORGIVE. M77 (xxix). A new Song. [London, *c.* 1750] fol.

    S.sh. Begins Forgive thou fairest of thy kind. *Includes arr. for Ger. Fl.*

148. FREDDI, Amadio. *D29 (i). Motecta Unica Voce Decantando Auctore Amadeo Freddo in Cathedrale Tarvisina Musicae Praefecto. Opus VII. . . . Sub Signo Gardani Ventiis MDCXXIII. Apud Bartholomeum Magni. fol.

    Pp. (1), 29, (1). Includes Ded. to Rev. D. Victoria Porto, Index. Music consists of motets, mostly for S. or T., with 2 for A., in score with BC.: Peccavi. Alma Redemptoris. Salve Regina. O Altitudo. Ave Regina. . . . Mater Regis. Anima mea . . . adiuro vos. Vulnerasti. Cupio dissolvi. Misericordias. Ave Regina . . . Ave Domina. Dominus regit me. Deus Deus meus. Anima mea . . . invenerunt. Iam quod quesivi. Ego flos campi. Regina Celi. Surge amica. Quam pulcri sunt. Omnes sitientes. Veni Sponsa Christi.

149. FRENCH, Richard. M77 (xxvi). The Reconciliation Set by Mr French. [London, *c.* 1750] fol.

    S.sh. Begins With scorn repuls'd, poor Damon sought. *Includes arr. for Ger. Fl.*

150. —— *M77 (xxvii). The Retirement a new Song The Words by T. F. Set by Mr. Rd. French. [London, *c.* 1750] fol.

    S.sh. Begins Come dissolving Softness come.

151. GALLIARD, Johann Ernst. D35. Songs in the Opera of Calypso & Telemachus as they are Perform'd at the Queens Theatre. Compos'd by Mr. Galliard. the Words by Mr. Hughes London Printed for J. Walsh . . . & J. Hare. . . . [1712] fol.

    Pp. (1), 62. Includes list of 15 aria colls. from operas published by Walsh. Singers are: Signra Margarit(t)a, Mrs. Barbier, Sigra Manina, Mr. Leveridge, Mrs. Pearson.

152. GALUPPI, BALDASSARE. M95 (i). [The Favourite Songs in the Opera Call'd Enrico ...] London. Printed for I. W[alsh ...] [1750?] fol.

> Pp. 25–46. Imp., t-p., pp. 25–30 defective. The 2nd bk. of two with consecutive pagination; the 1st bk. (pp. 1–24) missing.

153. GENTLEMAN. D94. A Cantata and Six Songs Set to Musick by a Gentleman of Oxford London Printed by John Johnson ... and by Wm. Cross in Oxford. ... [c. 1750] fol.

> Pp. 4, 17. Some songs have Fl. obbligato. List of subscribers.

154. —— M77 (viii). Another copy.

155. —— *M77 (xxx). A Hunting Song by C. L. Esqr. The Music by a Gentleman of Wigan. [London, c. 1745] fol.

> S.sh. Begins The Morning is charming, All Nature is gay. Includes arr. for Recorder or Ger. Fl.

156. GODEFRIDO, F. *B30. Fasciculus Musicus e Carmelo Collectus Tribus, Quinque, Sex Vocis, et Instrum. Concertatus ac totidem Replentibus Adiunctis. Auctore F. Godefrido A. B. M. Magd. de Pazzi Carmelita Strict. Obs. Cantus Primus. Antuerpiae, Apud Haeredes Petri Phalesii, Typographi Musices. MDCLII. 4°

> In 11 pt-bks. Cantus Primus, pp. (1), 22, (1); Cantus Secundus, pp. 23, (1); Cantus Primus & Cantus Secundus Rip., pp. 27, (1), 2 pts. placed on opposite pages; Altus (A., T. 2), pp. 23, (1); Tenor (T., T. 1), pp. 23, (1); Altus & Tenor Ripien., pp. 27, (1), 2 pts. placed on opposite pages; Bassus (BC.), pp. 19, (1); Violino Primo (Vl. 1, Va., Cornetti 1 & 2), pp. 26, (1); Violino secundo (Vl. 1 & 2, Tenor viol), pp. 26, (1); Fagotto seu Basso Viol. cum Basso Ripieno (Bass rip., Bass viol, T. 2 rip., Bsn.), pp. 23, (1); B. Continuus, pp. (1), 23, (1). Cantus I includes Ded. to D. Paschasio Francisco Van De Cruyce. Each pt. includes Index. Music consists of motets: SSATB conc. & rip., 2 Vls.—Quis est hic. Te Deum Laudamus. Litaniae Lorettaneae. SS conc., SSATB rip., 2 Vls.—Regina coeli. SSATB conc. & rip., 2 Vls., Bsn.—Tantum ergo sacramentum. Ave stella matutina. SSATB conc. & rip., 2 Vls., Va., 2 Viols—Salve Regina. SSATB conc., ATTTB rip., 2 Cornetti, 3 Viols—Tantum ergo veneremur. SSATTB conc. & rip., 2 Vls.—Iubilate Deo. All with BC.

157. GRANDI, ALESSANDRO. D29 (ii). Del Signor Alessandro Grandi Motetti a Voce Sola Novamente Ristampati. ... Stampa del Gardano. In Venetia MDCXXVIII. Appresso Bartolomeo Magni. fol.
    Pp. 48. Includes Ded. to Marc' Antonio Cornaro, senior Abbot of St. Mark, Index.

158. GREENE, MAURICE. *M158 (iv). Cantata by Dr. Greene. [London, 1750?] fol.
    Pp. 5. Imp., lacking t-p.; the above taken from p. 2. Begins Beneath a Beach as Strephon laid. *Consists of recit., aria, recit., aria, duet.*

159. —— M100 (i). A Cantata and Four English Songs Set to Musick [by Dr. Greene. London. Printed for I. Walsh ...] [c. 1742] fol.
    Pp. 12. Includes Licence dated 27. ii. 1741–2. Imp., t-p. defective.

160. —— M78 (xvii). The Snow Drop Set by Dr. Greene. [London, c. 1735] fol.
    S.sh. Begins With Head reclin'd. *Includes arr. for Fl.*

161. HANDEL, GEORGE FRIDERIC. E1–40. *Arnold's Collected Edition. fol. London, 1787–97.*
    M1–44. *Another copy in larger format and differing in contents of vols. and in some other respects:* E1, M1—Athalia, *pp. 192;* E2, M2—Theodora, *pp. 192;* E3, M3—Messiah, *pp. 219;* E4 (i), M4 (v)—Dettingen Te Deum, *pp. 104;* E4 (ii), M4 (iv)—Utrecht Jubilate, *pp. 44 (in M4 (iv) the 'Symphony' is misplaced between the 'Dettingen Te Deum' and the 'Te Deum 1720');* E4 (iii), M4 (i)—Te Deum 1737, *pp. 22;* E4 (iv), M4 (ii)—Te Deum 1719, *pp. 88;* E4 (v), M4 (iii)—Utrecht Te Deum, *pp. 48;* E4 (vi), M4 (vi)—Te Deum 1720, *pp. 31;* E5 (i), M5—Sosarme, *pp. 116;* E5 (ii), M8—Acis and Galatea, *pp. 103;* E6, M7—Semele, *pp. 191;* E7, M9—Teseo, *pp. 159;* E8, M10—Hercules, *pp. 248;* E9, M11—Judas Maccabaeus, *pp. 195;* E10, M12—Giulio Cesare, *pp. 170, (2), includes List of subscribers;* E11, M16—Joshua, *pp. 169, (2), includes ibid.;* E12, M14—Samson, *pp. 216;* E13 (i), M15 (i)—An Ode for Queen Anne 1713, *pp. 44;* E13 (ii), M13 (i)—Six Sonatas for Two Violins, *pp. 60;* E13 (iii), M13 (ii)—Seven Sonatas or Trios, *pp. 59;* E14 (i), M17 (i)—

VOCAL WORKS

Twelve Grand Concertos, *pp. 220;* E14 (ii), M17 (ii)—The Music in the Alchymist, *pp. 8, but pp. 4–8 missing in M17 (ii), another copy E22 (v);* E15 (i), M15 (ii)—The Choice of Hercules, *pp. 80;* E15 (ii), M18—Alexander's Feast, *pp. 141, (2), includes List of subscribers;* E16, M19—Belshazzar, *pp. 219;* E17, M20—Anthems Composed for the Duke of Chandos, *paginated separately: 42, 32, 52, 39, 59, 31;* E18, M21—*ibid., paginated separately: 47, 40, 66, 48, 60, 30, the last missing in E18;* E19 (i), M38 (i)—Anthem for the Wedding of Frederick and the Princess of Sax-Gotha, *pp. 87;* M39 (i)—Anthem for the Victory at Dettingen 1743, *pp. 44;* E19 (ii), M39 (ii)—Anthem for the Coronation of George IId. *pp. 18;* E19 (iii), M39 (iii)—*ibid., pp. 28;* E19 (iv), M39 (iv)—*ibid., pp. 44, (2), includes List of subscribers;* E19 (v), M39 (v)—*ibid., pp. 56;* E20, M24—Israel in Egypt, *pp. 282,* (**2**), *includes List of subscribers;* E21, M26—The Occasional Oratorio, *pp. 270;* E22 (i), M27—Ode on St. Cecilia's Day, *pp. 74;* E22 (ii), M22—Alcides, *pp. 80;* E22 (iii), M6 (i)—The Celebrated Water Musick, *pp. 56;* E22 (iv), M6 (ii)—The Musick for the Royal Fireworks, *pp. 20;* E23, M28—Joseph, *pp. 214, t-p. missing in M28;* E24, M29—Saul, *pp. 252,* (1) = *Index;* E25, M30—Jephtha, *pp. 230,* (1) = *Index;* E26, M31 (i)—Six Concertos for the Organ, *paginated separately: 52, 23, 30, 16, 11, 13;* E27, M31 (ii)—A Second Set of Six Concertos for the Organ, *pp. 184, (2), includes List of subscribers;* E28 (i), M32 (i)—Lessons for the Harpsichord, *pp. 60;* E28 (ii), M32 (ii)—A Second Set of Lessons for the Harpsichord, *pp. 60, pp. 42–44 missing and supplied in MS in E28 (ii);* E28 (iii), M32 (iii)—A Third Set of Lessons for the Harpsichord, *pp. 20;* E28 (iv), M32 (iv)—Six Fugues for the Organ, *pp. 16;* E28 (v), M25—Concertante in Nine Parts, *pp. 45;* E29, M33—Susanna, *pp. 205;* E30, M34—Esther, *pp. 185;* E31, M35 (ii)—Deborah, *pp. 272,* (3) = *Index, List of subscribers;* E32, M36—Agrippina, *pp. 174, including 1p. copy of excerpt in Handel's MS.;* E33, M37—L'Allegro, *pp. 149;* E34, M23—Solomon, *pp. 344;* E35, M40—Alexander Balus, *pp. 210;* E36, M41—The Triumph of Time and Truth, *pp. 199;* E37 (i), M42 (ii)—Concertos (commonly called the Hautboy Concertos), *pp. 100;* E37 (ii), M35 (i)—Twelve Sonatas for the German Flute, *pp. 44;* E38 (i), M42 (i)—La Resurrezione, *pp. 105;* E38 (ii), M39 (vi)—Masque, *pp. 54;* E39 (i), M44 (i)—Thirteen Chamber Duetto's and Twelve Cantatas, *pp. 58;* E39 (ii), M43 (i)—Two Trios and Four Cantatas, *pp. 77;* E39 (iii), M43 (ii)—Thirteen Chamber Duetto's and Twelve Cantatas, *pp. 92;* E40 (i), M44 (ii)—

VOCAL WORKS 27

Concertos &c. for the Organ, *pp. 80;* E40 (ii), M38 (ii)—
Anthem for the Funeral of Queen Caroline, *pp. 81.*

OPERAS

162. —— D49. The Favourite Songs in the Opera Call'd Alcina Compos'd by Mr. Handel Second Collection London Printed & Sold by I. Walsh. . . . [1735] fol.

Pp. 24. In score. Singers are: Sigr. Carestini, Sigra Strada, Mr. Beard, Mr. Savage, Miss Young, the Boy.

163. —— D47. Arminius an Opera. . . . Compos'd by Mr. Handel. London, Printed for and Sold by I. Walsh. . . . [1737] fol.

Pp. (*1*), *91. In score. Includes list of Handel's works published by Walsh. Singers are:* Sigra. Strada, Sigr. Hannibali, Sigra. Negri, Mr. Beard, Mr. Reinhold, Sigr. Conti, Sigra. Bertolli.

164. —— D32. The Favorite Aires in the Opera of Flavius London, Printed for R. Meares. . . . [1723] fol.

Pp. 24. Overture and 8 arias in score. Singers are: Sigra. Cuzzoni, Sigr. Senesini, Mrs. Robinson, Sigr. Berenstatt.

165. —— D42 (i). Il Radamisto Opera. . . . Composta dal Sigre, Georgio Frederico Handel London Publisht by the Author. Printed and Sold by Richard Meares . . . & by Christopher Smith. . . . [1720] fol.

Pp. (*1*), *121. In score. Includes Licence.*

166. —— D42 (ii). Arie Aggiunte di Radamisto Opera Rapresentata nel Regio Teatro. . . . Composta dal Sigre, Georgio Frederico Handel London Publisht by the Author. Printed and Sold by Richard Meares . . . & by Christopher Smith. . . . [1721] fol.

Pp. 38. In score.

167. —— D43. Rodelinda. An Opera Compos'd by Mr. Handel. Engrav'd Printed and Sold by J. Cluer. . . . [*c.* 1728] fol.

Pp. (*3*), *108. In score. Includes List of subscribers and of pubs. by Cluer and B. Creake. Singers are:* Sga. Cuzzoni, Sgr. Borossini, Sga. Dotti, Sgr. Boschi, Sgr. Senesino, Sgr. Paccini.

168. —— *D44. Rodelinda. Regina de' Longobardi. Drama. Da Rapresentarsi nel Regio Teatro di Hay-Market, per La Reale

Academia di Musica. London. Printed and Sold at the Opera-Office in the Hay-Market. MDCCXXV. sm. 8º

Pp. (5), 77. *Libretto only, in Italian and English, printed on opposite pages. Includes* Ded. in Italian to My Lord Conte di Essex *by* Haym, Argument *in Italian and English, and* Dramatis Personae *ditto.*

169. —— M77 (x). [The Favourite Songs in the Opera call'd Sosarmes. London Printed for and sold by I: Walsh. . . .] [1732] fol.

Pp. 26. Imp., only pp. 16–22 remaining. In score. Singers are: Sigra. Strada, Sigr. Bertolli, Sigr. Montagnana.

169a. —— *M98 (lxxxiii). Sung by Signra Francesca Vanini Boschi in the Opera of Pyrrhus Compos'd by Mr Handell [London, c. 1711] fol.

S.sh. Begins Houn non so che nel cor.

170. —— *M98 (lxxxiv). The Famous mock Song, to Houn non so che nel cor. Sung by Signra Boschi, in the Opera Pyrrhus, Corectly Engrav'd. [London, c. 1710] fol.

S.sh. Begins Good folks come here, I'll sing. *Voice pt. only, with bass ritornelli. Includes arr. for Fl.*

171. —— M94 (iii). Handel's Bass Songs from all the Operas Price 5s. London Printed for & sould by I: Walsh. . . . [c. 1745] fol.

Pp. 47. In score. Irregular pagination. Operas are: Ariodante, Atalanta, Berenice, Deidamia, Ezio, Faramondo, Orlando, Ottone, Parthenope, Ptolomy, Siroe, Sosarmes, Tolomeo. Singers are: Sigr. Boschi, Mr. Savage, Mr. Reinhold, Mr. Waltz, Sigr. Montagnana, Sigr. Riemschneider. *All songs in Italian save last one, which has an English translation by H. Carey.*

ORATORIOS

172. —— M80 (ii). Alexander Balus an Oratorio Set to Musick by Mr. Handel. London. Printed for I. Walsh. . . . 1748. fol.

Pp. 96, though no. 94, as there are 2 unno. pages between pp. 26, 27. Imp., lacking p. 34, and with pp. 1–33 bound in after p. 94. In score. Includes Licence, List of recent pubs. by Walsh. Singers are: Mr. Lowe, Mr. Reinhold, Sigra Casarini, Sigra Galli, Mrs. Sibilla.

VOCAL WORKS

173. —— M80 (iii). Songs in Alexander Balus The Remainer of this Oratorio in Score will be Publish'd next week. Printed for J. Walsh ... 1748. fol.

Pp. 33, though no. 31, as there are 2 unno. pages between pp. 26, 27. Singers are: Sigra Casarini, Sigra Galli, Mr Lowe, Mr Reinhold, Mrs. Sibilla.

174. —— D45. Alexander's Feast Or The Power of Musick. An Ode Wrote in Honour of St. Cecilia by Mr. Dryden. Set to Musick by Mr. Handel. Together with the Cantata ... as Perform'd at the Theatre Royal, ... Publish'd by the Author. London. Printed for & Sold by I. Walsh.... [1738] fol.

Pp. (2), 193. In score. The cantata, pp. 168–90, begins Cecilia volgi un sguardo *and is in Italian throughout; the singers are:* Sigr. Aragoni, Signra Strada. *The oratorio singers are:* Mr. Beard, Sigra. Strada, Miss Young, Mr. Erard. *There is an* Additional Song Sung by Sigr. Hannibali, *pp. 192–3.*

175. —— M81 (i). Songs in L'Allegro ed Il Penseroso. The Words taken from Milton. Set to Musick by Mr. Handel. London Printed for & sould by I: Walsh.... [1740] fol.

Pp. 36. In score. Singers are: Sigra. Francessina, Mr. Beard, Mr. Reinhold.

176. —— M81 (ii). Songs in L'Allegro ed Il Penseroso [etc., as above] by Mr. Handel. 2d. Colln. London [etc., as above].

Pp. 29, double pagination. In score. Singers are: Sigra. Francessina, Mr. Beard, Mr. Reinhold, Mr. Savage.

177. —— M77 (xxxiv). Sung by Mr. Beard in L'Allegro e Penseroso by Mr. Handel. [London, *c.* 1745] fol.

S.sh. Begins Let me wander not unseen. *Imp. Includes arr. for Fl.*

178. —— M81 (xi). The Most Celebrated Songs in the Oratorio Call'd Athalia Compos'd by Mr. Handel. London. Printed for & Sold by I. Walsh. [1733] fol.

Pp. 29. In score. Singers are: Sigra. Strada, Sigr. Carestini, Mr. Beard, the Boy, Miss Young, Mr. Waltz.

179. —— M79 (iii). Belshazzar an Oratorio Set to Musick by Mr. Handel. London. Printed for I. Walsh. . . . [1745] fol.

> Pp. (1), 85. In score. Singers are: Sigra. Francessina, Mr. Beard, Mr. Reinhold, Miss Robinson. Includes List of Walsh's pubs.

180. —— *M81 (iv). The Most Celebrated Songs in the Oratorio Call'd Deborah Compos'd by Mr. Handel. London. Printed for & Sold by I. Walsh. [1733] fol.

> Pp. 15. In score. Singers are: Sigra. Strada, Sigr. Carestini.

181. —— *M81 (v). The Most Celebrated Songs [etc., as above, with '2d. Colln.' written in ink below 'Deborah']

> Pp. 23–42. In score.

182. —— *M81 (vi). The Most Celebrated Songs [etc., as above, with '3d.' written in ink below Plate No.]

> Pp. 12. In score.

183. —— *M81 (vii). The Most Celebrated Songs [etc., as above, but in fact 4th Coll.]

> Pp. 1–22. In score.

184. —— M81 (vi a). [Esther. An Oratorio in Score. . . . London, Printed for Wright & Co. . . .] [1780] fol.

> Pp. (6). Imp., only 3 of 5 songs included at the end of the above and printed from Walsh's plates of c. 1750. Singer is Sigr (sic) Strada.

185. —— M79 (iv). Hercules in Score. Compos'd by Mr. Handel. Printed for I. Walsh. . . . [1745] fol.

> Pp. (2), 97. Imp., pp. 95–97 defective. Singers are: Mrs. Cibber, Miss Robinson, Mr. Beard, Sigra Francesina, Mr. Reinhold. Includes Licence, List of Walsh's pubs.

186. —— M79 (i). Joseph and his Brethren an Oratorio Set to Musick by Mr. Handel. London. Printed for I. Walsh. . . . [1744] fol.

> Pp. (1), 85. In score. Includes List of Walsh's pubs., Index.

187. —— M93. Another copy, with List and Index placed between Pts. I and II.

VOCAL WORKS

188. —— M92 (i). Joshua an Oratorio Set to Musick by Mr. Handel London. Printed for I. Walsh. . . . [1748] fol.

    Pp. (2), 66. Imp., pp. 3–20, 63–66 missing or defective. In score. Singers are: Mr. Reinhold, Sigra Galli, Sigra. Casarini, Mr. Lowe.

189. —— E42. Messiah An Oratorio In Score As it was Originally Perform'd. Composed by Mr. Handel To which are added His additional Alterations. London. Printed & Sold by H. Wright Successor to the late Mr. J. Walsh. . . . [1800?] fol.

    Pp. (3), 188, 35. Includes List of subscribers, Index, Appendix. T-p. preceded by engraving of Handel.

190. —— A5 (ii). Messiah in Three Parts. Durham: Printed by George Sowler [1770?] 8°

    Pp. 16, with pp. 11, 12 placed before pp. 9, 10. Words only. (See No. 70.)

191. —— M92 (ii). [The Occasional Oratorio. London. Printed for I. Walsh.] [1746] fol.

    Imp., only pp. 21–38 remaining. In score. Singers are: Sigra. Galli, Sigra. Frasi, Mr. Lowe, Mr. Reinhold, Sigra. Sibilla.

192. —— M91. Samson an Oratorio The Words taken from Milton Set to Musick by Mr. Handel London Printed for I. Walsh. . . . [1743] fol.

    Pp. (1), 91. In score. Overtures and arias only. T-p. preceded by engraving of Handel. Includes Index. Singers are: Sigra. Avolio, Mr. Lowe, Miss Edwards, Mr. Beard, Mrs. Clive, Mr. Reinhold, Mrs. Cibber, Mr. Savage.

193. —— M82. Samson an Oratorio The Words taken from Milton Set to Musick by Mr. Handel London Printed for I. Walsh. . . . [c. 1763] fol.

    Pp. 178, irregular pagination. Imp., with many pages missing or defective. In score. T-p. preceded by engraving of Handel. Singers are: Sigra. Aviolo, Mr. Lowe, Miss Edwards, Mr. Beard, Sigra. Frasi, Mrs. Clive, Mr. Reinhold, Mrs. Cibber, Mr. Savage. *Same plates as No. 192 but including recits. and choruses.*

194. —— M81 (viii). The Most Celebrated Songs in the Oratorio

VOCAL WORKS

Call'd Saul Compos'd by Mr. Handel. London. Printed for & Sold by I. Walsh. . . . [1735] fol.

Pp. 11. In score. Consists of the Overture.

195. —— M81 (ix). [The Most Celebrated Songs etc., as above, but 2nd Coll.]

Pp. 20. Imp., lacking t-p. In score. Singers are: Sigra. Francessina, Mr. Russell, Mrs. Arne.

196. —— M81 (x). [The Most Celebrated Songs etc., as above, but 3rd Coll.]

Pp. 17. Imp., lacking t-p. In score. Singers are: Mr. Beard, Mr. Russell, Sigra. Francessina, Mrs. Arne.

197. —— M79 (ii). Semele. . . . Set to Musick by Mr. Handel. London Printed for I. Walsh. . . . [1744] fol.

Pp. (2), 85. In score. Includes Licence, List of pubs. Singers are: Sigra. Francessina, Mr. Sullivan, Sigr. (*sic*) Avolio, Miss Young, Mr. Beard, Mr. Reinhold.

198. —— M80 (i). [Susanna. An oratorio. . . . Printed for I. Walsh. 1749] fol.

Pp. (1), 94. Imp., with t-p., pp. (1), 1–62, 73–90 missing or defective. Includes Licence.

199. —— M86. [Handel's Songs Selected from His Latest Oratorios For Concerts. For Violins &c. in Six Parts . . . London. Printed for I. Walsh. . . .] [1749–59] obl. fol.

Pp. 170, (1). Imp., lacking t-p., pp. 1–92, 121–32 missing or defective. In 4 Vols., Vol. IV pp. 137–70. Vocal pt. and fig. bass. Includes Index.

200. —— M84. [Handel's Songs etc., as above]

Pp. 61, (1). Imp., lacking t-p., pp. 1–50. Vl. I and Fls. I and II pt-bks. Includes Index.

201. —— M87. [Handel's Songs etc., as above]

Imp., lacking all pages. Vl. II pt-bk.

202. —— M94 (ii). A Second Set of Favourite Bass Songs Collected from the Late Oratorios Compos'd by Mr. Handel. These songs

VOCAL WORKS 33

are proper for two violoncellos. . . . London. Printed for I. Walsh. . . . [c. 1750] fol.

Pp. 45, double pagination. In score. Singers are: Mr. Reinhold, Mr. Savage.

MISCELLANEOUS

203. —— E62. Thirteen Celebrated Italian Duets, Accompanied with the Harpsichord or Organ. never before Printed. Composed by the late Mr. Handel. . . . London. Printed for Wm. Randall (successor to the late Mr. John Walsh). . . . [1775] fol.

Pp. 3, 91. Includes List of Subscribers, Index.

204. —— *M81 (iii). The Songs in the Ode wrote by Mr. Dryden for St. Cecilia's Day. Set by Mr. Handel. London Printed for & sould by I. Walsh. . . . [1739] fol.

Pp. 23. In score. Singers are: Sigra. Francessina, Mr. Beard.

205. HARK. M77 (xv). A new Song Sung by Mr. Lowe & Mrs. Arne at Vaux Hall. [London, c. 1746] fol.

S. sh. Begins Hark, hark, o'er the Plains.

206. HARMONIA. B4. Harmonia Sacra: Or Divine Hymns and Dialogues: With a Thorow-Bass. . . . Composed by the Best Masters of the Last and Present Age. . . . Printed by Edward Jones, for Henry Playford. . . . MDCLXXXVIII. [London] fol.

Pp. (4), 79, (1). 1st Bk., 1st ed. Includes Ded. to Thomas, Bishop of Bath and Wells, To the Reader *(both by Playford), List of Playford's pubs. Composers are:* [Anon.], Dr. John Blow, Mr. Pelham Humphreys, Mr. Matthew Locke, Mr. Henry Purcell, Mr. William Turner.

207. —— *B3 (ii). Harmonia Sacra: [etc., as above] The Second Book. . . . [etc., as above] MDCXCIII. [London] fol.

Pp. (4), 74. 1st ed. Includes Ded. to Henry Aldrich, Dean of Christ Church by Playford, Verses, Index. Composers are: [Anon.], Mr. Barrincloe, Dr. John Blow, Signior Giacomo Carissime, Mr. Jeremiah Clarke, Signior Gratiani, Mr. Robert King, Mr. Daniel Purcell, Mr. Henry Purcell.

208. —— B3 (i). Harmonia Sacra: Or Divine Hymns and Dialogues; With a Thorough-Bass. . . . Composed by the Best Masters of

the Last and Present Age. . . . The first Book. The 2d Edition very much enlarged and corrected; also four Excellent Anthems by the late Mr. Henry Purcell's never before Printed. . . . London; Printed by William Pearson, for Henry Playford . . . and John Sprint . . . 1703. fol.

Pp. (*1*), *130*, (*2*). *Includes Ded. to Queen Anne,* To the Reader (*both by Playford*), *Index. Composers are:* Dr. John Blow, Mr. John Church, Mr. Pelham Humphryes, Mr. Matthew Lock, Mr. Henry Purcell, Dr. William Turner, Mr. John Weldon.

209. HARMONIA SACRA GLOCESTRIENSIS. D18. Harmonia Sacra Glocestriensis. or Select Anthems. . . . a Te-Deum and Jubilate Together with a Voluntary for the Organ. Compos'd by Mr. William Hine. . . . [London, 1731] fol.

Pp. (*4*), *53. Includes Ded.* To all Lovers of Divine Harmony by A. H., *List of subscribers, and a* Te Deum, set by Mr. Henry Hall.

210. HADYN, FRANZ JOSEPH. D12. [Die Schoepfung. Ein Oratorium. . . . The Creation. An Oratorio. . . . Vienna 1800] fol.

Pp. 303. Imp., lacking t-p. Text in German and English.

211. HAYM, NICCOLÒ FRANCESCO. M98 (lxxii). Climene. Sung by Mrs. Toft in ye Opera of Pyrrhus & Demetrius Signr. Nicolini Haym. fol.

S. sh. Begins Gentle Sighs, a while releive (sic) us. *Includes arr. for Fl. P. 14. From same Coll. as No. 266.*

212. —— *M98 (lxxiv). Sung by the Barroness in the Opera call'd Pyrrhus and Demetrius Compos'd by Signr. Nicolino Haym fol.

S.sh. Begins Soft Ioys young loves gay pleasure. *Includes arr. for Fl. P. 51 of Coll. No. 265.*

213. —— M98 (lxxvii). Sung by Signra Margarita, in the Opera call'd Pyrrhus & Demetrius. Compos'd by Sigr Nicolino Haym. fol.

S. sh. Begins Too lovely Cruel Fair. *Includes arr. for Fl. P. 8 of Coll. No. 265.*

214. HEIGHINGTON, MUSGRAVE. *M78 (xiv). The Dream on Anacreon A Greek Ode publish'd by Milius Portius. translated into English, and set to Musick by Dr. Musgrave Heighington. [London, *c.* 1745] fol.

S.sh. Begins When gentle Sleep had charm'd my Breast. *Paginated* 26.

215. —— M77 (xviii). Upon a Lady being drown'd ... set by Dr. M. Heighington. [London, *c.* 1760] fol.

S. sh. Begins Fast by the Margin of the Sea.

216. HENNIO, AEGIDIO. *B32. Moteta Sacra Duarum, Trium, Quatuor cum vocum, tum instrumentorum cum Basso Continuo, Authore Aegidio Hennio, ... Musicae Praefecto, Canonico, & Cantore Ecclesiae Collegiatae S. Ioannis Evangelistae Leodii. Liber Primus. Cantus. Antuerpiae, Apud Haeredes Petri Phalesii Typographi Musices ad insigne Davidis Regis. MDCXLIX. fol.

In 5 pt-bks. Cantus Primus (*S., S. 1, A., T., T. 1*), *pp. 31, (1);* Altus (*A., Vl., Vl. 1*), *pp. 16;* Tenor (*S. 2, T., T. 2, B.*), *pp. 31, (1);* Bassus (*T., B., Vl., Vl. 2, Bass viol or Bsn.*), *pp. 20;* B. Continuus, *pp. 30, (1). Each pt. includes Ded. to Virgin Mary, Index (but no Index in Bassus pt.). Music consists of motets: a2*—Tota pulchra es. Ignis aeterne. Fulcite me floribus. Quaesivi te. Tenelle mi. Silens tacet. Iesu mi tu Amores. O Scava sanctae. In lectulo meo. Quam dilecta. *a3*—Virgo decora. Cantantibus Organis. O Sponse mi. Cantate. Salve Maria. O Bone Iesu. *a4*—Exultate. Exurgat Deus. Ecce dies Domini. Congregatae sunt. O Caeli Rex. *a2, Vl., Bass viol or Bsn.*—Siste gressum. *a2, 2 Vls.*—Qui Mariam adamatis. *a3, Vl.*—Terra & caelestis Chori. *All with BC.*

217. HOWARD, SAMUEL. *M78 (xii). The Generous Confession. set by Mr. Howard. Printed for J. Simpson in Sweetings Alley Royal Exchange. [London, 1750?] fol.

S. sh. Begins Too plain dear youth. *Includes arr. for Fl. Printer's colophon occurs at foot of page; backing in BUCEM entries.*

218. —— M78 (xix). Rural Life. Set by Mr. Howard. [London, *c.* 1750] fol.

S. sh. Begins How happy is the Maid. *Includes arr. for Fl.*

219. —— *M78 (xx). The Lass of St. Osyth. Set by Mr. Howard. Printed for Elizabeth Hare at the Viol & Hautboy in Cornhill near the Royal Exchange. . . . [London, c. 1740?] fol.

> S.sh. Begins At St. Osyth by the Mill. Includes arr. for Fl. Printer's colophon occurs at foot of page.

220. HUDSON, ROBERT. M158 (v). Autumn: A New Song. Set by Mr. Hudson, for the Lady's Magazine. [London, 1770] 4°

> S. sh. Begins Where e'er I turn my eyes around.

221. HUNTING SONG. *M77 (xxxvi). A hunting Song for two Voices. [London, c. 1750] fol.

> S. sh. Begins When Phoebus the tops of the Hills. Doubtfully ascribed to Handel. 2 voice parts only.

222. —— *M78 (xxi). Another copy.

223. IDASPE. D38. Songs in the New Opera Call'd Hydaspes. . . . Sold by I. Walsh . . . & P. Randall . . . & I. Hare. . . . [Music by F. Mancini] [London, 1710] fol.

> Pp. (1), 72. In score. Includes Overture, Table, List of Walsh's pubs. Preceded by engraved t-p. Singers are: Sigr. Nicolini, Sigr. Valentini, Sigra. Isabella, Sigra. Margaretta, Sigr. Cassani.

224. INCOSTANZA DELUSA. M77 (ix). The Favourite Songs in the Opera Call'd L'incostanza Delusa London. Printed for I. Walsh. . . . [1745] fol.

> Pp. 20. In score. Composers are: M. le Comte de St. Germain, Sigr. Brivio. Singers are: Sigra. Frasi, Sigra Galli.

225. IN PRAISE. *M77 (xxxv). In Praise of Wine A two Part Song. [London, c. 1750] fol.

> S. sh. Begins Bacchus he it is who fires me. Imp. Includes arr. for Fl., partly defective.

226. ISAAC, (?) BARTHOLOMEW. M98 (xliii). A Song in the Opera call'd the British Enchanters Sung by Mrs Hodgson Set by Mr. Isack. [London, c. 1710] fol.

> S. sh. Begins Listning she turns. Includes arr. for Fl.

227. JACKSON, William. *D17 (xvii). Time has not thin'd my flowing Hair.... Composed by Mr William Jackson of Exeter. Printed & Sold by J. Dale.... [London, c. 1795] fol.

Pp. 4. A duet. Acc. for Kb., Ger. Fl., or Guitar. No. 1 from Canzonets, Op. 9.

228. —— M155. Hymns in three Parts;... by William Jackson of Exeter. Opera Sesta. London; Printed for the Author.... [1768] fol.

Pp. 63. In score.

229. JOCKEY. *M78 (xiii). Jockey. Sung by Miss Stevenson at Vauxhall. Within Compass of the German Flute. [London, c. 1755] fol.

S. sh. Begins I'll sing of my Lover all Night and all Day.

230. KENT, James. E63 (ii). Twelve Anthems Composed by James Kent.... Printed for the Author 1773. Published by William Randall.... London. fol.

Pp. (9), 100. Includes Ded. to Dean and Chapter of Winchester and Warden and Fellows of Winchester College, List of subscribers, Words of anthems, Index.

231. —— *E49. A Morning & Evening Service with Eight Anthems ... by the late James Kent.... Vol. 2d. Revised and arranged by Joseph Corfe.... Printed for the Editor.... [c. 1777] fol.

Pp. 6, 121. Includes an account of Kent by Corfe, List of subscribers.

232. LAMPE, Johann Friedrich. *M77 (xxxii). Paternal Love. A New Song set to Musick by Mr. Lampe. [London, c. 1750] fol.

S. sh. Begins The Parent Bird whose little Nest. *Includes arr. for Ger. Fl.*

233. LAMPUGNANI, Giovanni Battista. D50. The Favourite Songs in the Opera Call'd Alceste by Sigr. Lampugnani. Printed for I. Walsh.... [1744] fol.

Pp. 18. In score. Singers are: Sigr. Monticelli, Sigr. Visconti, Sigra. Frasi.

235. —— M95 (ii). The Favourite Songs in the Opera Call'd Alfonso

by Sigr Lampugnani. London. Printed for I. Walsh. . . . [1744] fol.

Pp. 21. Imp., pp. 15–21 missing. In score. Singers are: Sigr. Monticelli, Sigr. Visconti, Sigra. Caselli, Sigra. Mancini.

236. LAWES, HENRY. B10 (i). Ayres and Dialogues, for One, Two, and Three Voyces. By Henry Lawes. . . . The Third Book. London, Printed by W. Godbid for John Playford. . . . MDCLVIII. fol.

Pp. (4), 48, (2). Includes Ded. to Lord Colrane, Ode, Table, List of Playford's pubs.

237. LE CAMUS, SEBASTIAN. *B21a. Airs, A Deux et Trois Parties. De feu Monsieur Le Camus, Maistre de la Musique de la Reyne. A Paris, Chez Christophe Ballard. . . . MDCLXXVIII. . . . obl. 4°

Pp. (5), 68, (4). In score. Includes Ded. to Duc de Richelieu, 'To the Reader', Privilege (dated 16/iv/1678), Index. Bk. I only. Music consists of 32 airs, 3 of which are a3.

238. LEGRENZI, GIOVANNI. B33. Prima Parte. Sentimenti Devoti. Espressi con la Musica di Due e Tre Voci. Da Gio. Legrenzi. . . . Libro Secondo. Opera Sesta. In Anversa, Presso i Heredi di Pietro Phalesio. . . . MDCLXV. 4°

In 4 pt-bks. Pt. I, pp. 50, (1); Pt. II, pp. 53, (1); Pt. III, pp. 35, (1); Pt. IV, pp. 43, (1). Index in each pt.

239. LEVERIDGE, RICHARD. M98 (xi). [Set by Mr Leveridge] [London, c. 1715] fol.

S.sh. Begins Albacinda Drew the Dart. *Imp., page heading cut off.*

240. ——— *M98 (xxi). A Song Sett and Sung by Mr Leveridge at the Theatre. [London, c. 1715] fol.

S. sh. Begins Fill the Glass. *Includes arr. for Fl.*

241. ——— M98 (xxix). The Mountebank, A Song in the Quacks or Farewell Folly. Sett and Sung by Mr Leveridge. [London, 1707] fol.

S. sh. Begins See Sirs, see here a Doctor rare. *Includes arr. for Fl. Paginated 6.*

242. LOCKE, MATTHEW. B34. The English Opera; or The Vocal Musick in Psyche. ... To which is Adjoyned The Instrumental Musick in The Tempest. By Matthew Lock. ... London, Printed by T. Ratcliff, and N. Thompson for the Author and are to be Sold by John Carr. ... MDCLXXV. 4°
 Pp. (5), 72. The Tempest begins p. 62. In score. Excludes the instrumental music composed by Draghi.

243. LOVE. *M77 (xxxviii). Love and Wine A two Part Song. [London, c. 1750] fol.
 S. sh. Begins Night and Day let's Drink and Kiss.

244. LOVE'S TRIUMPH. *M98 (lxiii). Sung by Mrs Tofts in the Opera call'd the Tryumphs of Love. fol.
 S.sh. Begins Kindly thus my Treasure. Paginated 11. From Songs In The New Opera, Call'd Love's Triumph as they are Perform'd at the Queens Theatre. Sold by I: Walsh. ... and I. Hare. ... [Music by C. F. Cesarini, Giovanni del Violone, F. Gasparini] [London, c. 1708]

245. —— M98 (lxiv). Sung by Mrs Lindsey, in the Opera call'd Love's Triumph. fol.
 S. sh. Begins Gay kind and airy. Includes arr. for Fl. Paginated 23. From same Coll. as No. 244.

246. —— *M98 (lxv). Sung by Mrs. Toft, in ye Opera of Loves Triumph. fol.
 S. sh. Begins Go Shepherd you're a Rover. From same Coll. as No. 244.

247. —— *M98 (lxvii). Sung by Mr Leveridge in the Opera call'd Love's Triumph fol.
 S. sh. Begins I Love a plain lass. Includes arr. for Fl. Paginated 5. From same Coll. as No. 244.

248. LUCIO, FRANCESCO. *B35. Canto Primo. Motetti Concertati a Doi, e Tre Voci. Di Francesco Lucio. ... Opera Seconda ... In Rotterdamo. Appresso Giovanni van Geertsom. MDCLVIII. fol.
 In 4 pt-bks. Canto Primo, pp. 31; Canto Secondo, pp. 27; Basso, pp. 24; Organo, pp. 23. Includes Index.

249. LULLY, JEAN-BAPTISTE. B20. Persée, Tragedie Mise en Musique, Par Monsieur de Lully. . . . A Paris, Par Christophe Ballard. . . . MDCLXXXII. . . . fol.

Pp. (2), xviii, 328. In score. Includes Ded. to Louis XIV.

252. MAID IN THE MILL. M98 (xx). A Song Sung by Mrs. Prince in the Maid in the Mill. [London, c. 1705] fol.

S. sh. Begins A Bonny Lad there was. Includes arr. for Fl.

253. MARENZIO, LUCA. B35b (i). Basso Madrigali a Quattro Voci di Luca Marenzio. . . . Libro Primo. In Venetia Appresso Angelo Gardano. MDLXXXXII. sm. 4°

Pp. (1), 29, (1). Imp., bass pt. only. Includes Ded. to Marc' Antonio Serlupi, Index.

254. MONTEVERDI, CLAUDIO. *B35b (ii). Basso di Claudio Monteverde Il Terzo Libro de Madrigali a Cinque Voci. . . . In Venetia appresso Ricciardo Amadino. MDXCIII. sm. 4°

Pp. (1), 22, (1). Imp., bass pt. only. Includes Ded. to Duke of Mantua, Index.

255. MONTHLY MASKS. *D34. The Whole Volume Compleat Intituled The Monthly Masks of Vocal Musick Containing all the Choisest Songs by the Best Masters made for the Play-houses Publick Consorts and other Occasions for the Year 1703 with a Through Bass to Each Song. . . . London Printed for & sould by I. Walsh. . . . fol.

Pp. (71). Stated incorrectly in BUCEM as imp. Includes Ded. to William Marquis of Hartington by Walsh. Index of all the songs (wrongly inserted between t-p. for November and first song), List of works pub. by Walsh, including Table of stage songs with source and composer. Extends from November 1702–October 1703 inclusive. Each month has separate t-p., all but November and February as follows: The Monthly Mask of Vocal Music or the New-est Songs Made for the Theatre's and other Occasions Publish'd for December. . . . These Collection's will be Continued Monthly for ye Year 1703. . . . London Printed for and sold by I. Walsh and I. Hare . . . *with the month pasted in on printed slip (but lacking for June). November's t-p. same as above except that* November *is engraved as part of a different design and is followed by* These Collection's. ... Year 1704 The whole Volume of Monthly Collection's being now Compleat for ye Year 1703 London. ... *February's t-p. is simply the following arranged in an oval:* The Songs and Symphonys Perform'd before Her Majesty at. ... St. James on New-years day. Compos'd by Mr. J. Eccles. ... February 1703. ... [London etc., as above]. *The stage works and composer of each are:* She wou'd and she wou'd not—*Weldon;* Love betraid—*Eccles;* The Fair Penitant—*Eccles;* The Agreeable Disappointment—*Weldon;* As you find it—*Eccles. Other composers are:* Mr. John Barrett, Mr. Berenclow, Mr. Courtivill, Mr. Wm. Crofts, Mr. John Eccles, Mr. Gillier, Mr. Phillip Hart, Mr. Hickes, Mr. D. Purcell, Mr. John Weldon. *Singers are:* Mrs. Bracegirdle, Mrs. Campion, Mr. Cooke, Mr. Davis, Mr. Elford, Mrs. Hodgson, Mrs. Hudson, Mr. Hughs, Mr. Laroon, Mr. Leveridge, Mr. Robert, Mrs. Shaw.

256. MORGAN, George. *M77 (xxxvii). A Two Part Song By Mr. Morgan. [London, *c.* 1725] fol.

    S. sh. *Begins* By shady Woods and purling streams. *Paginated* 43 (?).

257. MORNING HYMN. E63 (i). The Morning Hymn. taken from the Fifth Book of Milton's Paradise Lost. Set to Music by the late John Ernest Galliard. The Overture, Accompanyments & Chorusses added by Benjamin Cooke. ... London Printed by Welcker. ... [1773] fol.

    Pp. (1), 2, 70. *Includes Ded. to Academy of Ancient Music by Cooke, List of subscribers.*

258. OSWALD, James. *M77 (xxxi). The Tears of Scotland. [London, *c.* 1750] fol.

    S. sh. *Begins* Mourn Hapless Caledonia Mourn.

259. PARSON. M98 (lxxxvi). The Parson among the Pease A new Song the words by Mr. Durfey. [London, *c.* 1710] fol.

    S .sh. *Begins* One Long Whitson Holliday. *Includes arr. for Fl.*

260. PEPUSCH, Johann Christoph. D33. The Songs and Symphony's in the Masque of Venus & Adonis ... by Dr. Pepusch.

... Carefully Corected by the Author. London Printed for J. Walsh ... & J. Hare. ... [1716] fol.

> *Pp. (1), 41. In score. Includes Table and statement that 3 of the songs were composed by an Italian. Singers are:* Mrs. Margaritta de L'Epine, Mrs. Barbier, Mr. Turner.

261. —— D27. Six English Cantatas. . . . Compos'd by Mr. J. C. Pepusch London Printed for J. Walsh. . . . & J. Hare. . . . [1720] fol.

> *Pp.(2),31., mostly unpaginated. Includes* To the Lovers of Musick, *Ded. to Marchioness of Kent.*

262. —— D28. Six English Cantatas for one Voice Four for a Flute and two with a Trumpet and other Instruments Compos'd by J. C. Pepusch Book ye Second London Printed for J. Walsh ... & J. Hare. ... [1720] fol.

> *Pp. (1), 46. Includes Ded. to James Duke of Chandos.*

263. —— M98 (lxxix). A Cantata compos'd by Signr. Pepusch. [London, c. 1715] fol.

> *Pp. (2). Begins recit.* See from ye silent Grove Allexis Flyes. *The same as No. 2 from No. 261.*

264. —— *M158 (ii). Alexis. A Cantata [London, c. 1740] fol.

> *Pp. 4. Different ed. from No. 263.*

265. PIRRO E DEMETRIO. D36. Songs In The New Opera, Call'd Pyrrhus and Demetrius. . . . Sold by I: Walsh ... & P. Randall ... and I. Hare. ... [London, 1709] fol.

> *Pp.(3),58. Preceded by engraving which gives Walsh only as publisher. In score. Singers are:* Sigr. Nicolini, Mrs. Toft, The Barronness, Mr. Cook, Sigra. Margarita, Mr. Ramondon, Sigr. Valentini. *The only named composer is Haym.*

266. —— *M98 (lxviii). Pyrrhus. Sung by Sigr. Cavaliero Nicolino Grimaldi in the Opera of Pyrrhus & Demetrius. fol.

> *S.sh. Begins* Come O Sleep. *Includes arr. for Fl. Italian text given at end. From* Songs In The New Opera of Pyrrhus and Demetrius. ... London Printed for John Cullen. [1709]

VOCAL WORKS

267. —— *M98 (lxix). Pyrrhus. Sung by Signr. Cavaliero Nicolini. fol.

> S. sh. Begins Her bright Eyes are Stars that charm us. Italian text beneath English begins Du pupille che sono due stelle. Includes arr. for Fl. Page heading imp. From same Coll. as No. 266.

268. —— *M98 (lxx). [Marius. Sung by M. D'lapine] in Pyrrhus & Demetrius. fol.

> S. sh. Begins Blushing Violets sweetly smelling. Includes arr. for Fl. Page heading imp. From same Coll. as No. 266.

269. —— *M98 (lxxi). Sung by Signra Margaritta, in the Opera call'd Pyrrhus and Demetrius. fol.

> S. sh. Begins May I tell you that I'me dyeing. Includes arr. for Fl. Paginated 36. From Songs In The New Opera, Call'd Pyrrhus and Demetrius. . . . Sold by I: Walsh: . . . and I. Hare. . . . [London, c. 1712]

270. —— M98 (lxxiii). Sung by Mr. Ramondon, in the Opera call'd Pyrrhus and Demetrius. fol.

> S. sh. Begins Love thou airy vain Illusion. Includes arr. for Fl. Paginated 45. From same Coll. as No. 269.

271. —— *M98 (lxxv). Climene. Sung by Mrs. Toft in ye Opera of Pyrrhus & Demetrius. fol.

> S. sh. Begins Rise O Sunn. Includes arr. for Fl. T. Cross Junr. Sculp. at foot of page. Paginated 2. From same Coll. as No. 266.

272. PLEASANT. B43. The Second Book of the Pleasant Musical Companion: Being a Choice Collection of Catches, for Three and Four Voices. . . . Compos'd by Dr. John Blow, the late Mr. Henry Purcell, and other Eminent Masters. The Fourth Edition, corrected and much Enlarged. London Printed by W. Pearson, for Henry Playford. . . . 1701. obl. 4°

> Pp. (6). Unpaginated, pieces numbered 1–98. Composers apart from above are: [Anon], Mr. Samuel Ackeroyd, Mr. Richard Brown, Mr. John Eccles, Mr. John Gilbert, Mr. Gillier, Mr. Barth Isaak, Mr. John Jackson, Mr. John Lenton, Mr. John Reading, Mr. J. Roffee, Mr. Tho. Tudway, Dr. John Wilson, Mr. Mich. Wise.

273. POLIDORI, ORTENSIO. D29 (iv). Motetti a Voce Sola, et a Doi di Ortensio Polidori da Camerino. . . . Opera Decima Terza. . . . In Venetia MDCXXXVI Appresso Bartolomeo Magni. fol.

>   *Pp. 51. Includes Ded. to Mother Superior* Catarina Francesca Cartocci.

274. PORPORA, NICOLÒ ANTONIO. M153 (v). [12 Cantatas by] nicolò porpora Londra nel MDCCXXXV. obl. fol.

>   *Pp. 82. Most of t-p. taken up with Ded. to Frederick, Elector of Hanover.*

275. PORTA, FRANCESCO DELLA. B38. Libri Primi Cantionum Francisci Della Porta Duarum, Trium Quatuor et Quinque vocum Pars Secunda Cum Basso Continuo ad Organum. Cantus. Antuerpiae, Apud Magdalenam Phalesiam & Cohaeredes. MDCL. 4°

>   *In 5 pt-bks.* Cantus, *pp. 42, (1);* Altus, *pp. 35, (1);* Tenor, *pp. 33, (1);* Bassus, *pp. 26, (1);* B. Continuus, *pp. 31, (1). Each pt. includes Index.*

276. PSALMS. A19. Psalmi Davidis Metrorhythmici ad Ambrosii Lobwasseri melodias concinnati Apud Paltenium in Francofurto venales. MDCXII. 12°

>   *Pp. 16, 827 (last 3 unpaginated),(7). Includes Ded. to* Frederick, Count Palatine of the Rhine, Holy Roman Emperor *etc. by* Andreas Spethe, *and to* Maurice, Landgrave of Hasse, *by Spethe, Epigrams, Notes, Index.*

277. —— A18. The Whole Booke of Psalmes: . . . Composed unto 4. parts by sundry Authors. . . . Newly corrected and enlarged by Tho: Ravenscroft. . . . Printed at London for the Company of Stationers, 1621. 8°

>   *Pp. (8), 273, (5). Includes Preface, List of composers,* Of the Praise . . . of the Psalmes, *Index, Prayers, Table.*

278. —— A14. The Psalmes of King David Translated by King James Cum Privilegio Regiae Maiestatis. Oxford, Printed by William Turner, Printer to the famous University: MDCXXXI. 12°

>   *Pp. 319. Printer's colophon occurs on last page. Words only.*

VOCAL WORKS

279. —— A10. The Whole Book of Psalmes: Collected into English meeter, by Thomas Sternhold, John Hopkins, and others. . . . Printed by the printers to the Universitie of Cambridge. . . . 1633. 8°

    Imp., pp. 11, 12, 39 to end defective or missing.

280. —— *B36. Canto Opera Prima, e Libro Primo di Salmi Musicali a tre, quattro, e cinque Voci, con Sinfonia et in fine. Una Letania della Beata Vergine di Marcello Minozzi. . . . In Venetia; Apresso Alessandro Vincenti. MDCXXXVIII. 4°

    In 5 pt-bks. Canto, pp. (1), 44, (1); Alto (A. [Vl. 1]), pp. (1), 44, (1); Tenore (T., B., [Vl. 2]), pp. (1), 31, (1); Basso, pp. (1), 43, (1); Basso Continuo, pp. (1), 43, (1). *Each pt. includes Ded. to Oratory of St. Philip of Carpi, Index. Music consists of a3—* Confitebor. Beatus vir. Laudate Pueri. Laudate Pueri del Sig. Galeazzo Sabbatini. Letatus sum. Nisi Dominum. Credidi. Beati omnes. Inconvertendo. *a4—*Dixit Dominus. In Exitu. Domine probasti me. De profundis. Letaniae. *a5—*Magnificat. *a3, Vls. 1 and 2—*Lauda Hierusalem.

281. —— †*B37. Psalmi Francisci Petrobelli. . . . Venetius MDCLXII. Apud Franciscum Magni. 4°

    In 7 pt-bks. Canto, pp. 34, (1); Alto, pp. 31, (1); Tenore, pp. 43, (1); Basso, pp. 34, (1); Violino, pp. 31, (1); Violino, pp. 32; Organo, pp. 41, (1). *Each pt. includes Ded. to Emperor Leopold 1, Index. Music consists of: a2—*Nisi Dominus. *a3—* Confitebor; Letatus sum; Lauda Ierusalem. *a4—*Dixit Dominus; Beatus vir; Laudate pueri; Magnificat; *all with 2 Vls. and BC.*

282. —— M169. Psalms & Hymns in Solemn Musick of Foure Parts. . . . Also Six Hymns for One Voyce to the Organ. By John Playford. London, Printed by W. Godbid for J. Playford. . . . 1671. fol.

    Pp. (1), (1), (8), 97, (3). *Imp., pp. 85–97 and (2) from Index missing or defective. Includes Preface, Index, List of Playford's pubs., Ded to William Sancroft, the text of* A Hymn on the Divine Use of Musick Composed to Musick for Three Voyces By Mr. John Jenkins.

283. —— *B31. Cantus Psalmi Vespertini Dominicales Quinque vocibus cum Organo, & sine Organo decantendi Auctore Rev. Bonifacio

VOCAL WORKS

Gratiano.... Lib. I Opus Quartum. Romae, Excudebat Mascardus, MDCLXXIIII.... 4°

> In 6 pt-bks. Cantus, pp. 16; Altus, pp. 16; Tenor Primus, pp. 15, (1); Tenor Secundus, pp. 16; Bassus, pp. 16; Organum, pp. 14. Each pt. includes Index. Music consists of Dixit Dominus. Confitebor. Beatus vir. Laudate pueri Dominum. In exitu. Magnificat.

284. —— *B28. Airs a Quatre Parties, sur la Paraphrase des Pseaumes de Messire Antoine Godeau, Composez par Monsieur Jaques de Gouy. Dessus. A Amsterdam, chez Estienne Roger.... [c. 1697] obl. 8°

> In 4 pt-bks. Dessus, Haute-Contre, Taille, Basse-Contre, all pp. 55. Settings are of Psalms 1 to 50.

285. —— *A13 (i). A New Version of the Psalms of David, Fitted to the Tunes used in Churches. By N. Tate and N. Brady. London, Printed by T. Hodgkin, for the Company of Stationers, 1699.... 12°

> Pp. 229. Words only. Includes Privilege (dated 3/xii/1696), Directions about the Tunes and Measures, Advertisement of the Supplement, Table.

286. —— A13 (ii). A Supplement to the New Version of Psalms by N.Tate and N. Brady.... London, Printed by J. Heptinstall, and Sold at Stationers Hall... by D. Brown...J. Wild.... 1700. 12°

> Pp. 69, (3). Words only. Includes Tables.

287. —— B42. Tunes to the Psalms of David, in Four Parts.... The like never before Published. By S. S. and J. H. London: Printed by William Pearson, for Henry Playford... and Sold by John Richardson.... 1700. sm. obl. 8°

> Pp. (29), 77, (2). Includes Preface, Introduction, Table. The only composer mentioned is John Playford. Music contained in a Second Part.

288. —— A8 (i). The Whole Book of Psalms.... By John Playford. The Seventh Edition, Corrected and Amended. London, Printed by J. Heptinstall, for the Company of Stationers: And are to be sold by Henry Playford.... 1701. 8°

> Pp. (14), 276. Includes Preface, Of the Virtue... of the Psalms,

VOCAL WORKS

Solmisation examples by Mr. James Cutler, *the Gamut, Instructions, Table, List of Playford's pubs.*

289. —— *B41. The Metre Psalm Tunes, in Four Parts. Compos'd for the Use of the Parish-Church of St. Michael's of Belfrey's in York. By Thomas Wanless, . . . Organist of the Cathedral . . . of St. Peter in York. . . . London, Printed by J. Heptinstall, for A. and J. Churchill. . . 1702. obl. 4°

> Pp. (2), 92. *Includes* Rules to be observed or got without Book, Solmisation examples, Table.

290. —— A17. A New Version of the Psalms of David, Fitted to the Tunes used in Churches. By Sir Richard Blackmore. . . . London: Printed by J. March, for the Company of Stationers, 1721. . . . 8°

> Pp. (8), 330. *Words only. Includes* Ded. to George I, Recommendations, Preface.

291. —— D19–26. Estro Poetico-Armonico Parafrasi Sopri li primi Venticinque Salmi Poesia di Girolamo Ascanio Giustiniani, Musica di Benedetto Marcello. . . . Tomo Primo [etc.] Appresso Domenico Lovisa Venezia MDCCXXIV. fol.

> 8 vols., *each with t-p. identical to above apart from vol. no.* Vol. I, pp. 30, 130, (1); Vol. II, pp. 22, 148, (1); Vol. III, pp. 8, 22, 141, (1); Vol. IV, pp. 8, 27, 197, (1); Vol. V, pp. 20, 133, (1); Vol. VI, pp. 23 (with 4 pp. duplicated), 146, (1); Vol. VII, pp. 28, 168, (1); Vol. VIII, pp. 8, 24, 181, (1). *Each vol. includes* Address or Preface, Letters from various individuals including Mattheson and Telemann, Index. *(See No. 295.) Printer's colophon occurs on last page.*

292. —— *A15. The Psalms of David, Imitated in the Language of the New Testament, and apply'd to the Christian State and Worship. By I. Watts. The Fifth Edition. . . . London; Printed for John Clark and Richard Hett . . . and Richard Ford. . . . MDCCXXV. 12°

> Pp. viii, 8, (21), 319. *Includes* Address to the reader, Tunes in The Tenor Part Fitted to the Several Metres, Index, Table, List of books by Watts.

293. —— M75 (i). [Number VII] The Whole Book of Psalms For One, two, three, four & five Voices with a Thorough Bass Set to

Music by Mr. John Travers. . . . London Printed for John Johnson. . . . [*c.* 1750] fol.

> *Pp. 309–53. Imp., pp. 315, 316, 335–53 missing. All or most of previous 6 monthly issues missing. No. of issue added in MS. Psalms 119–37.*

294. —— M75 (ii). [Number VIII] [etc., as above]

> *Pp. 354–407. Imp., pp. 385–96, 405–7 missing. Settings of Psalms 138–50. Includes Index. No. of issue added in MS.*

295. —— D1–8. The First Fifty Psalms. Set to Music by Benedetto Marcello . . . and adapted to the English Version, By John Garth. Vol. I. London, Printed for John Johnson. . . . MDCCLVII. fol.

> *8 vols., each with t-p. identical to above apart from vol. no. Vol. I, pp. (1), (1), 2, (16), 130; Vol. II, pp. (1), (1), 2, (1), 131, (2); Vol. III, pp. (2), 4, 2, 144, (2); Vol. IV, pp. (2), 2, (1), 154, (2); Vol. V, pp. 4, (1), 123, (2); Vol. VI, pp. 4, (3), 127; Vol. VII, pp. 4, (1), 148, (2); Vol. VIII, pp. 4, (1), 150, (1). Each vol. includes the same Ded. to Richard Lord Bishop of Durham, Licence, List of subscribers; also a translation of the original Preface, different for each vol. Vol. I only includes remarks on his translation by Garth, memoirs of Marcello, and remarks on Marcello's settings by Avison. 2 copies of each vol. (see No. 291).*

296. —— A9. Psalms, Hymns and Anthems; for the Use of The Children of the Hospital for the Maintenance and Education of Exposed and Deserted Young Children. [London, *c.* 1770] 8°

> *Pp. 28, (1). Composers are:* [Anon], Mr. Green, Dr. Heighington, Mr. Scott, Mr. Smith, Mr. Worgan. *Includes Index.* Caulfield Sculp.

298. —— M164. Psalm Tunes Composed in Four Parts for Choirs of Singers . . . by Edward Miller. . . . London. Printed & Published by W. Miller. [*c.* 1805] 8°

> *Pp. (1), 45. Imp., p. 45 missing. Composers are:* Arne, Emanuel Bach, Brentbank, Burney, Carey, J. Clark, Croft, Denby, Dibdin, G. Green, Handel, Heighington, Dr. Howard, Luther, Miller, John Milton, Purcell, Rathiel, Ravenscroft, Wainwright, Wm. Wheall, Whitton.

299. —— M163. *Another copy. Imp., only pp. 3–6 remaining.*

VOCAL WORKS

300. —— *A12. Recueil des Psaumes de David, suivi des Cantiques Sacrés; Le tout mis en musique sur les anciens airs, rhythmés mis en harmonie, et arrangés pour l'orgue ou le piano-forte. Précédé des Psaumes et des Cantiques, selon l'usage de L'Eglise Anglicane, marqués pour le plein-chant: Jersey: R. Gosset, Imprimeur-Libraire, Queen Street. [n.d.] 8°

Imp., pp. iv, 128 only, lacking final pages containing Psalms 139–150. Each Psalm has music on 2 staves. Includes Preface, Morning and Evening Prayers.

301. PURCELL, DANIEL. M98 (vii). The Serenading Song in the Constant Couple; or a Trip to the Jubilee, written by Mr George Farquhar, Set by Mr Daniel Purcel, Sung by Mr Freeman, and exactly engraved by Tho: Cross. [London, c. 1700] fol.

S. sh. Begins Thus Damon knock'd. Includes arr. for Fl.

302. —— M98 (xxvi). A Song in the Tender Husband, Sung by Mr Hughes Set by Mr Dan Purcell Within the Compass of the Flute. [London, c. 1707] fol.

S. sh. Begins Why Belvidera tell me why.

303. PURCELL, HENRY. B2 (i). Orpheus Britannicus. A Collection of all the Choicest Songs for One, Two, and Three Voices, Compos'd by Mr. Henry Purcell. . . . London, Printed by J. Heptinstall, for Henry Playford. . . . MDCXCVIII. fol.

Pp. vi, (2), 30, 248. Includes List of books sold by Playford, Ded. to Lady Howard by Playford, Address by Playford, Odes, Table, An Ode on the Death of Mr. Henry Purcell. . . . The Words by Mr. Dryden, and Sett to Musick by Dr. Blow. London, Printed by J. Heptinstall, for Henry Playford. . . . 1696. T-p. preceded by engraved portrait of Purcell.

304. —— B2 (iii). Orpheus Britannicus. A Collection of the Choicest Songs, for One, Two, and Three Voices. . . . The Second Book, which renders the First Compleat. . . . London: Printed by William Pearson, for Henry Playford. . . . 1702. fol.

Pp. (2), iv, (2), 176. Includes Ded. to Charles, Lord Halifax, by Playford, Address by Playford, Odes, List of books sold by Playford, Table. Preceded by same portrait as above.

305. —— M97 (ii). Another copy. *Imp., pp. 147–50, 173–6 defective.*

VOCAL WORKS

306. —— M97 (i). [Orpheus Britannicus. A Collection of all The Choicest Songs for One, Two, and Three Voices. . . . The Second Edition with Large Additions. . . . London: Printed by William Pearson, and Sold by John Cullen, . . . 1706.] fol.

Pp. 286. Imp., t-p. and pp. to p. 24 inclusive missing, p. 25 defective.

307. —— M158 (i). [Orpheus Britannicus. A Collection of Choice Songs for One, Two, and Three Voices with a Through Bass for the Harpsicord. . . . London. Printed for I. Walsh. . . .] [c. 1745] fol.

Pp. 120. Imp., includes only pp. 1–8, 19–26, 31–42, 49–52, 60, 59 (53 in error), 63, 64, 83, 84, 91, 92, 101–8, 113–16. (See No. 308.)

308. —— M103. *Another copy. Imp., includes only pp. 11–18, 27–30, 43–48, 53–58, 61, 62, 65–82, 85–88. Nos. 307 and 308 together nearly form a complete copy of this ed.*

309. —— B1. The Vocal and Instrumental Musick of The Prophetess, or The History of Dioclesian. Composed by Henry Purcell. . . . London, Printed by J. Heptinstall, for the Author, and . . . sold by John Carr. . . . MDCXCI. fol.

Pp. (2), 173, (2). In score. Includes Ded. to Charles, Duke of Somerset, List of Carr's pubs.

310. —— D48. *Another copy. Imp., lacking pp. 173, (2).*

311. —— *M98 (ii). A New Song sung by Mrs. Dyer in the last new Play called Henry the Second King of England. [London, c. 1693] 8°

S. sh. Begins In vain gainst Love, in vain I strove. Mr. Henry Purcell *occurs at foot of page.*

312. —— D30. Te Deum & Jubilate, for Voices and Instruments, made for St. Caecilias's Day, 1694. By the late Mr. Henry Purcell. London, Printed by J. Heptinstall, for the Author's Widow, and . . . Sold by Henry Playford. . . . 1697. fol.

Pp. (1), 48. In score. Includes Ded. to Nathaniel, Bishop of Durham by Frances Purcell, List of Purcell's works sold by Playford. On t-p. Henry Playford *is crossed out in ink, and after 1697 is*

VOCAL WORKS

added her at her house in great Deans yard Westminster, *also in ink.*

313. RADCLIFFE, JAMES. *D9. Church Music, Consisting of Ten Anthems in Score for the use of Cathedrals and other Choirs, with a Collection of Chants, a Sanctus Gloria in Excelsis, Composed and arranged for the Organ, Harpsichord or Forte Piano, by James Radcliffe, of the Cathedral Church Durham. . . . London Engraved Printed & Published for the Author by E. Riley. . . . [1801] fol.

Pp. (iv), 109. Includes Ded. to James, Bishop of Lichfield and Coventry and to the Dean and Chapter of Durham, Preface (dated October, 1801). Also issued From the Press of L. Pennington, Durham. *8 copies.*

314. RAMONDON, LEWIS. *M98 (lxxxiib). Set by Mr. Ramondon. [London, c. 1716] fol.

Pp. (2). Begins At noon in a Sultry Summers day. *Vocal pt. occupies the lower half of a page, with Weldon's setting in the upper half (see No. 369). Includes an arr. for Fl. on reverse side.*

315. RILEY, WILLIAM. M78 (x). Roger of the Dale A Favourite English Song. [London, c. 1750] fol.

S. sh. Begins Ye gentle Winds that fan the Sea. *Includes an arr. for Fl.*

316. ROUSSEAU, JEAN JACQUES. B45 (i). The Cunning-Man a Musical Entertainment in Two Acts. . . . Taken from the Devin du Village of Mr. J. J. Rousseau, and Adapted to his Original Music. by C. Burney. . . . London. Printed and Sold by R. Bremner. . . . [c. 1767] obl. fol.

Pp. 34. Text in French and English. In score. Singers are: Mrs. Arne, Mr. Champness, Mr. Vernon. *Includes list of Bremner's pubs.*

317. ROVETTA, GIOVANNI. *B39. Bicinia Sacra sive Cantiones Sacrae Duabus Vocibus, Suavissime Concertantibus cum Basse Generali canendae Autore Ioanne Rovetta Vice-Magistro Capellae Serenissimae Venetiarum Reipublicae. Liber Tertius. Vox Prima. Antuerpiae, Apud Haereded Petri Phalesii Typographi Musice. MDCXLVIII. 4°

In 3 pt-bks. Vox Prima, pp. 28, (1); Vox Secunda, pp. 26;

B. Continuus, *pp. 20*, (*1*). *Index in each pt. except Vox II. Music consists of motets:* Dominus illuminatio mea. Exultavit cor meum. Alma redemptoris Mater. Nulla scientia melior est illa. Gaudete patres. O pretiosum. Deus in nomine tuo, Iubilate Deo. Dies sanctificatus. Surge propera. Lauda Sion. Ave Regina caelorum. Salve Regina. Quam Pulchra amica mea.

318. SABBATINI, GALEAZZO. *B40. Sacrae Laudes Musices Concentibus a Galeatio Sabbatino Contextae, Binis, Ternis, Quaternis, Quinisque Vocibus ad Organum concinendae. Liber Primus Opus Tertium Decennali cultu elaboratum. Cantus I. Antwerpiae, Typis Haeredum Petri Phalesii. MDCLVI. 4°

> *In 5 pt-bks.* Cantus I, *pp. 30*, (*1*); Cantus II, *pp. 27*, (*1*); Tenor, *pp. 19*, (*1*); Bassus, *pp. 19*, (*1*); B. Continuus, *pp. 23*, (*1*). *Index in each pt. Music consists of motets: a2*—Audi Maria. Domine Dominus noster. Beatus vir. Hoc est praeceptum. Domine ne in furore. O Bona Crux. Iesu Domine. O verum Christi corpus. Leva ejus. *a3*—O dulce nomen Iesu. Cum Palma. Domine Iesus. O Nomen Iesu. O Clementissime. Corpora Sanctorum. *a4*—Ego dix. Omnes Sancti. Adoramus te. *a5*—Veni electa me. Audi Maria.

319. SACRED. M165. [Sacred Music, Containing Two Hundred and Fifty of the most Favorite Tunes . . . adapted to a New Selection of Hymns by . . . Mr. Boden; and Dr. Williams & also the Psalms and Hymns of Dr. Watts . . . Composed by Edward Miller. . . . London: Printed for the Author by T. Williams . . . sold also by Broderip & Wilkinson, . . . by W. Miller . . . & by Wm. Sheardown. . . .] [1800?] 8°

> *Unpaginated. Imp., lacking t-p, 4 pp. List of subscribers, first 19 pieces, and Index. Each piece is numbered.*

320. —— M166. *Vol. 2 of the above. Unpaginated. Imp., lacking t-p.*

321. SAINT GERMAIN CONTE DE. *M77 (xix). A New Song. Set to Musick by Comte De St. Germain. [London, *c.* 1745] fol.

> *S. sh. Begins* Gentle Love this Hour befriend me.

322. —— *M78 (ix). *Another copy.*

VOCAL WORKS

323. —— M77 (xx). The Maid that's made for Love & me Set by Comte de St German. [London, c. 1750] fol.

   S. sh. Begins O wouldst thou know what Sacred Charms.

324. SCELTA. *B29. Scelta di Motetti di diversi Eccellentissimi Autori Raccolti da Gio. Van Geertsom a due, e tre, voci. Con il Basso Continuo per l'Organo Clavicembalo Spinetto, o altro Instrumente simile. Cantus Primus. In Rotterodamo Appresso Giovanni van Geertsom all' ensegna de la Reyna di Pologna in de Meulesteegh. MDCLVI. 4°

   In 4 pt-bks. Cantus Primus, *pp.* 47, (1); Cantus Secun., *pp.* 47, (1); Bassus, *pp.* 29, (1); B. Continuus, *pp.* 34, (1). Index in each *pt. Contents are:* Auton Maria Abbatini—Dilatatae sunt (a2); Horatio Benevoli—Fortitudo mea. Venite (a3); Iacomo Carissimi—Laudemus virum (a2). Surgamus eamus. Audite sancti (a4); Silvestro Durante—Bellica defixos (a3); Stephano Fabri—Inquietum est (a2). Sideus pro nobis (a3); Francisco Foggia—Adiuva me domine. Terribili sonitu (a2), Alleluja Beatus vir. Hodie apparuerunt (a3); Bonifatio Gratiani— Quousque (a2). Dilectus deo. O bone Jesu (a3); Gio. Franc. Marcorelli—Iubilate gentes (a2); Paolo Tarditi—Laudabo nomen tuum (a3); Giuseppe Tricario—Repleatur os meum (a3).

325. SCHNEIDER, JOHANN CHRISTIAN FREDERICK. D96. Missa Solis Vocibus Humanis. . . . A Frederico Schneidero. . . . Lipsiae ex Officina musica C. F. Peters. [1820?] fol.

   Pp. 51. Ded. to Frederick Augustus King of Saxony.

326. SELECT. B10 (ii). Select Ayres and Dialogues for One, Two, and Three Voyces. . . . Composed by John Wilson Charles Colman Doctors in Musick. Henry Lawes William Lawes Nicholas Laneare William Webb Gentlemen and Servants to his late Majesty. . . . And other Excellent Masters of Musick. London, Printed by W. Godbid for John Playford . . . 1659. fol.

   Pp. (4), 114. T-p. bound in error before H. Lawes's *Ayres and Dialogues (q.v.), the rest of the book follows. Includes Address by Playford, Table, List of Playford's pubs. which gives 1659 ed. as Reprinted with large Additions. The list in Lawes's Ayres gives the 1st ed. as 1652. Composers other than in t-p. are:* [Anon.], Mr. Tho. Brewer, Mr. William Caesar, alias Smegergill, Mr. John Cobb, Mr. Edward Colman, Lady Deerings, Mr. John Goodgroome, Mr. Jenkins, Mr. Robert Johnson, John

VOCAL WORKS

Playford, Mr. Jeremy Savil, Mr. William Tompkins, Mr. Warner.

327. —— B10 (iii). Select Ayres and Dialogues to Sing to the Theorbo-Lute or Basse-Viol. Composed by Mr. Henry Lawes. . . . And other Excellent Masters. The Second Book. . . . London, Printed by William Godbid for John Playford. . . . 1669. fol.

Pp. (6), 120. Includes List of Playford's pubs., Address by Playford, Table, Odes. Composers other than H. Lawes are: [Anon.], Tho. Blagrave, Dr. Charles Colman, Mr. Edward Colman, Mr. John Goodgroome, Mr. Will. Gregorie, Mr. Roger Hill, J. Hilton, Mr. Simon Ives, Mr. John Jenkins, Mr. Nich. Lanier, Mr. Will. Lawes, Mr. Alphon. Marsh, Mr. John Moss, John Playford, Dr. John Wilson.

328. STANLEY, JOHN. M67 (i). Six Cantata's For A Voice and Instruments: Set to Musick by John Stanley MB. . . . London. Printed for John Stanley. [1742] fol.

Pp. (4), 49. Includes Preface, Licence dated 24.viii.1742.

329. —— M68 (ii). *Another copy.*

330. —— M68 (i). Six Cantata's for a Voice and Instruments, Set to Music by John Stanley MB. London: Printed for John Stanley. . . . [1748] fol.

Pp. (1), 45. A second set. Includes Licence as above. Imp., lacking pp. 1–4.

331. SUBLIGNY, MADAM. *M98 (xv). A Song in praise of Punch to the tune of Mdm. Sublignys Minuet. [London, 1702?] fol.

S. sh. Begins Come fill up the Bowl. *Includes an arr. for Fl. Paginated* 31.

332. TAYLOR, J. M78(xv). A Song Sung by Miss Falkner. [London, c. 1750] fol.

S. sh. Begins Had I but the Wings of a Dove. *Includes an arr. for Ger. Fl.*

333. THOMYRIS. B5. [Songs in the New Opera call'd Thomyris Collected out of the Works of the most Celebrated Itallian

Authors viz. Scarlatti Bononcini and other great Masters. ... London Printed for I. Walsh ... and P. Randall. ...] [1707] fol.

Pp. 57. *Imp., lacking t-p., pp. 1–16, 20, 21, 23, 32, 33, 43, 47, 49, 53–55, 57. Singers are:* Signra Margaritta, Mrs. Toft, Mr. Hughs, Signr. Valentino, Mrs. Lindsey, Mr. Leveridge, Mr. Lawrance.

334. —— *M98 (li). Sung by Mrs Lindsey in the Opera call'd Thomyris, at the Theatre Royall. fol.

S. sh. Begins What Lover ever can hope for Favour. *Paginated 23. From Coll. No. 333.*

335. —— *M98 (lii). Sung by Signra Margaritta in the Opera call'd Thomyris, at the Theatre Royall. fol.

S. sh. Begins Pleasure calls fond hearts recover. *Includes an arr. for Fl. Paginated 56. From Coll. No. 333.*

336. —— *M98 (liii). Sung by Mrs. Lindsey in the Opera call'd Thomyris, at the Theatre Royall. fol.

*S. sh. Begin s*Can you leave ranging. *Includes an arr. for Fl. Paginated 43. From Coll. No. 333.*

337. —— *M98 (liv). Sung by Mr. Leveridge in the Opera call'd Thomyris at ye Theatre Royall. fol.

S. sh. Begins Farewell Love and all soft Pleasure. *Paginated 45. From Coll. No. 333.*

338. —— M98 (lv). Sung by Mr Lawrence in the Opera call'd Thomyris at the Theatre Royall. fol.

S. sh. Begins In vain is Complaining. *Includes an arr. for Fl. Paginated 15. From Coll. No. 333.*

339. —— *M98 (lvi). Cleora. Sung by Mrs. Toft in ye Opera of Thomyris. fol.

S. sh. Begins Pritty warbler cease to hover. *Includes an arr. for Fl. Imp., lacking most of the last stave of the Fl. pt. From* Songs in the New Opera of Thomiris. ... London. Printed for John Cullen. ... [1707]

340. *M98 (lvii). Cleora. Sung by Mrs. Toft in ye Opera of Thomyris. fol.

   S. sh. Begins I revive now you're turning. Includes an arr. for Fl. From same Coll. as No. 339.

341. —— *M98 (lviii). [Baldo. Sung by Mr. Leveridge in ye Opera of Thomyris.] fol.

   S. sh. Begins My delight, my Dear, my Princess. Includes an arr. for Fl. Imp., lacking most of heading. From same Coll. as No. 339.

342. —— *M98 (lix). Sung by Mrs Lindsey in the Opera call'd Thomyris, at the Theatre Royall. fol.

   S. sh. Begins Ever Merry gay and Airy. From Coll. No. 333.

343. —— *M98 (lx). Sung by Mrs. Lindsey in the Opera call'd Thomyris, at ye Theatre Royall. fol.

   S. sh. Begins When one's gone ner'e Keep a pother. Includes an arr. for Fl. Paginated 49. From Coll. No. 333.

344. —— *M98 (lxi). Sung by Mrs. Lindsey in the Opera call'd Thomyris at ye Theatre Royall. fol.

   S. sh. Begins Away you Rover, for shame give over. Includes an arr. for Fl. From Coll No. 333.

345. —— *M98 (lxii). [Orontes, Sung by Sigr. Valentini in ye Opera of Thomyris.] fol.

   S. sh. Begins Bright Wonder of Nature. Includes an arr. for Fl. Imp., lacking most of heading and part of last stave of Fl. pt. From same Coll. as No. 339.

346. —— *M98 (lxvi). Sung by Mrs Lindsey in the Opera call'd Thomyris, at ye Theatre Royall. fol.

   S. sh. Begins Shoud ere the fair disdain you. Includes an arr. for Fl. From Coll. No. 333.

347. —— *M98(lxxx). [Cleora. Sung by Mrs. Toft, in ye opera of Thomyris.] fol.

   S. sh. Begins Oh I must fly, cease to try. Includes an arr. for Fl. Imp., lacking most of heading. From same Coll. as No. 339.

348. —— *M98 (lxxxi). [Tigranus. Sung by Mr. Lawrance in ye Opera of Thomyris.] fol.

> S. sh. Begins Since in vain I strive to gain you. Includes an arr. for Fl. Imp., lacking heading. From same Coll. as No. 339.

349. TRAVERS, JOHN. M94 (i). Eighteen Canzonets for Two, and three Voices. . . . Set to Musick by John Travers. . . . London Printed for the Author by John Simpson. . . . [c. 1745] fol.

> Pp. (6), 64. Includes Ded. to Pepusch, List of subscribers, Table.

350. TWELVE. M153 (iv). Twelve Duets or Canzonets for two German Flutes or Voices Compos'd by Sigr. Hasse &c. To which is added the favourite Song of Sigra Galli London. Printed for I. Walsh. . . . [1748] obl. fol.

> Pp. 13. Short score. Includes List of Walsh's pubs. Hasse only composer named (1 duet).

351. TWO. B3 (iii). Two Divine Hymns: being a Suppliment to the Second Book of Harmoniae Sacra. London: Printed by W. Pearson . . . for Henry Playford. . . . 1700. fol.

> Pp. 8. Composers: Clarke, Croft.

352. VENETIAN. M153 (i). Venetian Ballads Compos'd by Sigr. Hasse And all the Celebrated Italian Masters Printed for Jno Walsh. . . . [London, 1742] obl. fol.

> Pp. (1), 40. In score. Includes Ded. to Charles Sackville Count of Middlesex by Adam Scola. On v⁰ of t-p. occurs Raccolta di Gondoliere &c. . . . Composers: Auletta, Lampugnani, Pergolesi, the remainder presumably by Hasse. Texts in Italian.

353. —— M153 (ii). A Second Set of Venetian Ballads For the German Flute, Violin, or Harpsicord. Compos'd by Sigr. Hasse [etc. as above]. . . . London. Printed for and Sold by I. Walsh. . . . [1742] obl. fol.

> Pp. 40. In short score. No composers named. Texts in Italian.

354. —— M153 (iii). A Third Set of Venetian Ballads [etc., as for No. 353]

> Pp. 39. In short score. No composers named. Texts in Italian.

VOCAL WORKS

355. VENTURI, STEFANO. *B35b (iii). Basso di Stefano Venturi del Nibbio Il Quarto Libro de Madrigali a Cinque Voci. . . . In Venetia, MDXCVIII. Appresso l'Herede di Girolamo Scoto. sm. 4°

Pp. (*1*), *22,* (*1*). *Includes Ded. to Angelo Menervetti, Index. Imp., B. pt. only.*

356. WALOND, WILLIAM. M76. Mr. Pope's Ode on St. Cecilia's Day Compos'd by Willm. Walond. . . . London Printed for the Author. [*c.* 1760] fol.

Pp. (*2*), *84. In score. Includes List of subscribers.*

357. WATTS, ISAAC. *A16. Hymns and Spiritual Songs. In Three Books. I. Collected from the Scriptures. II. Compos'd of Divine Subjects. III. Prepar'd for the Lord's Supper. By I. Watts. The Ninth Edition. . . . London: Printed for Richard Ford. . . . 1725. 12°

Pp. xxiv, 326, (*4*), *xxv–xxviii,* (*2*). *Includes Preface* (*1st ed.*), *ditto* (*2nd ed.*), *List of Watts's pubs., Tables. Words only.*

358. WEBBE, SAMUEL (The Elder). *E56. Eight Anthems in Score. For the use of Cathedrals, and County Choirs. composed by Samuel Webbe. . . . London, Printed for F. Linley. . . . [1797/8] fol

Pp. (*1*), *59. Includes Ded. to Dean of Lincoln on t-p., Advertisement, Index. 8 copies.*

359. WELDON, JOHN. M77 (xxxix). A Song for four Voices Set by Mr John Welldon Engrav'd from the Original Coppy. [London, *c.* 1730] fol.

S. sh. Begins Let Ambition fire thy mind.

360. —— M98 (v). Panthea A Song Set by Mr. John Weldon. Sung by Mrs Campion at the Theater Royall. [London, *c.* 1700] fol.

Pp. (*2*) *bound in reverse order. Begins* Panthea all the Senses Treats. *Includes an arr. for Fl.*

361. —— M98 (vi). Celia A Song Set by Mr John Weldon. [London, *c.* 1710.] fol.

S. sh. Begins Celia you in Vain deceive me. *Includes an arr. for Fl.*

VOCAL WORKS

362. ——— *M98 (viii). The Marriage Song Sung by Mrs Hudson in the agreeable Disapointment Set by Mr John Weldon. [London, c. 1703] fol.

   S. sh. Begins Love in her bosome. Includes an arr. for Fl.

363. ——— M98 (xvi). The Wakefull Nightingale a Song Sett by Mr. Iohn Weldon. [London, c. 1705] fol.

   S. sh. Begins The Wakefull Nightingale that takes no Rest. Includes an arr. for Fl.

364. ——— M98 (xvii). A Song Set by Mr. John Weldon, & Sung by Mrs Campion. [London, c. 1700] fol.

   S. sh. Begins Cupid instruct an am'rous Swain. Includes an arr. for Fl.

365. ——— *M98 (xviii). A Song Sung by Mrs Campion in the Comedy call'd she wou'd and she wou'd not, Set by Mr Welldon. [London, c. 1703] fol.

   S. sh. Begins Celia my heart has often Rang'd. Includes an arr. for Fl.

366. ——— M98 (xxii). S.sh. Begins From grave Lessons and Restraint. Imp., lacking heading. Includes an arr. for Fl.

367. ——— M98 (xxvii). A Song On a Beauteous Lady, who had bin playing, before the Author came in, Sett by Mr. John Welldon. [London, c. 1700] fol.

   S. sh. Begins When your Angellick Face I'd Seen.

368. ——— M98 (xlviii). A Song Set by Mr Welldon, after the Itallian Maner, The Words by a Lady. [London, c. 1700] fol.

   Pp. (2). Begins In softest Musick. Includes an arr. for Fl.

369. ——— *M98 (lxxxiia). Set by Mr. John Weldon. [London, c. 1716] fol.

   Pp. (2). Begins At Noon in a Sultry Summers day. Half page with Ramondon's setting of the same words (see No. 314). T. Cross Sculp. at foot of page. Includes an arr. for Fl. on reverse side.

370. WHILST. M98 (xlix). A New Song made for the Theatre ye words by Mr. Hill. [London, c. 1710] fol.

  S. sh. Begins Whilst Joyless light conveying.

371. WORGAN, JAMES (The Elder). M78 (viii). Sappho's Hymn to Venus Set to Musick by Mr. James Worgan. [London, 1749] fol.

  Pp. 11. In score. Begins Venus beauty of the Skies.

372. WORGAN, JOHN. M77 (xi). Jockey and Jenny. A favourite Dialogue Set by Mr. John Worgan and Sung by Mr Lowe, and Mrs Arne, at Vaux-Hall. [London, 1748] fol.

  Pp. (2). Begins When Jockey was blest with your love.

373. —— M77 (xiii). The Fair Thief Set by Mr. Worgan, Sung by Mr. Lowe at Vaux Hall. [London, c. 1760] fol.

  S. sh. Begins I tell with equal Truth and Grief. Includes an arr. for Ger. Fl.

374. —— *M77 (xiv). The Shepherds Wedding Set by Mr. Worgan. [London, 1748] fol.

  S.sh. Begins Pastora's come with Myrtle Crown'd.

375. —— M77 (xvii). A Song to an Air in an Organ Concerto for Vauxhall Gardens set by Mr. Worgan. [London, c. 1740] fol.

  S. sh. Begins The Meads and the Groves.

376. WYNNE, JOHN. M77 (vi). Twelve English Songs Set to Musick by Mr. John Wynne. . . . London engrav'd printed & sold by J. Simpson. . . . [1748] fol.

  Pp. 14. Imp., lacking pp. 13, 14.

377. —— M78 (vi). Another copy. Imp., lacking t-p., pp. 1–4, 13, 14.

378. —— *M77 (xxxiii). Love Triumphant over Reason. A new Song Set to Musick by Mr Wynne. . . . [London, c. 1750] fol.

  S. sh. Begins Fond Reason, ah! where art thou fled.

379. YOUNG, ANTHONY. *M98 (xxviii). A Song Sung by Mr Davis at the Theatre, Sett by Mr Anthony Young. [London, c. 1715] fol.

  S. sh. Begins Damon Restrain your Wand'ring Eyes.

II. INSTRUMENTAL WORKS

380. AGUS, GIUSEPPE. M156 (i). [Six solos for a violin with a thorough bass for the harpsichord. . . . Opera seconda. . . . London. Printed for John Johnson.] [c. 1765] fol.

    Pp. 39. Imp., lacking t-p.

381. AIRES. C93. Aires & Symphonys for ye Bass Viol being a choice Collection of ye most favorite Song tunes, Aires & Symphonys out of the late Operas . . . fitted to the Bass Viol by the best Masters. also some excellent Lessons made purpose for yt Instrument. . . . London, Printed for J. Walsh . . . & J. Hare. . . . [c. 1710] obl. fol.

    Pp. (1), 14. Includes Index. Operas are: Almahide, Camilla, Clotilda, Hydaspes, Love's Triumph, Pyrrhus.

382. ALBERTI, DOMENICO. M109 (ii). VIII Sonate per Cembalo Opera Prima da Dominico Alberti. London. Printed for I. Walsh. . . . [1748] obl. fol.

    Pp. 27.

383. —— M154 (i). Another copy.

384. ALBINONI, TOMMASO. C27 (i). Albinoni's Aires in 3 Parts for Two Violins and a Thorough Bass. . . . London Printed for I. Walsh . . . and I. Hare. . . . [1703] obl. 4°

    In 3 pt-bks. Violino Primo, pp. 8; Violino Secondo, pp. 8; Basso Continuo, pp. 7. Vl. II has no t-p.

385. ANDERS, HENDRIK. C55 (i). Trioos Allemande, Courante, Sarabande, Gigue &c. Gecomponeerd door H. Anders. tot Uytreht by Klaas Klaase Knol. [c. 1700] obl. 8°

    In 3 pt-bks. Violino Primo; Violino Secondo; Basso Continuo (all pp. 12).

386. APOLLO. *C75. Apollo's Banquet, Newly Reviv'd: Containing New and Easie Instructions for the Treble-Violin. With Variety of the Best and Choicest Ayres, Tunes, Jiggs, Minuets,

Sarabands, Chacones and Cybells, that have been Perform'd at both Theatres, and other Publick Places. To which are added the Newest French Dances, now in use at Court, and in Dancing-Schools. Several of the Tunes being in the Compass of the Flute. [The Eighth Edition:] entirely New. London, Printed by W. Pearson, for Henry Playford. . . . 1701. obl. 4°

Unpaginated; pp. (64). Pieces No. 1–143. For Vl. solo. Includes Address by Playford, Instructions for the Violin, *List of Playford's pubs. (pp. 7), two Errata. Composers are:* [Anon.], Mr. Jeremy Clarke, Mr. Courtivillee, Mr. J. Eccles, Mr. [S. ?] Eccles, Mr. Finger, Mr. Keene, Mr. King, Mr. Lenton, Mr. Montford, Mr. Morgan, Mr. Motley, Mr. Peasable, H. Purcell, Mr. Teenoe, Mr. Tollett, Mr. Wroth. *Dancer* Mr. Eaglesfield *mentioned. Plays:* Measure for Measure. the Pillgirm (*sic*).

387. ARNE, THOMAS AUGUSTINE. M124 (iii). Mr Arne's Medley Overture. fol.

Imp., 1 p. of Vl. I pt. only. The above is the page heading. From Six Medley or Comic Overtures in seven parts. . . . Compos'd by Dr. Arne, Lampe, Clarke &c. . . . London. Printed for I. Walsh. [1763].

388. AVISON, CHARLES. D92. Six Concerto's in Seven Parts . . . by Charles Avison. . . . Opera Secunda Newcastle: Printed by Joseph Barber. . . . And Sold by Benjamin Cooke. . . . London. . . . MDCCXL. fol.

Imp., lacking Vl. II rip., viola. Remaining pts. are: Violino Primo Concertino, *pp. (5), 13;* Violino Secondo Concertino; Violino Primo Ripieno *(both pp. 9);* Violoncello; Basso Ripieno *(both pp. 8). Vl. I conc. includes Ded. to Colonel Blathwayt, List of subscribers.*

389. —— C12. Six Concertos in Seven Parts for Four Violins, one Alto Viola, a Violoncello and a Thorough Bass with general Rules for Playing Instrumental Compositions in Parts. . . . By Charles Avison. . . . Opera Terza. London. Printed for John Johnson. . . . MDCCLI. fol.

In 7 pt-bks. As for above, plus Violino Secondo Ripieno; Alto Viola; Basso. *Vl. I conc., pp. (1), vi, (1), 16; Vl. II conc.; Vl. I rip.; Vl. II rip.; Viola (all pp. 13); Vc., pp. (1), 14; Bass, pp. (1), 13.*

INSTRUMENTAL WORKS

Last 2 pts. contain short rules for realising from fig. bass; only Vl. I conc. includes Rules for Playing, *Ded. to* Mrs. Ord, *List of subscribers.*

390. —— D64. Six Sonatas for the Harpsichord with Accompanyments for Two Violins and Violoncello. . . . by Charles Avison. . . . Opera Quinta. London Printed for John Johnson. . . . 1756. fol.

Imp., lacking Vl. I pt. 3 remaining pt-bks. are: Violino Secondo; Violoncello *(both pp. 13);* [Harpsichord], *pp. (2), 37. Hpsi. pt. includes Ded. to* Lady Blackett, Advice on Performance.

391. —— M110 (i)-112 (i). *Another copy. Imp., lacking hpsi. pt., and most pp. in M111 (Vl. I) and M112 (Vc.), with remainder defective.*

392. —— M110 (ii)-112 (ii). Six Sonatas for the Harpsichord With Accompanyments for two Violins & a Violoncello Composed by Charles Avison. . . . Opera Settima. London. Printed for R. Bremner. . . . [*c.* 1765] fol.

Imp., lacking hpsi. pt., and most pp. in M111 (Vl. I), and last 3 in M112 (Vc.), remainder defective. Violino Secondo *(M110), pp. 9.*

393. —— M110 (iii)-112 (iii). Six Sonatas, for the Harpsichord, With Accompanyments For two Violins and a Violoncello . . . by Charles Avison. . . . Opera Ottava. London, Printed for the Author, and sold by R. Johnson. . . . J. Walsh, and R. Bremner. Edin. 1764. fol.

Imp., lacking hpsi. pt., and most pp. in M112 (Vc.), remainder defective. Violino Primo *(M111);* Violino Secondo *(M110) (both pp. 11). Each pt. includes Ded. to* Miss Bowes.

394. —— M117 (i)-121 (i). Twelve Concertos for Two Violins, One Alto-Viola, and a Violoncello. . . . Opera Nona. Set I. 1766. London, Printed for the Author . . . by R. Johnson. . . . fol.

In 5 pt-bks. Comprising 6 concertos. Imp., Violino Primo *(M119), pp. 13;* Violino Secondo *(M118), all pp. missing or defective;* Viola *(M120), pp. 10;* Violoncello *(M117), pp. 12, but t-p. and pp. 1-4 missing or defective;* Organ *(M121), pp. 25, but t-p. and pp. 1-4, 7-25 missing or defective. T-p. includes List of Avison's pubs.*

395. —— *M184 (v), 185 (v), 186 (vi)–189 (vi). Two Concerto's The First for an Organ or Harpsichord, in Eight Parts. The Second for Violins, in Seven Parts ... by Charles Avison. ... Newcastle: Printed by Joseph Barber; ... 1742. fol.

> Imp., lacking Vl. I rip. and Vc. pt-bks. Violino Primo Concertino (M185),pp.3; Violino Secondo Concertino (M186); Violino Secondo (M184); Viola (M187) (all pp. 2); Basso, Vc. / Basso ripieno (M188), pp. 3; Keyboard (M189), pp. (1), 9. T-p. lacking in all but M189. M189 includes List of subscribers.

396. BACH, JOHANN CHRISTIAN. *M83 (viii). Canzonette With Variations, Compos'd by Sigr. Bach. Printed and Sold by A. Hummell. ... [c. 1785?] fol.

> Pp. 6. Above is page heading (t-p. lacking?). 15 variations for Kb.

397. BACH, JOHANN SEBASTIAN. C5. Exercices pour le Clavecin par J. S. Bach. Oeuvre I [Partie I] à Vienne, chez Hoffmeister & Comp. à Lepsic, au Bureau de Musique. [1801/2] obl. fol.

> 6 pts. bound together, each with above t-p. and the pt. no. added in ink. The 6 Partitas. Pt. I, pp. 11; Pt. II, pp. 16; Pt. III, pp. 12; Pt. IV, pp. 19; Pt. V, pp. 15; Pt. VI, pp. 23.

398. —— C6. Exercices pour le Clavecin par J. S. Bach. Oeuvre I [I] à Vienne, chez Hoffmeister [etc. as above] [1803] obl. fol.

> Pp. 35. T-p. has Oeuvre I, with the addition in pencil. The Goldberg Variations.

399. —— C7. Le Clavecin bien tempéré ou Preludes et Fugues dans tous les Tons et Demitons du Mode majeur et mineur par J. Seb. Bach I Parthie à Vienne, chez Hoffmeister [etc. as above] [1802] obl. fol.

> Pp. 87. Many of the Preludes and some of the Fugues have been altered and shortened.

400. —— C8. Le Clavecin bien tempéré [etc. as above] I [I] Parthie [etc. as above] [1802] obl. fol.

> Pp. 97. T-p. has Parthie I, with the addition in ink. A more accurate ed. than the above.

401. —— C9. VI Suites pour le Clavecin composées par J. S. Bach.

Oeuvre [I] No. [I] a Leipsic au Bureau de Musique (Hoffmeister et Kühnel). [1802] obl. fol.

> 6 pts. bound together, each with above t-p. and the figure after Oeuvre and No. left blank and added in ink or pencil. Each Pt., pp. 7.

402. —— C10 (i). Six Preludes á l'Usage des Commençants pour le Claveçin composées par J. S. Bach. à Vienne chez Hoffmeister & Compf.: à Leipsic chez Hoffmeister & Kühnel /: Bureau de Musique: / [1802] obl. fol.

> Pp. 7.

403. —— C10 (ii). XV Inventions pour le Clavecin composées par Mr. J. S. Bach. à Vienne chez Hoffmeister & Comp. à Leipsic, au Bureau de Musique. (Nouvelle Edition.) [1801] obl. fol.

> Pp. 15. *Two-part Inventions.*

404. —— *C10 (iii). XV Symphonies pour le Clavecin composées par J. S. Bach. à Vienne chez Hoffmeister [etc. as above] [1801] obl. fol.

> Pp. 20. *Three-part Inventions.*

405. —— *C10 (iv). Fantaisie pour le Clavecin Composées par J. S. Bach No. I â Leipsic au Bureau de Musique /: Hoffmeister et Kühnel: / [1815] obl. fol.

> Pp. 4. *Fantasia in C minor.*

406. —— C10 (v). Fantaisie chromatique composée par J. S. Bach. à Vienne chez Hoffmeister & Compf: à Leipsic au Bureau de Musique. [1802]. obl. fol.

> Pp. 15. *Chromatic Fantasia and Fugue.*

407. BARBANDT, CARL. M109 (vii). A Sonata for the Harpsichord Composed for and Presented to His Present Majesty by Charles Barbandt. London Printed by Authority at Welcker's Musick Shop 1764. obl. fol.

> Pp. 6. *The above is the heading on p. 2. BUCEM has 'Dedicated to His Present Majesty' in error.*

408. BARSANTI, FRANCESCO. D56 (i). Sonatas or Solos for a Flute with a Thorough Bass for the Harpsicord or Bass Violin

Compos'd by Francesco Barsanti London. Printed for & sold by I. Walsh ... and Ioseph Hare.... [1727] fol.

> Pp. 35. In score.

409. BATES, WILLIAM. *M83 (v). Eight Easy Lessons for the Organ or Harpsichord Compos'd by William Bates. London Printed and Sold by Peter Welcker.... [c. 1765] fol.

> Pp. 24. Each Lesson comprises 2 or more mvts.

410. BECKER, DIEDRICH. *C72. Erster Theil Zwey-stimmiger Sonaten und Suiten Nebest einem gedoppelten Basso Continuo gesetzet von Dietrich Beckern Bestalten Rahts-Violisten in Hamburg Violino Primo. Hamburg Gedruckt bey Georg Rebenlein ... 1674. In Verlegung des Autoris bey welchen es auch zu finden. 4°

> In 3 pt-bks. all unpaginated: Violino Primo, pp. (3, 54); Violino Secondo, pp. (57); Basso Continuo, pp. (49, 1). Vl. I includes Ded. to Elders and Council Members of Hamburg, patrons of Becker. BC. includes Errata for all pts. Music consists of 9 sonatas each followed by a suite.

411. BEILBY, THOMAS. *M190, 191. Six Sonatas for the Harpsichord or Forte Piano with Accompanyments of a Violin and Violoncello ... by Thomas Bielby. London Printed by Welcher. ... [1772] fol.

> Vl. pt. is included on a 3rd stave in the Kb. pt. Violoncello (M190), pp. 6; Keyboard (M191), pp. (4), 30. Kb. pt. includes List of Welcker's pubs. (pp. 4). Sonatas consist of either 3 mvts. with slow middle mvt., or 2 quick mvts.

412. BERG, GEORGE. *M167 (iv). XXIV Duets for Frenchhorns Trumpets or German Flutes ... by George Berg. London Printed for John Johnson.... [c. 1764?] obl. 8°

> Pp. 24. Imp., lacking pp. 17–24.

412a. BESARDUS, JOANNES BAPTISTA. B8. Thesaurus Harmonicus. .... Coloniae Agrippinae, Excudebat Gerardus Greuenbruch, sumptibus Authoris.... MDCIII. fol.

> Pp. (10), ff. 172, pp. (7). Includes Privilege, Ded. to Philippo Gulielmo Auraniae Principi, Preface, Verses, Errata, De modo, intestudine studendi libellus.

INSTRUMENTAL WORKS

413. BETTI, Martino. *C30 (viii). A Solo in A♯ for a Violin by Sigr Martino Betti. The Solo Proper for the Harpsicord or Spinnet. [London, c. 1705] fol.

> Paginated 13–16; from a Coll. published by Walsh and Hare. In score.

414. ——— *C30 (xi). Violino Solo a♯ del Martino Betti Perform'd by Sigr. Gasperini at the Theater Royall The Solo Proper for the Harpsicord or Spinnett. [London, c. 1705] fol.

> Pp. 4. In score. From same Coll. as No. 413.

415. BIBER, Heinrich Johann Franz von. *C42. Fidicinium Sacro-Profanum, Tam Choro, quam Foro Pluribus Fidibus concinnatum, & concini aptum, sub Auspiciis Celsissimi Maximiliani Gandolphi. . . . Henrici J. F. Biber Capellae Vice-Magistro ejusdem Celsissimi. Violino Primo. Sumtibus Authoris, apud Wolfgangum Mauritium Endterum, Bibliopol. Norimbergens. [1680] fol.

> In 6 pt-bks. Violino Primo, pp. (3), 28, (1); Violino Secondo, pp. 14; Viola Prima; Viola Secunda (both pp. 28, (1)); Violone, pp. 25, (1); Basso Continuo, pp. 29. Vl. I pt. includes the Ded. and Errata for all pts., and engraved portrait of Biber aged 36. Each pt. includes Index. Music consists of 6 sonatas for 2 Vls., 2 Violas, Violone, and BC., and 6 for Vl., 2 Violas, Violone, and BC.

416. BIRCKENSTOCK, Johann Adam. D59. XII Solos for a Violin with a Thorough Bass for the Harpsicord or Bass Violin Composed by Gio. Adamo Birckenstok Opera Prima London. Printed for and sold by I. Walsh . . . and Ioseph Hare. . . . [c. 1732] fol.

> Pp. 71. In score.

417. BLOW, John. *C14. A Choice Collection of Lessons for the Harpsichord, Spinnet, &c. Containing four Sett's. . . . By Dr. Iohn Blow, Ingrav'd for, and Sold by Henry Playford. . . . [London, 1701] obl. 4°

> Pp. 21. Music consists of 3 suites in D minor, A minor, C major.

418. BONONCINI, Giovanni Maria. C38. Bononcini's Ayres In 3 Parts, As Almands Corrants Preludes Gavotts

Sarabands And Jiggs. With A Through Bass For The Harpsicord. London Printed and Sold by I: Walsh . . . and I: Hare. . . . [1701] obl. fol.

> In 3 pt-bks. Violino Primo; Violino Secondo (*both pp. 6*); Bassus, *pp. 5. Music consists of 24 pieces, mostly dances.*

419. BORUNLASKI, JOSEPH. *C11. The Volunteer; A New Sonata for the Piano Forte or Harpsichord Composed by Joseph Count Borunlaski. . . . James Johnson Entered in Stationers Hall. Sculpt. Edinburgh. [*c.* 1800?] fol.

> *Pp. 7. Ded. on t-p. to Hon. Mrs. Buchanan.*

420. BOYCE, WILLIAM. M113 (iv), 115 (iv), 116 (iv). Twelve Sonatas for Two Violins; With a Bass for the Violoncello or Harpsichord. By William Boyce. . . . London, Printed for the Author . . . by I. Walsh. . . . 1747. fol.

> *In 3 pt-bks. Violino Primo (M116) pp. (9), 34, (2); Violino Secondo (M115), pp. 34; Basso e Violoncello (M113), pp. 30. M116 includes List of Walsh's pubs. (pp. 2), Privilege, List of subscribers.*

421. BROENNEMULLER, ELIAS. *D57. Fasciculus Musicus Sive Tabulae Varii Generis Modorum ac Concentum Musicorum Notis Consignatae et Compositae ab Elia Brunnemullero. Leovardiae Excud. F. Halma. . . . [1710] fol.

> *Pp. (1), 41. In score. Includes Ded. to Queen Anne, Privilege dated 30. iv. 1710. Music consists of dances for Kb., solos with fig. bass for Ob., Recorder, or Vl., and 4 arias in Italian with Ob. obbligati.*

422. BURGESS, HENRY (the Younger). D61. Six Concertos, for the Organ and Harpsichord, also for Violins & other Instruments in 5 Parts Compos'd by Mr. Hen. Burgess Junr. London Printed for J. Walsh. . . . [*c.* 1740] fol.

> *In 5 pt-bks. Violino Primo, pp. 9; Violino Secondo, pp. 8; Tenore, pp. 7; Basso, pp. 8; all with above t-p. 5th pt-bk., pp. 38, has different t-p.:* Six Concertos for the Harpsichord or Organ Compos'd by Mr. Henry Burgess Junr. London. Printed for the Author, Sold by I. Walsh. . . . *i.e. the 6 concertos arr. for Kb. solo. Imp., Vl. I pt. t-p. defective. Concerto VI has Ob. pt. for last mvt. printed separately and inserted in Vl. I pt.*

423. BURTON, JOHN. M109 (vi). A Favourite Lesson Compos'd by Mr. Burton. Printed for Henry Thorowgood. [London, *c.* 1765] obl. fol.

Pp. 5. The above is the heading on p. 2. For Kb.

424. CALEDONIAN. M182A (i). Caledonian Country Dances Being A Collection of all the Celebrated Scotch Country Dances now in Vogue. ... for the Violin, Hoboy, or German Flute; with their Basses for the Bass Violin or Harpsicord. 3d. Edition carefully Corrected. ... London. Printed for ... I. Walsh. ... [1750] obl. 8°

Pp. 100.

425. —— *M182A (ii). Caledonian Country Dances Book the Second. Being A Collection [etc. as above] [*c.* 1752] obl. 12°

Pp. 100. Imp., pp. 1–12, 65–70 missing or defective.

426. CASTELLO, DARIO. †*C45. Sonate Concertate in Stil Moderno per Sonar nel Organo Overo Spineta con Diversi Instrumenti. A II & III Voci con il Basso Continuo. Di Dario Castello Venetiano Libro Primo. ... Canto Primo. En Anversa Presso i Heredi di Petro Phalesio. ... MDCLVIII. fol.

In 4 pt-bks. Canto Primo (Soprani, Violini); Canto Secondo (Soprani, Trombone overro Violeta, Fagotto), (both pp. 25); Basso (Fagotto), pp. 9; Basso Continuo, pp. 13. Canto Primo t-p. has Voci crossed out in ink and inst. added instead. Each pt. includes Index. Music consists of 12 sonatas, 1–3 for two Soprani, 4–6 for two Soprani e Trombon overo Violeta, 7–8 for two Sopran & Fagotto, 9–11 for two Violini e Fagotto, 12 for two Violini & Trombon overo Violetta; all with BC.

427. CAZZATI, MAURITIO. *C64. Suonate a Due Violini con suo Basso Continuo per l'Organo. Di Mauritio Cazzati Maestro di Capella in S. Maria Maggiori di Bergamo. Opera Decima Ottava. Violino I. En Anversa, Pressa i Haeredi di Pietro Phalesio. ... MDCLXXIV. 4°

In 3 pt-bks. Violino I; Violino II (both pp. 28); Bassus Contin., pp. 25. Each pt. has Index. Music consists of 12 sonatas and a capriccio.

428. CLAGGET, WALTER. M156 (ii). Six Solos and Six Scots Airs With Variations for the Violin or Violoncello with a Thorough Bass for the Harpsichord. . . . Walter Claget Opra 2da. London Printed for the Author, and Sold by him. . . . And Messrs Thompson & Sons. . . . [1763?] fol.

Pp. 39. In score.

429. CLARKE, JEREMIAH. M124 (iv). Mr. Clarke's Medley Overture. fol.

Imp., 1 p. of Vl. I pt. only. The above is the page heading. From Six Medley or Comic Overtures in seven parts. . . . Compos'd by Dr. Arne, Lampe, Clarke &c. . . . London Printed for I. Walsh. [1763].

430. COLLECTION. *C67. A Collection of Musick in Two Parts. Consisting of Ayres, Chacones, Divisions, and Sonata's, for Violins or Flutes. By Mr. G. Finger. To which is Added a Sett of Ayres in Four Parts, By Mr. John Banister. The First Book. London, Printed by J. Heptinstall, for Mr. John Banister, and are to be sold at his House. . . . Mr. Carr's Shop. . . . Mr. Playford's. . . . 1691. obl. 4°

In 2 pt-bks. One contains the First Treble *pt. of a sonata and short pieces, a solo sonata with fig. bass in score, dances for* First *and* Second Treble *by Banister on adjacent pages. The other contains the* Second Treble *pt. of the sonata and short pieces, various pieces for a solo instr., and* Tenor *and* Bass *pts. for the dances placed on adjacent pages (both pp. 21).*

431. COMIC. M182 (i). [The Comic Tunes to all the Late Opera Dances. . . . Vol. III. Part I] Londo[n. Printed for I. Walsh. . . .] [*c.* 1750?] obl. 8°

Pp. 20. Imp., lacking most of t-p., and pp. 1–6. Dancers are: Sigra. Auretti, Sigra. Campioni, Sigr. Nardi, Sigra. Sodi. *In short score with occasional indications of instrumentation.*

432. —— M182 (ii). The Comic Tunes to all the Late Opera Dances As Perform'd by Siga. Auretti, Sodi. Campioni &c. at the King's Theatre in the Hay Market. Set for the German Flute, Violin, or Harpsicord. Compos'd by Sigr. Hasse, and ye most Eminent Italian Authors. Vol. III. Part II London. Printed for I. Walsh. . . . [*c.* 1750?] obl. 8°

Pp. 21–40. Imp., lacking p. 22. Dancers in addition to those on t-p.: Sigr. Bronorio, Sigr. Campioni, Sigra. Nardi. *Details as for No. 431.*

433. —— M182 (iii). The Comic Tunes [etc. as for No. 432]. . . . Vol. III. Part III. London. Printed for I. Walsh. . . . [*c.* 1750?] obl. 8°

Pp. 41–58. Imp., lacking p. 50. Dancers are: Sigra. Auretti, Sigra. Bronorio, Sigr. Campioni, Sigra. Nardi, Sigr. Sodi. *Details as for No. 431.*

434. —— M182 (iv). The Comic Tunes [etc. as for No. 432]. . . . Vol. III. Part IV. London. Printed for I. Walsh. . . . [*c.* 1750?] obl. 8°

Imp., only pp. 59–69 remaining. Dancers are: Sigra Auretti, Sigr. Bronorio, Sigra. Nardi, Sigr. Sodi. *Details as for No. 431.*

435. —— M181. [The Comic Tunes to all the Late Opera Dances etc.] [as for No. 432?] [*c.* 1750?] obl. 8°

Pp. c. 41. Imp., lacking t-p. and pp. 32 to end. Dancers are: Sigra. Barberini, Mons. Desnoyer, Sigr. *and* Sigra. Fausan. *Details as for No. 431.*

436. CORBETT, WILLIAM. M113 (i)–116 (i). Le Bizzarie Universali, a Quatro cio Due Violini, Viola e Basso Continuo Concerto's in four Parts. . . . Composed by William Corbett. . . . Opera VIII. . . . London; Printed for the Author. . . . [*c.* 1728] fol.

In 4 pt-bks. Imp. M116 *(Vl. 1);* M115 *(Vl. 2) (both pp. 13);* M114 *(Viola), all pages missing;* M115 *(Organ, Vc.), pp. 13, but p. 13 missing. Ded. to Queen Christiana.*

437. CORELLI, ARCANGELO. D53. The Score of the Four Setts of Sonatas Compos'd by Arcangelo Corelli. For two Violins & a Bass. . . . Vol. 1st. . . . The Whole Carefully Corrected by several most Eminent Masters, and revis'd by Dr. Pepusch. Engraved . . . by Tho. Cross. London. Printed for and Sold by Benjamin Cooke. . . . [1732] fol.

Set I (Op. 1), pp. (1), 43; Set II (Op. 2), pp. 34; Set III (Op. 3), pp. 54; Set IV (Op. 4), pp. 43. Includes Ded. to Sir Richard Corbet by Cooke. The publisher's imprint has paper pasted over it on which occurs Sold by Iohn Walsh. . . .

438. *M62. The Score of the Four Setts of Sonatas Compos'd by Arcangelo Corelli. [etc. as above] London. Printed for and sold by John Johnson. . . . [c. 1740] fol.

Pp. of each Set as above. Includes portrait of Corelli by J. Cole, Ded. to Sir Richard Corbet by Cooke.

439. —— †*C50. Violino I. Suonate a Tre, Due Violini, e Violone, col Basso per l'Organo. Di Arcangelo Corelli da Fusignano detto il Bolognese. Opera Prima. . . . In Anversa, Stampata in Casa di Henrico Aertssens. . . . MDCLXXXXIII. 4°

In 4 pt-bks. Violino I, pp. 40; Violino II, pp. 39; Violone; Organo (both pp. 32). Each pt. includes Index.

440. —— M129 (i), 130 (i), 132 (i). Archangelo Corelli Opera Prima XII Sonatas of three parts for two Violins and a Bass with a Through Bass for ye Organ Harpsicord or Arch Lute Engrav'd from ye Score and Carefully Corected by ye best Italian Masters. . . . London Printed for I. Walsh. . . . [1733] fol.

In 3 pt-bks. M130 (Vl. 1); M132 (Vl. 2); M129 (Vc) (all pp. 24).

441. —— *C49. Violino Primo. Suonate da Camera a Tre, Due Violine, e Violone, o Cimbalo. Del Sig. Arcangelo Corelli. Opera Seconda. In Anversa. Appresso Henrico Aertssens. . . . MDCLXXXIX. 4°

In 3 pt-bks. Violino Primo; Violino Secondo; Violone o Cimbalo (all pp. 35). Each pt. includes Index.

442. —— C80. Suonate da Camera a Tré Composta de Arcangelo Corelli. Opera Seconda. In Amsterdam per Etienne Roger. [c. 1695] obl. 8°

In 3 pt-bks. Vl. 1; Vl. 2 (both pp. 18); BC., p. 16.

443. —— M129 (ii), 130 (ii), 132 (ii). Archangelo Corelli Opera Secunda XII Sonatas of three parts [etc. as for No. 440] [1733] fol.

In 3 pt-bks. M130 (Vl. 1); M132 (Vl. 2); M129 (BC.) (all pp. 18).

444. —— M129 (iii), 130 (iii), 132 (iii). Archangelo Corelli Opera Terza XII Sonatas of three parts [etc. as for No. 440] [1733] fol.

In 3 pt-bks. M130 (Vl. 1); M132 (Vl. 2); M129 (BC.) (all pp. 25).

445. —— *C33. Violino Primo. Suonate da Camera, a Tre, Doi Violini, Violoncello, e Cembalo. Da Arcangelo Corelli. Da Fusignano, detto il Bolognese. Opera Quarta. Prima Parte. ... In Anversa, da Henrico Aertssens. ... 1692. ... fol.
> *In 4 pt-bks.* Violino Primo, pp. 24; Violino Secondo, pp. 20; Violoncello; Cembalo (*both pp. 20*). Each pt. includes Address by Corelli and Index.

446. —— M129 (iv), 130 (iv), 132 (iv). Archangelo Corelli Opera Quarta XII Sonatas of three parts [etc. as for No. 440] [1733] fol.
> *In 3 pt-bks. M130 (Vl. 1); M132 (Vl. 2); M129 (BC.) (all pp. 16). BC. pt.* = *Vc. and cembalo pts. in No. 445.*

447. —— D68. XII Sonata's or Solo's for a Violin a Bass Violin or Harpsicord Compos'd by Arcangelo Corelli. His fifth Opera. This Edition has ... ye Graces to all ye Adagio's ... by Arcangelo Corelli. ... London Printed for J. Walsh. ... [*c.* 1733] fol.
> *Pp. 92. In score. On p. 62 occurs 2nd t-p.:* The Second Part Containing Preludes, Allemands ... & ye Follia. by Arcangelo Corelli Printed for J. Walsh. *i.e. sonatas 7–12. The Graces are added on a 3rd stave above the Vl. pt.*

448. —— M150. Sonate a Violino e, Violono o Cimbalo da Arcangelo Corelle (*sic*). ... Opera Quinta Parte Prima, London. Printed for and Sold by John Johnson. ... [*c.* 1750] fol.
> *Pp. 69. In score. Includes 2nd t-p.:* Preludi, Allemande. ... Follia. ... Parte Seconda. London, [etc. as above].

449. —— M143–9. Concerti Grossi con duoi Violini e Violoncello di Concertino obligati e duoi altri Violini, Viola e Basso si Concerto Grosso ad arbitrio. ... Opera Sesta. Parte Prima. A Amsterdam Chez Estienne Roger. ... [1712] fol.
> *In 7 pt-bks. Imp. M143 (Vl. 1 conc.), pp. 34, but t-p. and pp. 1–16 missing; M144 (Vl. 2 conc.), pp. 33; M149 (Vc. conc.), pp. 34; M145 (Vl. 1 rip.); M146 (Vl. 2 rip.) (both pp. 27); M147 (Viola), pp. 25 (?), but lacking pp. 17–25 (?); M148 (BC.), pp. 27. Ded. to Giovanni Guglielmo, Prince Palatine of the Rhine on t-p. Each pt. includes 2nd t-p.:* Preludii, Allemande, ... Parte Seconda per Camera. A Amsterdam Chez Estienne Roger. ...

450. —— D54. The Score of the Twelve Concertos Compos'd by Arcangelo Corelli. For two Violins & a Violoncello, with two Violins more, a Tenor & Thorough Bass for Ripieno Parts, which may be doubled at pleasure. . . . Vol. IId. The Whole Carefully Corrected by several most Eminent Masters, and revis'd by Dr. Pepusch. . . . London Printed for and sold by Benjamin Cooke. . . . Where also may be had . . . the Four Setts of Sonatas by the same Author. vol. 1st. [1732] fol.

Pp. (1), 139. Imp., lacking pp. 134–9. Includes Ded. to Ralph Jenison of Walworth Hall, Co. Durham, by Cooke.

451. —— D69 (i). Concerti Grossi con duoi Violini, e Violoncello di Concertino obligati, e duoi altri Violini, Viola, e Basso di Concerto Grosso. . . . Da Arcangelo Corelli. . . . Opera Sesta. XII Great Concertos, or Sonatas . . . being the Sixth and last work of Arcangelo Corelli. . . . London Printed for I. Walsh . . . and I. Hare. . . . [c. 1735] fol.

Imp., only 3 pt-bks. Vl. 2 conc., pp. 33; Vl. 2 rip., pp. 27; Vc. conc., pp. 34, but lacking t-p. and pp. 1–2. Each pt. includes 2nd t-p.: Preludii, Allemande. . . . Parte Seconda per Camera London Printed for I. Walsh.

452. —— M63. The Score of the Twelve Concertos Compos'd by Arcangelo Corelli. For two Violins and a Violoncello, with two Violins more, a Tenor and Thorough Bass for Ripieno Parts, which may be doubled at pleasure. . . . Vol. IId. The whole Carefully Corrected by several most Eminent Masters, and revis'd by Dr. Pepusch. . . . London Printed for and sold by John Johnson. . . . [c. 1740] fol.

Pp. 139. Imp., pp. 10, 11, 52, 53, 138, 139 defective. Includes same portrait and Ded. as No. 438.

453. —— *C30 (vii). A Solo in A♯ for a Violin by Arcangelo Corelli The Solo Proper for the Harpsicord or Spinnet. [London, Printed for Walsh and Hare. c. 1705] fol.

Pp. 9–12. In score. From the same Coll. as No. 413.

454. COURT. C73. Court Ayres: Or, Pavins, Almains Corant's, and Sarabands, of two parts, Treble & Basse, for Viols or Violins. Which may be perform'd in Consort to the Theorbo Lute, or Virginalls. Treble. London, Printed for John Playford. . . . 1655. obl. 4°

In 2 pt-bks. Treble, pp. (2), 112; Basse, pp. (2), 90. Each pt. includes Ded. to William Ball, eldest son of Sir Peter Ball, Preface, (both by Playford). Composers are: [Anon.], Mr. John Carwarden, Mr. William Childe, Mr. Richard Cobb, Dr. Charles Colman, Mr. Richard Cook, Sir Edward Golding, Mr. William Gregory, Mr. George Hudson, Mr. Simon Ives, Mr. John Jenkins, Mr. William Lawes, Mr. Valentine Oldis, Mr. Benjamin Rogers, Mr. Ben. Sandley, Mr. Christopher Simpson, Mr. John Taylor, Capt. Silas Taylor, Mr. Vaux.

455. DEAN, THOMAS. *C30 (x). A Solo in A♯ for a Violin and a Bass by Mr Tho Dean of the New Theatre the Solo Proper for the Harpsicord or Spinnett. [London, Printed for Walsh and Hare. c. 1706] fol.

Pp. 5-7. In score.

456. DEMOIVRE, DANIEL. *C100. Aires made on purpose for a Flute as Allemands Gavotts Sarabands Minuets and Jiggs for the Improvement of the hand, with Great Variety of Aire Suitted to the Instrument Compos'd by Mr. Demoivre 3d. Collection. Printed for I. Walsh ... and I. Hare. ... [c. 1705] obl. 4°

Pp. 14. Music consists of 7 suites for Recorder solo.

457. DIESINEER, GERHARD. C81. [Instrumental Ayrs in Three, and four Parts, Two Trebbles, Tenor and Bass. ... By Gerhard Diesineer] [c. 1680] obl. 4°

In 3 pt-bks. Imp., each pt. lacking t-p. [First Treble]; [Second Treble] (both pp. 75); [Bass], pp. 71. Treble I pt. includes Address.

458. DIEUPART, CHARLES. *C31. Six Suittes Divisées en Ouvertures, Allemandes, Courantes, Sarabandes, Gavottes, Minuets, Rondeaux & Gigues Propres à jouer sur la flûte ou le Violon avec une Basse Continue Composées Par Monsieur Dieupart A Amsterdam chez Estienne Roger. ... [c. 1705] fol.

In 2 pt-bks. Recorder or Vl.; BC. (both pp. 16). For each suite there is a suggested transposition for either a flute de voix or a flute du quatre.

459. DIVISION-VIOLIN. *C74 (i). The First Part of the Division-Violin; A Collection of Divisions upon several Grounds for the Treble-Violin. The Fift Edition Corrected with Additions.

London, Printed on Copper-Plates and sold by H. Playford. . . . 1701. obl. 4°

> Pp. (2, 56). Items no. 1–36, but 1st 4 wrong—1, 4, 3, 2. The Ground is placed at the end of the Vl. pt. Concludes with a piece for 2 Vls. on a Ground. Includes List of Playford's pubs., Table. Composers are: [Anon.], Mr. John Banister, Signior Balshar (Batzar), Mr. Becket, Mr. Salomon Eccles, Mr. Farrinel, Mr. Frecknold, Mr. Baptist [Lully?] of France, Mr. Mell, Mr. Paulwheel, Mr. Anthony Pool, Mr. Reading, Col. Van Shmelt, Mr. Simpson, Mr. Robert Smith, Mr. Tollet.

460. DIVISION-VIOLIN. *C74 (ii). The Second Part of the Division-Violin: Containing the Newest Divisions to a Ground, and Scotch Tunes of Two Parts for the Treble-Violin, with several Solo's; by Signior Archangelo Correlli, and others. The Second Edition Corrected, with large Additions. London, Printed on Copper-Plates, and sold by H. Playford. . . . 1693. obl. 4°

> Pp. (1), 20. Music consists of 2 pieces for solo Vl., and 10 pieces for Vl. and bass (sometimes fig.) placed on adjacent pages, and facing opposite directions. Includes List of Playford's pubs.,Table. Composers are: [Anon.], Mr. Tho. Baltzar, Mr. Bullimore, Signior Archangelo Corelli, Mr. John Eccles, Mr. Salomon Eccles, Mr. Tho. Farmer, Mr. Finch.

461. DRAGHI, GIOVANNI BATTISTA. D55. Six Select Sutes (sic) of Leszons for the Harpsicord in Six Severall Keys. Consisting of Preludes, Allemands. . . . Compos'd by Signr. Giovani Baptista Draghi London Printed for I. Walsh . . . and I. Hare . . . and P. Randall. . . . [1707] fol.

> Pp. 35.

462. FELTON, WILLIAM. M83 (x). Six Concerto's for the Organ or Harpsichord With Instrumental Parts Compos'd by Mr. Felton Opera Prima. London Printed for John Johnson. . . . [c. 1745] fol.

> Pp. 45. Imp., Kb. pt. only.

463. FINGER, GOTTFRIED. *C36. Sonatae, XII. Pro diversis Instrumentis. . . . Authore Godefrido Finger. . . . Opus Primum Anno MDCLXXXVIII ce Livre se vend à Amsterdam chez Estienne Roger. . . . fol.

> In 4 pt-bks. I (Vl., Vl. 1); II (Vl. 2); III (Viola, Vl. 3, Viola

di Basso, Viola di Gamba); *IV* (BC.) (*all pp. 24*). *Each pt. includes Index, and an engraving preceding t-p.*

464. FIORE, ANGELO MARIA. *C39. Trattenimenti da Camera A Due Stromenti Violino e Violoncello e Violoncello e Cimbalo del Signore Angelo Maria Fiore Opera Prima A Amsterdam chez Estienne Roger.... [c. 1705] fol.

> *In 2 pt-bks. I (Vl., Vc.), pp. 16; II (Vc., Kb.), pp. 13. The music consists of 14 Trattenimenti, 1–10 for Vl. and BC., 11–14 for Vc. and BC., each with 3 or 4 mvts. Vl./Vc. bk. includes at end a Canon in 2 mvts. for 2 Vcs.*

465. FISCHER, JOHANN CHRISTIAN. *M156 (iv). Rondeau Perform'd on the Hautboy by Mr. Fischer at Vauxhall Adapted lso for the Harpsicord & Transpos'd for the German Flute. [London, c. 1765] fol.

> *Pp. (3). Above is page heading. Ob. pt. and fig. bass (in score). 2 pp.; transpositon for Ger. Fl. 1p. (lacking in BM. copy).*

466. —— *M83 (vii). A Favourite Concerto Adapted for the Harpsicord or Piano Forte Composed by Giovanni Christiano Fischer. London. Printed for and sold by the Author.... [c. 1770] fol.

> *Pp. 10. The piece is in 3 mvts.—Allegro, Adagio, Rondeau; the key E major (Adagio in G minor).*

467. FISHER, F. E. M113 (v), 115 (v), 116 (v). Six Sonatas for Two Violins with a Thorough Bass for the Harpsichord.... Composed by Mr. F. E. Fisher. Opera Prima London Printed for J. Johnson.... [c. 1755] fol.

> *In 3 pt-bks. M116 (Vl. 1); M115 (Vl. 2); M113 (Violoncello e Cembalo) (all pp. 11). Includes Ded. to the Musical Society at Cambridge, List of Johnson's pubs.*

468. —— M126 (iv)–128 (iv). *Another copy.*

469. GABRIELLI, DOMENICO. *C66. Balletti. Gighe, Correnti, e Sarabande, a due Violini, e Violoncello, con Basso Continuo, del Sigr. Domenico Gabrieli, Sonatore di Violoncello in S. Petronio di Bologna ... posta in lama, da Giov. Phill. Heus,

Musico. Opera Prima. Si Vendono in Amsterdam ... apresso Giov. Phill. Heus.... 1693. obl. 4°

In 4 pt-bks. Violino Primo; Violino Secondo; Violoncello; Basso Continuo (all pp. 12). Ded. on t-p. to Pietro Slicher. Music consists of 12 Balletti each of 2 mvts., the second being a dance.

470. GALLIARD, JOHANN ERNST. M96 (iii). Six Sonatas for the Bassoon or Violincello with a Thorough Bass for the Harpsicord Compos'd by Mr. Galliard London. Printed for, & Sold by Iohn Walsh.... [1733] fol.

Pp. 27. In score.

471. GARTH, JOHN. M117 (ii)-121 (ii). Six Concertos For the Violoncello with Four Violins, an Alto Viola, and Basso Repieno ... by John Garth. Printed for the Author ... by John Johnson ... J. Walsh ... and R. Bremner. [1760] fol.

Imp., lacking Vls. 1 and 2 rip. and Vc. conc. pt-bks. M119 (Vl. 1 conc.), pp. 13, but last 3 defective; M118 (Vl. 2 conc.), pp. 12; M120 (Viola), pp. 9, but lacking p. 9 and pp. 5, 6 defective; M121 (organ), all pp. missing or defective; M117 (Basso Repieno), pp. 10. Ded. to H.R.H. Duke of York on t-p.

472. —— M133-4. Another copy. Imp., lacking 6 pt-bks. M134 (Vl. 1), all pp. missing; M133 (Vl. 2), pp. 13, but pp. 1-6, 11-13 missing or defective.

473. —— M110 (iv)-112 (iv), M160 (i). Six Sonata's for the Harpsichord, Piano Forte, and Organ; with Accompanyments for two Violins, and a Violoncello; composed by John Garth, Opera Seconda. London, Printed for the Author, and sold by R. Bremner ... R. Johnson ... T. Smith ... T. Haxby .... MDCCLXVIII. fol.

In 4 pt-bks. Imp. M111 (Vl. 1); M110 (Vl. 2) (both pp. 13); M112 (Vc.), all pp. missing or defective; M160 (Kb.), pp. 2, 29, but pp. 13, 14 defective. M160 includes List of subscribers.

474. —— M109 (iii). Six Voluntarys for the Organ Piano Forte or Harpsichord Composed by John Garth Opera Terza. London Printed by Welcker.... [1771] obl. fol.

Pp. 27.

INSTRUMENTAL WORKS

475. —— M110 (v)–112 (v). A second Sett of Six Sonatas for the Harpsichord, Piano Forte, and Organ [etc. as for No. 473]. . . . Opera IV. London Printed by Welcker. . . . [1772] fol.

> Imp., lacking Kb. pt-bk. M111 (Vl. 1); M110 (Vl. 2) (both pp. 10); M112 (Vc.), all pp. missing or defective.

476. —— M160 (ii), 161 (i), 162 (i). Another copy. Imp., lacking Vl. 2 pt-bk. M161 (Vl. 1); M162 (Vc.) (both pp. 10); M160 (Kb.), pp. 4, 25. M160 includes List of Welcker's pubs. (pp. 4).

477. GEMINIANI, FRANCESCO. D95. Concerti Grossi con Due Violini Violoncello, e Viola di Concertino obligati, e due altri Violini, e Basso di Concerto grosso ad arbitrio il IV. V. e VI si potranno suonare con due Flauti traversieri, o due Violini con Violoncello. . . . Da Francesco Geminiani, Opera Seconda, London. Printed for the Author, and Sold by I. Walsh. . . . [1732] fol.

> In 7 pt-bks. Vl. 1 conc.; Vl. 2 conc., Vl. 1 rip.; Vl. 2 rip. (all pp. 11); Viola, pp. 9; Vc., pp. 11; BC., pp. 8. Only Vl. 1 conc. has t-p.

478. —— D66. Six Concertos, Composed by F. Geminiani. Opera Seconda. The Second Edition, Corrected and Enlarged . . . by the Author. . . . London. Printed for the Author by John Johnson. . . . [1757] fol.

> Pp. 47. In score.

479. —— *M83 (xi). A favourite Minuet with Variations by Mr. Geminiani. [London. John Johnson? c. 1750] fol.

> Pp. 4. The above is the page heading. For Kb.

480. GIARDINI, FELICE. M66 (ii). Sei Sonate a Violino solo e Basso Composte dall Sigr. Felice Degiardino. . . . Opera Prima. London. Printed for the author and sold . . . by J. Cox at Simpson's Musick Shop. . . . [c. 1751] fol.

> Pp. 25, 2. Includes Licence dated 27. ix. 1751, Ded. to Signor Conte di Turpin, List of Cox's pubs. (pp. 2).

481. GIBBS, JOSEPH. M66 (i). Eight Solos for a Violin with a Thorough Bass for the Harpsichord or Bass Violin compos'd

by Joseph Gibbs. . . . London Printed for the Author and sold by Peter Thompson. . . . [1746] fol.

> Pp. (3), 41. Includes Ded. to Sir Joseph Hankey, List of subscribers.

482. GLUCK, CHRISTOPH WILLIBALD VON. M126 (iii)–128 (iii). Six Sonatas for two Violins & a Thorough Bass compos'd by Sigr. Gluck Composer to the Opera. London Printed for J. Simpson. . . . [1746] fol.

> In 3 pt-bks. M128 (Vl. 1); M126 (Vl. 2); M127 (Vc.) (all pp. 13). Each pt. includes List of Simpson's pubs.

483. GORTON, WILLIAM. C94. Never Publish'd before a choice Collection of New Ayres Compos'd and Contriv'd for Two Bass-Viols. By Mr. William Gorton. . . . London. Printed for John Young. . . . 1701. obl. 8º

> In 2 pt-bks. 1st Part; 2nd Part (both pp. 7).

484. GREENE, MAURICE. M154 (iii). A Collection of Lessons for the Harpsicord Compos'd by Dr. Greene. 2d. Book. London. Printed for I. Walsh. . . . [c. 1755] obl. fol.

> Pp. 24. Imp., lacking pp. 9–24. Includes List of Walsh's pubs.

485. HACQUART, CAROLUS. *C41. Harmonia Parnassia, Sonatarum trium, & 4 Instrumentorum, Auctore Carolo Hacquart. . . . Opus secundum, Violino Primo. Trajecti ad Rhenum, Apud Arnoldum ab Eynden. 1686 Sumptibus Auctoris. 5 Partes. fol.

> In 5 pt-bks. Violino Primo, pp. (1), 27; Violino Secondo, pp. (1), 25; Alto Viola di Gamba, pp. (1), 10; Basso Viola di Gamba, pp. (1), 27; Bassus Continuus, pp. (1), 24. Each pt. includes Ded. to Guilielmo Hoogendorp, Index. BC. pt. has pp. bound in reverse order. Music consists of 10 sonatas.

486. ——— *C92. Chelys. Carolo Hacquart Opus Tertium Anno 1686 Hagae Comitis sumptibus auctoris Georg Seiller fecit. obl. 4º

> Pp. 56. T-p. preceded by full page engraving by Georg Seiller. T-p. includes Ded. to Petro Pittenio and Petro Kvysten. Music consists of 12 suites for gamba.

487. —— *C90. X Sonates a 2 Violes de Gambe & 1 Basse Continue egalement bons a jouer sur 2 Bassons ou Basses de Violon Composez par Mr Carolo A Amsterdam aux depens d'Estienne Roger. . . . [*c.* 1710] fol.

> In 3 pt-bks. Premiere Basse; Seconde Basse (*both pp. 13*); Basse Continue, *pp. 8.*

488. HANDEL, GEORGE FRIDERIC. D67. Twelve Grand Concertos in Seven Parts for Four Violins, a Tenor Violin, a Violoncello with a Thorough Bass for the Harpsicord. Compos'd by George Frederick Handel. Publish'd by the Author London Printed for and sold by Iohn Walsh. . . . [1740] fol.

> Imp., lacking Vls. 1 and 2 rip. pt-bks. Vl. 1 conc., pp. (3), 67, but pp. 61–67 missing; Vl. 2 conc., pp. 56; Viola, pp. 48; Vc., pp. 49, but pp. 48–49 missing; BC., pp. 42. Vl. 1 conc. pt. includes Privilege dated 31. x. 1739, List of subscribers. Op. 6.

489. —— M83 (i). Six Concertos For the Harpsicord or Organ Compos'd by Mr. Handel. These Six Concertos were Publish'd by Mr. Walsh from my own Copy Corrected by my Self, and to Him only I have given my Right therein. George Frideric Handel. . . . London. Printed for I. Walsh. . . . [1738] fol.

> Pp. 48. Op. 4. Includes List of Walsh's pubs.

490. —— *M183 (ii)–189 (ii). Handel's Six Overtures for Violins in all their Parts as they were Perform'd at the Kings Theatre in the Operas of Admetus Alexander Scipio Rodelinda Tamerlane Aggrippina the 3d. Collection. . . . London. Printed for . . . I. Walsh . . . and Ioseph Hare. . . . [*c.* 1728] fol.

> In 7 pt-bks. Imp., M183, 184, 186–9 lacking t-p. M185 (Vl. 1); M186 (Vl. 2); M183 (Ob. 1); M184 (Ob. 2, Vl. 3); M187 (Viola); M188 (Vc., Bsn.); M189 (BC.) (*all pp. 8–13*).

491. —— D69 (ii). XXIV Overture for Violins &c. in Eight Parts as they were Perform'd at the Kings Theatre in the Operas of Parthenope. . . . Rinaldo. Compos'd by Mr. Handel. . . . London. Printed for and sold by Iohn Walsh . . . and may be had at Ios: Hare's. . . . [*c.* 1730] fol.

> Imp., only 3 pt-bks. remaining: Vl. 2; Ob. 2; Bsn., Vc., BC. (*all pp. 27*). Vl. 2 and Ob. 2 pts. include an additional unnumbered page headed Overture in Elpidia, by [L. Vinci], from Walsh's print of c. 1720?

INSTRUMENTAL WORKS

492. —— M183 (iii)–189 (iii). Six Overtures for Violins &c. in Seven Parts as they are Perform'd at the King's Theatre in the Operas of Ariadne Orlando Sosarmes Ætius Porus Esther . . . by Mr. Handel. Fifth Collection. . . . London. Printed for I. Walsh. . . . [1734] fol.

> In 7 pt-bks. Imp., lacking t-p. in M185. M185 (Vl. 1), pp. 7; M186 (Vl. 2), pp. 6; M183 (Ob. 1), pp. 7; M184 (Ob. 2), pp. 6; M187 (Viola), pp. 6; M188 (Vc., Organ, BC.), pp. 7; M189 (Vc., Bsn., Organ, BC.), pp. 6. Each pt. includes List of Walsh's pubs. on t-p.

493. —— M183 (iv)–189 (iv). Six Overtures for Violins &c [etc. as above] in the Operas of Justin Arminius Atalanta Alcina Ariodante Pastor fido 2d . . . by Mr. Handel. Sixth Collection London. Printed for . . . I. Walsh. . . . [c. 1737] fol.

> In 7 pt-bks. M185 (Vl. 1); M186 (Vl. 2, Ob.) (both pp. 6); M184 (Vl. 2, Vl. 3, Ob. 2, Horn 2), pp. 7 (paginated 6); M183 (Ob. 1, Trumpet, Horn 1), pp. 9 (paginated 6); M187 (Viola); M188 (Bass, BC., Organ, Vc.); M189 (ibid.) (all pp. 6). Includes List of Walsh's pubs.

494. —— D46. Handel's Overtures in Score From all his Operas and Oratorios viz. [33 overtures with p. references] These Compositions . . . in Score are of great advantage to all Students and Practitioners in Musick. . . . London. Printed for & Sold by I. Walsh. . . . [1740] fol.

> Pp. 178.

495. —— M126 (i)–128 (i). VI Sonates à deux Violons, deux haubois ou deux Flutes traversieres & Basse Continue Composées Par G. F. Handel Second ouvrage. Printed . . . by Iohn Walsh. . . . Note: This is more Correct than the former Edition. [London, 1733] fol.

> In 3 pt-bks. Imp. M128 (Vl. 1, Fl. 1), pp. 25; M126 (Vl. 2), all pp. missing; M127 (Vc., BC.), pp. 22, but t-p. defective. Each pt. includes List of Walsh's pubs.

496. —— M126 (ii)–128 (ii). Seven Sonatas or Trios for two Violins or German Flutes with a Thorough Bass for the Harpsichord or Violoncello compos'd by Mr. Handel. Opera Quinta. London Printed for . . . I. Walsh. . . . [1739] fol.

In 3 pt-bks. Imp. M128 (Vl. 1), pp. 27; M126 (Vl. 2), all pp. missing; M127 (BC.), pp. 26. Each pt. includes List of Walsh's pubs.

497. —— M124 (i). *Another copy.* Imp., Vl. 1 pt. only.

498. —— C101. Suites de Pieces Pour le Clavecin. composées par G. F. Handel. Premier Volume. London Printed for the Author. And are to be had at Christopher Smith's. . . . And by R. Mears. . . . Engraved and Printed at Cluers Printing-Office. . . . [c. 1720] obl. fol.

>Pp. (1), 94. Includes a Preface by Handel in which he states that he has been obliged to publish this ed. because Surrepticious & incorrect copies *had been printed.*

499. —— C102 (i). Suites de Pieces Pour le Clavecin. composees par G. F. Handel. London Printed, & Sold by John Walsh. . . . [1733] obl. fol.

>Pp. 94. T-p. identical with No. 498 except for a blank space instead of Premier Volume.

500. —— C102 (ii). Suites de Pieces Pour le Clavecin. composées par G. F. Handel. Second Volume. London Printed, & Sold by John Walsh. . . . [1733] obl. fol.

>Pp. 83.

501. —— M83 (iii). The Water Musick, Compos'd by Mr. Handel. London, Printed for Thompson & Son. . . . [c. 1760] fol.

>Pp. 4. The above is the heading on p. 4. Consists of Largo, Allegro, March, all in D for Kb. Printer's colophon at foot of p. 4.

502. HARMONIA ANGLICANA. *C37 (i). Harmonia Anglicana Or The Musick of the English Stage, Containing Six sets of Ayers and Tunes in 4 Parts, made for the Operas Tragedys and Comedyes of the Theater Royal, The first Collection which will be continued with the sets of Tunes made for the Play Houses and other occasions, Engraven in a fair Character London Printed & Sold by I: Walsh . . . & I: Hare . . . . [1701] obl. fol.

>In 4 pt-bks. 1st Treble; Second Treble; Tenor; Bass (*all pp. 13*). Includes A New set of Ayres for the Conserts of the Musicall Society the Tunes for all sorts of Instruments. Plays and

composers are: *Lovers Stratagem (Comedy)*—Peasable; *Courtship a la mode (Comedy)*—Croft; *Love's at a Loss (Comedy)*—Finger; *Ambitious Stepmother (Tragedy)*—Lenton; *Unhappy Penitent (Tragedy)*—D. Purcell.

503. —— *C37 (ii). Harmonia Anglicana [etc. as above]. . . . The [2nd.] Collection [etc. as above]. . . . [1701] obl. fol.

In 4 pt-bks. First Treble; Second Treble; Tenor; Bass *(all pp. 12)*. Plays and composers are: *The Mad Lover (Opera)*—Mr. Iohn Eccles; *Virgin Prophetess or the Fate of Troy (Opera)*—Mr. Finger; *Love Makes a Man or Fops Fortune (Comedy)*—Mr. Finger; *Sir Harry Wildair (Comedy)*—Mr. Finger; *Humours of the Age (Comedy)*—Mr. Finger; *Alexander the Great (Opera)*—Mr. Finger.

504. HARMONIA MUNDI. M183 (v), 185 (v)–189 (v). Harmonia Mundi The 2d. collection Being VI Concertos in Six Parts for Violins and other Instruments. . . . [by] Vivaldi, Tessarini, Albinoni, Alberti never before Printed London Printed for and sold by I: Walsh . . . and Ioseph Hare. . . . [1728] fol.

In 6 pt-bks. Imp. M185 *(Vl. 1 conc.), only defective t-p. remaining;* M186 *(Vl. 2 conc., Vl. 2 rip., Vl. 3, Ob.), pp. 12;* M183 *(Vls. 1 and 2 rip.), pp. 12, but pp. 8–12 missing;* M187 *(Viola);* M188 *(Organ, Vc.);* M189 *(ibid.) (all pp. 11).*

505. HART, PHILIP. *C13. Fugues for the Organ or Harpsichord with Lessons for the Harpsichord Compos'd by Philip Hart. London. Printed by Tho. Cross for the Author. . . . [1705?] obl. 4°

Pp. (1), 50. *Includes Ded. to John Jeffreys of Llywell, Brecknockshire.*

506. HAYES, PHILIP. M161 (iii)–162 (iii). Six concertos, with Accompaniments; for the Organ, Harpsichord or Forte-Piano; to which is added a Harpsichord Sonata . . . by Phil: Hayes. . . . London, Published for the Author. . . . [1769] fol.

Imp., *lacking Kb. pt.* M161 *(Vl. 1), pp. 12;* M162 *(Vc.), pp. 11.*

507. HELY, BENJAMIN. C95. The Compleat Violist. or An Introduction to ye Art of Playing on ye Viol. . . . With a Collection of the Psalm Tunes set to the Viol. . . . To which are added some select Aires & Tunes. . . . Also several lessons. . . .

Compos'd ... by ye late famous Master Mr. Benjamin Hely. London. Printed for & Sould by I. Hare ... also sould by B. Norman.... [1699] obl. 8°
Pp. (3), 16.

508. HERSCHEL, FRIEDRICH WILHELM. M161 (ii)–162 (ii). Sei Sonate per il Cembalo, cogli Accompagnamenti di Violino e Violoncello ... composte da Federico Herschel e publicate in Bath.... MDCCLXIX fol.
Imp., lacking Kb. pt. M161 (Vl.), pp. 14; M162 (Vc.), pp. 13.

509. HEUDELINE. *C40. Trois Suittes de Pieces à Deux Violes Propres à jouer sur le violon & le Clavessin Composées par Monsieur Heudeline Livre Premier Seconds Édition Corrigée par l'Autheur de quantité de fautes qui se sont glisées dans l'édition de Paris.... A Amsterdam chez Estienne Roger.... [c. 1708] fol.
In 2 pt-bks. Dessus, pp. 16; Basse, pp. 9.

510. HOBEIN, JOHANN FRIEDRICH. *M109 (ix). A Favorite Lesson for the Harpsichord or Piano Forte Compos'd by I. F. Hobein Senior. Printed for John Rutherford. ... London. [c. 1785?] obl. fol.
Pp. 4. Imp., lacking t-p. The above is the heading on p. 2.

511. KEMPIS, NICOLAUS . C44. Symphoniae Unius, Duorum, Trium, IV, et V. Instrumentorum Adjunctae quatuor 3 instrumentorum & duarum vocum. Auctore Nicolao A Kempis. ... Operis Secundi Liber Primis.... Pars Prima. Antuerpiae apud Magdalenam Phalesia.... MDCXLVII. fol.
In 6 pt-bks. Pt. I (Vl. solo, Vl. 1, Vl. or cornetto, cornetto), pp. (1), 35, (1); Pt. II (Vl. 2, Bass Viola or Bsn., Instr. 2, Vl. 1), pp. (1), 30, (1); Pt. III (Trombone, Bass Viola, Bsn., Vl. 2, Tenor Viola, Alto, Instr. 3), pp. (1), 12, (1); Pt. IV (Bass Viola, Bass, Tenor), pp. (1), 9. (1); Pt. V (unspecified instr. in tenor clef, Cantus), pp. (1), 7, (1); [Pt. VI] (BC.), pp. (1), 29, (1). Each pt. includes Ded. to Jacob Boonen, Archbishop of Mechlin, Index.

512. KONINK, SERVAAS VAN. *C56. Trios pour la Flute le Violon le Hautbois et toutes Sortes d'Instruments faits par Monsieur Servaas de Konink de Musique a Amsterdam.... Premier

Oeuvre. A Amsterdam ches I. L. Delorme et E. Roger. . . . . [1696] obl. sm. 8°

> In 3 pt-bks. Premier Dessus; Second Dessus; Basse (all pp. 32). T-p. includes Ded. to Guillaume de Lanaye. Music consists of 30 Trios, some in the form of suites. The 1st pt. of No. 513.

513. —— *C55 (ii). Trioos voor de Fluyten Hautbois en Violen. . . . door Servatius de Konink Tweede Trioos Boek Vierde Werk tot Amsterdam ten Koften vanden Autheur et se vendent aussi chcs Estienne Roger. . . . [c. 1700] obl. 4°

> In 3 pt-bks. Dessus; Second Dessus; Basse (all pp. 16). Music consists mainly of dance mvts. with a few song arr. The 2nd pt. of No. 512.

514. LA BARRE, MICHEL DE. *C54. Pieces en Trio pour les Violons, Flustes et Haubois, par le Sieur De La Barre. Premier Dessus. a Amsterdam ches I. L. Delorme et E. Roger. . . . [c. 1696] obl. sm. 8°

> In 3 pt-bks. Premier Dessus; Second Dessus; Basse (all pp. 47). Music consists mainly of dance mvts. with a few fantasias, fugues, etc.

515. LADYS BANQUET. *C16. The Ladys Banquet. Being A Choice Collection of the newest & most Airy Lessons for the Harpsichord or Spinett, very usefull for Beginners & all others that are Lovers of these Instruments, set by our best Masters. To be Annualy continued . . . engrav'd on Copper Plates. London Printed for and Sold by I. Walsh . . . and Iohn Hare. . . . 1704. obl. 4°

> Pp. 28. Composers are: Mr. Barrett, Mr. Ier: Clarke, Mr. Courtiville, Mr. Croft, Mr. King, Mdm. Subligny, Mr. Weldon.

516. LADYS ENTERTAINMENT. *C17 (ii). The Ladys Entertainment or Banquet of Musick being a Choice Collection of the Newest and most Airy Lessons for the Harpsichord or Spinet Together with several Excellent Preludes Tocatas and the most favourite Song Tunes in the Opera's all Fairly Engraven. . . . Note these Lessons are likewise proper for the Lute Harp or Organ by Mr. Ramondon. London Printed for I. Walsh. . . . I. Hare . . . and P. Randall. . . . [1708?] fol.

> Pp. 24. T-p. preceded by full page engraving. Composers are: [Anon.], Signr Amadori, Sigr Simonelli.

517. —— *C17 (i). The 2d Book of The Ladys Entertainment or Banquet of Musick [etc. as above] ... for the Lute Harp or Organ by Mr. Ramondon London [etc. as above] [1708] fol.

> Pp. (1), 24. T-p. preceded by engraving as above. Composers are: [Anon.], Signr Fontana, Mr. Henr Hall of Hereford, Mr. Dan: Purcell, Mr. Richardson of Winton. *Stage work:* Camilla.

518. LAMPE, JOHANN FRIEDRICH. M184(vi), 185(vi), 186(vii)–189 (vii). The Cuckoo, A Celebrated Concerto in [Seven] Parts, Viz. Traversa, [Traversa Ripieno], Violin 1, Violin 2, Te'nor, Violoncella, and Bass ... by Lampe. London. Printed for John Wilcox. ... [c. 1740] fol.

> Imp., *lacking* Traversa, i.e. solo Fl., *and printed* Fl. rip. *and* BC. *pts.* M184 (Fl. rip.), 1 MS fol.; M185 (Vl. 1); M186 (Vl. 2); M187 (Viola); M188 (Vc.) (all pp. (2)); M189 (Organ), 1 MS fol. *In t-p.* Seven *and* Traversa Ripieno *have been added by hand, the former above a crossed out* Five. *T-p. of M185 has '*Thomas Sharp 1741*'.*

519. —— M124 (vii). Lampe's Original Medley Overture. fol.

> Imp., 1p. of Vl. 1 pt. only. The above is the page heading. From Six Medley or Comic Overtures in seven parts. ... Compos'd by Dr. Arne, Lampe, Clarke &c. ... London. Printed for I. Walsh. [1763]

520. LANZETTI, SALVATORE. M96 (ii). Six Solos for two Violoncellos or a German Flute and a Bass. Compos'd by Sigr. Salvatore Lanzetti. Opera Seconda. London. Printed for I. Walsh. ... [c. 1740] fol.

> Pp. 34. *In score.*

521. —— M96 (i). Six Solos for two Violoncellos [etc. as above] Lanzetti. [Op. 1] London. Printed for I. Walsh. ... [c. 1745] fol.

> Pp. 41. *In score.*

522. LECLAIR, JEAN MARIE. M126 (vii)–128 (vii). Sonates en Trio Pour Deux Violons Et la Basse Continue Composées Par Mr. Leclair l'Aine. ... Oeuvre IV. Se vend a Paris Chez L'auteur, ... Sr. Boivin. ... Sr. Leclerc. ... Avec Privilége du Roy. [c. 1730] fol.

> *In 3 pt-bks.* M128 (Vl. 1), pp. 28; M126 (Vl. 2), pp. 24; M127 (Organ, Vc.), pp. 27.

523. LEGRENZI, GIOVANNI. *C62. Violino Primo. Suonate dà Chiesà, a dà Camera, Correnti, Balletti, Allemande, e Sarabande à tre, doi Violini, e Violone, con il Basso Continuo. Del Sig. Giovani Legrenzi. Opera Quarta. In Venetia. Apresso Gioseppe Sala. MDCLXXXII. 4°

> In 4 pt-bks. Violino Primo; Violino Secondo; Violone; Basso Continuo (all pp. 28). Music consists of 12 sonatas, 3 sarabandes, 6 courantes, 6 balletts, and 3 allemandes. Each pt. includes Index.

524. ——— †*C63. Violino Primo. Sonate a Due Violini, e Violone. Con il suo Basso Continuo per l'Organo. Del Signor D. Giovanni Legrenzi Opera Ottava. In Venetia. Apresso Gioseppe Sala. 1677. 4°

> In 4 pt-bks. Violino Primo, pp. 32; Violino Secondo, pp. 23; Violone, o Viole, pp. 22; Organo, pp. 24. Each pt. includes Index. Music consists of 6 sonatas a2 and 4 sonatas a3.

525. LESSONS. M109 (v). A Collection of Lessons for the Harpsichord Compos'd by Sigr. Kunzen, Kellery, Agrell & Hoppe. London. Printed for Thompson and Sons. . . . [1762] obl. fol.

> Pp. 33.

526. ——— C18. A Collection of Lessons and Aires for the Harpsichord or Spinnett Composed by Mr: J: Eccles Mr: D: Purcell and others Fairly Engraven London Printed for I. Walsh . . . and I. Hare. . . . [1702] obl. fol.

> Pp. 10, (4). Includes Rules for Playing a Thorough Bass with Examples and Explinations of Cords in General and Rules for Tuning a Harpsichord or Spinnett. The only composers named in the text are: Mr. D. Purcell and Mr. Iohn Eccles.

527. ——— *C77. Select Lessons for the Violin, as Preludes Almands Sarabands Corants Minuets and Iiggs as also the Newest country Dances now in use Fairly Engraven London Printed for and sold by I. Walsh . . . and I. Hare. . . . 1702. obl. sm. 8°

> Pp. (12), 18. Music begins with A Florish or Prelude in every Key on the Violin; the keys are actually the major and minor of C, D, E, F, G, A, and B flat major and B minor. Composers are: Mr. Clark, Mr. Eccles, Mrs. Evans, Mr. Finger, Mr. Keen. Mr. Lenton.

528. —— M109 (iv). Six Easy Lessons for the Harpsichord Compos'd by Sigr. Binder, Mazzinghi, Ritstchel, Legne, Galluppi, Zamperelli Book I. London Printed for Joseph Hill. . . . [*c*. 1765] obl. fol.

> Pp. 25.

529. LOCKE, MATTHEW. C68. Matthew Locke His Little Consort of Three Parts: Containing Pavans . . . for Viols or Violins. . . . To be performed either alone or with Theorbo's and Harpsechord. Treble. London, Printed by W. Godbid for John Playford. . . . 1656. obl. 4°

> *In 3 pt-bks. Unpaginated.* Treble, Tenor; Second Treble, Tenor *(both pp. (11)); Bassus, (pp. (12)). Each pt. includes Address. Bass pt. includes List of Playford's pubs.*

530. LOEILLET, JEAN BAPTISTE. M99. [Sonatas or Solos for a Flute with a Through Bass for the Harpsicord or Bass Violin. . . . Parte Prima London, Printed for J. Walsh . . . & J. Hare. . . .] [*c*. 1712] fol.

> Pp. 53. *Imp., lacking t-p. and pp. 1–4, 37, 38. In score.*

531. —— M124 (ii). XII Sonatas in three Parts Six . . . for two Violins and a Bass, three for two German Flutes and three for a Hautboy & common Flute. . . . Compos'd by Mr. John Loeillet Opera secunda. London Printed for . . . I. Walsh. . . . Ino. and Ioseph Hare. . . . [1725] fol.

> *Imp., only 1 pt-bk. containing Vl. 1, Fl.,* Traversa I *pts., pp. 24.*

532. LONATI, CARLO AMBROGIO. *C30 (ix). A Solo in G♭ for a violin by Carlo Ambrogio The Solo Proper for the Harpsicord or Spinnet. [London, Printed for Walsh and Hare. *c*.1705] fol.

> Pp. 17 20. *In score.*

533. LULLY, JEAN-BAPTISTE. C55(iii). Ouve[r]ture du Triomphe de l'Amour avec tous les Airs de Violons. Composez par Monsieur de Lully. . . . Se Vandent int Musick stuck inde Jonge Roeless steeg. t Amsterdam. [*c*. 1685] obl. 4°

> *In 3 pt-bks., instr. unspecified, 2 with G clef, 1 with F clef, all pp. 16. The above is taken from p. 1 of Vl. 1 pt. only, with insertions or corrections in ink (= square brackets).*

533a. —— B35a (i). Les Trio des Opera de Monsieur de Lully, Mis en ordre pour les concerts. . . . Premier Dessus. A Amsterdam, dans l'Imprimerie de P. & J. Blaeu. . . . 1690. obl. 4°

> In 3 pt-bks. Premier Dessus, pp. (8), 51; Second Dessus, pp. (8), 51; Basse, pp. (8), 82. Two upper pts. have text incipits, Bass pt. has full text. Each pt. includes Ded. to M. Philibert de la Tour, Baron de Bourdeaux by Le Chevalier B, Address to reader, Privilege, Index.

533b. —— B35a (ii). Les Trio des Opera [etc., as above]. . . . 1691. obl. 4°

> In 3 pt-bks. Premier Dessus, pp. (2), 104; Second Dessus, pp. (2), 104; Basse, pp. (2), 88. Each pt. includes Index.

534. MARAIS, MARIN. C82. Pieces a une et a deux Violes Composées par M. Marais. . . . A Paris chez l'Autheur . . . et Jean Hurel. . . . [1686] obl. fol.

> Pp. 120. Includes Privilege dated 20. viii. 1686, Ded. to Lully, Instructions on playing the Viol. Imprint occurs below Privilege. (Cf. No. 535.)

535. —— C83. Basse-continuës des pieces a une et a deux Violes. Avec une augmentation de plusieurs pieçes particulaieres en partition a la fin des dittes Basse-continuës. Composées par M. Marais. . . . A Paris chez l'Autheur . . . et Jean Hurel. . . . [1689] obl. fol.

> Pp. 101. Includes Privilege dated 1. iii. 1689, Preface with remarks on 1686 pub. of which this is the fig. bass pt. Imprint as above.

536. —— *C57. Pieces en Trio pour les Flutes, Violon, & Dessus de Viole Composées par M. Marais . . . 1er Dessus. A Paris chez l'Autheur. . . . Je. Hurel. . . . Hi. Bonneüil. . . . H. Foucault. . . . 1692. obl. 4°

> In 3 pt-bks. 1er Dessus; 2me Dessus; Basse-Continue (all pp. 114). Each pt. includes Privilege, Ded. to Mme. Roland. Imprint occurs below Privilege. Music consists of 67 mvts., mostly dances.

537. —— *C85. Pieces de Viole composées par Mr. Marais. . . . Livre Second A Amsterdam chez Estienne Roger. . . . [c. 1701] obl. fol.

INSTRUMENTAL WORKS

Pp. (*1*), *75. Includes instructions on performance. Music consists of 142 pieces, mostly dances.* (*Cf. No. 538.*)

538. —— *C84. Pieces de Viole [etc. as above] [c. 1701]* obl. fol.
Pp. (*1*), *49. Includes instructions as above. The BC. pt. of No. 537.*

539. MARCELLO, BENEDETTO. M96 (iv). Six Solos for a Violoncello with a Thorough Bass for the Harpsicord Compos'd by Benedetto Marcello Opera Seconda. ... London. Printed for & Sold by Iohn Walsh. ... [1732] fol.
Pp. 25. In score.

540. MATTEIS, NICOLÀ. C29. Senr. Nicola's first and Second Book's of Aire's in 3 Parts Containing Preludes ... and Jigg's with divers Fancye's and Vollentary's in Every Key for two Violins and a Bass The Second Treble. ... Composed by Nicola Matteis Napolitano Libro Primo ett Secundo London Printed for I. Walsh ... and I. Hare. ... [1703] obl. fol.
In 3 pt-bks. Vl. 1, pp. 25; Vl. 2, pp. 23; B.C., pp. 18. Vl. 1 pt. has full page engraving preceding t-p. Each pt. has 2nd. t-p.: The Second Booke of Aire's Containing Preludes ... &c. more Difficult then the Former for the Improvement of the Hand on the Violin Composed by Senr. Nicola Matteis Napolitano Libro Secundo London [etc. as above]. *Vl. 1, pp. 22; Vl. 2, pp. 13; BC., pp. 9.*

541. —— *C30 (vi). A Solo in a♯ for a Violin Compos'd by Mr Nicola The Solo Proper for the Harpiscord or Spinnett.* [London, Printed for Walsh and Hare, *c. 1705*] fol.
Pp. 5–8. In score. See PURCELL, *No. 561.*

542. MAZZAFERRATA, GIOVANNI BATTISTA. *C65. Violino Primo Sonate a Due Violini con un Basetto di Viola se piace del Sig. Gio. Battista Mazzeferrata Maestro di Capella dell' Illustrissima Accademia della Morte di Ferrara. Libro Primo Opera Quinta. In Venetia* MDCLXXVIII. 4°
In 4 pt-bks. Violino Primo, pp. 39, (1); Violino Secondo, pp. 38, (1); Bassetto Viola, pp. 31, (1); Basso Continuo, pp. 37, (1). Each pt. includes Index. Music consists of 12 sonatas. A different ed. from that in BM.

543. MERULA, Tarquinio. †*C51. Violino Primo il Secondo Libro delle Canzoni da Suonare a Tre, Duoi Violini, & Basso del Cavalier Tarquinio Merula gia Maestro Capella in S. Maria Maggior di Bergamo con il Basso Generale Opera Nona. . . . In Venetia Appresso Alessandro Vincenti MDCLV. 4°

> In 4 pt-bks. Violino Primo; Violino Secondo; Basso; Basso Continuo (all pp. 23, (1)). Each pt. includes Index. Music consists of 12 canzone.

544. —— †*C52. Primo Violino. Il Quarto Libro Delle Canzoni Da Suonare A Doi, & à Tre. Del Cavre. Tarquinio Merula Opera XVII. . . . In Venetia. Appresso Alessandro Vincenti. MDCLI. 4°

> In 4 pt-bks. Primo Violino, pp. 62, (1); Secondo Violino, pp. 44; Violone, pp. 39, (1); Basso Continuo, pp. 47, (1). Each pt. includes Index. Ded. on t-p. to Count Nicolo Ponzoni. Music consists of 25 canzone—9 for 2 Vls.; 8 for Vl., Violone; 8 for 2 Vls., Violone— and 3 sonatas and a Sinfonie (sic) di tutti gli tuoni, all for 2 Vls., Violone; all the pieces have BC. in addition.

545. MONDONVILLE, Jean Joseph Cassanea de. M83 (ix). Six Sonates or Lessons for the Harpsicord which may be Accompanied with a Violin or German Flute. Compos'd by Mr. Mondonville. London. Printed for I. Walsh. . . . [1753] fol.

> Pp. 51. In score.

546. MUDGE. D60. Six Concertos in Seven Parts. . . . Compos'd by Mr. Mudge. To which is added Non Nobis Domine, in 8 Parts. London. Printed for I. Walsh. . . . [1749] fol.

> In 7 pt-bks. Vl. 1 conc., pp. 18; Vl. 2 conc., pp. 14; Vl. 1 rip., pp. 16; Vl. 2 rip., pp. 14; Viola, pp. 15; Vc., pp. 16; BC., pp. 26. Non nobis Domine is for instrs. with 2 Viola pts.

547. MUNNINCKX, P. F. *C43. Balletti Allemande, Corante Sarabande, cum Tribus Instrumentis Authore P. F. Munninckx. Violino I. Antuerpiae, apud Haeredes Petri Phalesii. . . . MDCLXXII. fol.

> In 3 pt-bks. Violino I; Violino II; Bassus Viol. vel Bass. Cont. (all pp. 25, (1)). Music consists of 70 mvts., mostly dances, plus 8 hymns with words. Each pt. includes Index.

548. MUSICK. C96. Musick's Recreation on the Viol Lyra-way . . . To which is added . . . some Brief Rules and Instructions for

INSTRUMENTAL WORKS 93

young Practitioners. The Second Edition, Enlarged with Additional New Lessons. London, Printed by A. G[odbid] and J. P[layford the Younger] for J. Playford.... 1682. obl. 4°

Pp. (6), 88. Includes List of Playford's pubs. In 2 Parts; Part II begins on p. 57. Composers are: [Anon.], Mr. T. B., Mr. Banister, Dr. Charles Colman, Mr. Baptist [Draghi], Mr. John Esto, Mr. Farmer, Mr. G. H., Mr. Simon Ives, Mr. Jenkins, Mr. Porter, Mr. William Young.

549. PELLEGRINI, FERDINANDO. M83 (iv). Six Lessons for the Harpsichord Composed by Sigr. F. Pellegrino Oper Vth. London. Printed for R. Bremner.... [*c.* 1763] fol.

Pp. 19.

550. PEPUSCH, JOHANN CHRISTOPH. *C30 (xii). A Solo in D♯ for a Violin by Signr Pepusch The Solo Proper for the Harpsicord or Spinnet. [London, Printed for Walsh and Hare, *c.* 1705] fol.

Pp. 21–24. In score. See PEZ, No. 555.

551. ——— D63. Solos for a Violin with a Through Bass for the Harpsicord or Bass Violin Compos'd by Signr. Pepusch Parti Secunda London Printed for I. Walsh... I. Hare.... [*c.* 1707] obl. fol.

Pp. 35. Imp., lacking Vl. pt. and Pt. I.

552. ——— M104 (iii). Mr. Pepusch's Aires for two Violins.... The whole Fairly Engraven and Carefully Corected. London Printed for J. Walsh.... [1733] fol.

Pp. 24. In score.

553. PERIODICAL. *C4. Periodical Overtures for the Harpsichord, Piano-Forte &c. No. 1 To be continued Monthly.... London Printed & Sold by Longman, Lukey & Co.... [*c.* 1775] obl. fol.

Pp. 51. Only No. 1 has t-p., the others were probably removed in binding. No composers named, but the fly-leaf contains Index in contemporary hand giving composers and p. references, the former are: [J. C.] Bach, [Christian] Cannabich, Crispi, Filtz, Pasquali Ricci, [K.] Stamitz. *Includes Nos. 1–12.*

554. PETERSEN, DAVID. *C35. Speelstukken Samengestelt Door David Petersen. Dese stükken werden gespeelt met een Viool en Bas Continuo. Waar by gervoegt kan werden een theorbe, of Viool dagamba. [Amsterdam, 1683] fol.

> Pp. (1), 32. In score. Includes Ded. to Joannes Hud, Burgomaster of Amsterdam. Music consists of 11 sonatas and 1 suite.

555. PEZ, JOHANN CHRISTOPH. C30 (iv). Sonata in D♯ for Violins in 3 Parts by Christophoro Pez As also a Solo for a Violin by Signr Pepusch neither of them before Printed Publish'd for June to be Continu'd Monthly with the Best and Choisest Sonatas and Solos by the Greatest Masters in Europe for the Year 1704. [London, Printed for Walsh and Hare.] fol.

> In 4 pt-bks. Vl. 1; Vl. 2; Vc.; BC. (all pp. 2). Only Vl. 1 pt. has above t-p. Imp., lacking the Pepusch piece, but see No. 550.

556. PICCINI, NICOLO. M83 (vi). [Overture to La Schiava. . . . London, c. 1768] fol.

> Pp. 5. Imp., lacking t-p. P. 1 has heading Overture La Schiava. For Kb.

557. PRELLEUR, PIERRE. M124 (v). Mr. Prelleur's Medley Overture, As it was Perform'd at the Theatre in Goodman's Fields in the Chymical Counterfeits or Harlequin turn'd Worm Doctor. fol.

> Imp., Vl. 1 pt. only, pp. 1. The above is the page heading. From Six Medley or Comic Overtures. . . . London. Printed for I. Walsh. [1763].

558. ——— M124 (vi). Mr. Prelleur's Second Medley Overture. Printed by Wm. Smith. . . . fol.

> Imp., 1 pt. only: Primo Tutti Oboi e Violin, pp. 1. The above is the page heading. From same Coll. as above.

559. PURCELL, HENRY. C28. A Collection of Ayres, Compos'd for the Theatre, and upon other Occasions. By the late Mr. Henry Purcell. Violino Primo. London, Printed by J. Heptinstall. for Frances Purcell . . . sold by B. Aylmer . . . W. Henchman . . . and Henry Playford. . . . 1697. fol.

> In 4 pt-bks. Vl. 1, pp. (2), 48; Vl. 2, pp. 48; Viola; BC. (both pp. 40). Vl. 1 pt. includes Ded. to Charles, Duke of Somerset by

INSTRUMENTAL WORKS

Frances Purcell. The incidental music comes from Dioclesian, King Arthur, Fairey Queen, Indian Queen, Married Beau, Old Bachelor, Amphitryon, Double Dealer, Distressed Innocency or The Princess of Persia, Gordian Knot Untied, Abelazor, Bonduca, Virtuous Wife.

560. ——— *C15. A Choice Collection of Lessons for the Harpsichord or Spinnet Composed by ye late M. Henry Purcell. . . . The third Edition with Additions & Instructions for beginners Printed on Copper Plates for Mrs. Frances Purcell. . . . 1699. obl. 8°

   Pp. (5), 63. Instructions include Rules for Graces.

561. ——— C30 (ii). That Excellent Sonata in F for Violins in 3 Parts call'd the Golden Sonata Compos'd by Mr. Henry Purcell Also Mr. Nicola's Favourite Solo in a Publish'd for Febr . . . to be Continu'd Monthly with the Best and Choisest Sonatas and Solos by the Greatest Masters in Europe for the Year 1704. [London, Printed for Walsh and Hare] fol.

   In 4 pt-bks. bound together: Vl. 1; Vl. 2; Vc.; BC. (all pp. 2). Only Vc. pt. has above t-p. Imp., lacking Nicola Matteis's piece, but see No. 541.

562. RAMEAU, JEAN-PHILIPPE. *M154 (ii). A [2d] Collection of Lessons for the Harpsicord Compos'd by Mr. Rameau. Opera [3za]. London Printed for I. Walsh. . . . [1765?] obl. fol.

   Pp. 27. Enclosures in brackets added by hand. Includes List of ornaments and their performance, List of Walsh's pubs.

563. REAL, JOSEPH. *M167 (ii). Twenty four Duets for two French-Horns two Guittars, or two German Flutes . . . by M. Joseph Real. London Printed for Thompson and Son. . . . [c. 1785?] obl. 4°

   Pp. 24. Imp., lacking pp. 23, 24. Op. 5 (?). List of Thompson's pubs. in BM. Hirsch IV. 1111 (15) includes Real's Ops. 1 and 5, each comprising 24 duets, under heading 'Military Music for French Horns, Clarinets, Hautboys, and Bassoons'.

564. ——— *M167 (i). [Twenty four Duets for two French-Horns etc. as above?] [London, c. 1780?] obl. 4°

   Pp. 24. Imp., lacking t-p. and pp. 1–4. Op. 1 (?), by Real (?). (See above.)

565. ROSEINGRAVE, THOMAS. D93. Voluntarys and Fugues made on purpose for the Organ or Harpsicord by Mr. Thomas Roseingrave.... London. Printed for and sold by I. Walsh ... and Ioseph Hare.... [1728] fol.

Pp. 29.

566. ROZELLI. *M167 (iii). Twenty One Duets For two French Horns or two Guittars To which is Added Three Trios for 3 Horns ... by Sigr. Rozelli Op. 4 London Printed for C. and S. Thompson.... [*c.* 1760?] obl. 4°

Pp. 17, though paginated 16.

567. RUSH, GEORGE. M109 (viii). A First Concerto for the Harpsichord with Accompanyments for Violins, French-Horns &c. Composed by Mr. Rush. London. Printed by Welcker. [*c.* 1733] obl. fol.

Pp. 5. Imp., Kb. pt. only.

568. SAINT GERMAIN, CONTE DE. M126 (v)–128 (v). Six Sonatas for two Violins with a bass for the Harpsicord or Violoncello compos'd by Ms. de St. Germain. London. Printed ... by I. Walsh.... [1750] fol.

In 3 pt-bks. M128 (Vl. 1), pp. 20; M126 (Vl. 2), pp. 17; M127 (BC.), pp. 16. M128 includes Privilege dated 27. xi. 1749.

569. SCARLATTI, DOMENICO. D62. Twelve Concerto's In Seven Parts for Four Violins, one Alto Viola, a Violoncello, & a Thorough Bass, done from two Books of Lessons for the Harpsicord. Composed by Sigr. Domenico Scarlatti with additional Slow Movements from Manuscript Solo Pieces, by the same Author ... by Charles Avison.... London. Engraved by R. Denson, and Printed for the Author, by Joseph Barber in Newcastle.... MDCCXLIV. fol.

Imp., lacking Vls. 1 and 2 rip. and BC. pt-bks. Remaining pt-bks.: Vl. 1 conc., pp. (3), 34; Vl. 2 conc., pp. 25; Viola, pp. 23; Vc., pp. 26. Vl. 1 conc. includes Ded. to Mrs. Bowes by Avison, List of subscribers.

570. SCHENCK, JEAN. *C86. Dese Sonaten worden best gespeelt met twee violen di Gamba oste ook wel met een Bas of Bas-Continuo. tot Amsterdam voor den Auteur. Konst Oeffeningen

INSTRUMENTAL WORKS

Van Schenk. Ce Livre se Vend a Amsterdam ches Estienne Roger.... [MDCLXXXVIII. Opera Seconda.] fol.
> In 2 pt-bks. [Gamba], pp. 37; [BC.], pp. 23. The above occurs, in a different order, in an engraving that precedes the t-p.; the latter includes the part in brackets and Ded. to Jakob Boreel and Nicolaas Witsen. Music consists of 15 sonatas.

571. —— C87. Scherzi Musicali per la Viola di Gamba con Basso Continuo ad libitum ... dal ... Giovanni Schenck ... Opera Sesta. [a Amsterdam ches Estienne Roger....] [c. 1708] obl. fol.
> In 2 pt-bks. [Gamba], pp. 49; [BC.], pp. 29. The part in brackets occurs on engraving preceding the t-p. T-p. includes Ded. to Giovanni Guglielmo, Count Palatine of the Rhine. Music consists of 101, mostly dance, mvts, arranged in suites.

572. —— *C32. Suonate a Violino e Violone o Cimbalo.... Da Giovanni Schenck Musico di Camera Comissario e cameriere di S. A. F. il Principe Palatino del Rheno Opera 7ma. A Amsterdam chez Estienne Roger.... [c. 1700] fol.
> In 2 pt-bks. Violino Solo, pp. (1), 30; Basso Continue, pp. (1), 20. Each pt. includes Ded. to Ionas Witsen, Secretary of the City of Amsterdam. Music consists of 18 suites.

573. —— *C88. Le Nymphe di Rheno per Due Viole di Gamba Sole ... dal ... Giovanni Schenck Musico di Camera Comissario & Cameriere di Sua Serenissma. Altezza Elettorale Opera Ottava A Amsterdam chez Estienne Roger.... [c. 1710] fol.
> In 2 pt-bks. Viola Prima; Viola Seconda (both pp. 29). T-p. preceded by engraving similar to that in No. 571. Ded. on t-p. to Giovanni Guglielmo. Music consists of 12 sonatas.

574. —— C89. L'Echo du Danube Contenant six Sonates dont les deux prémiéres sont à 1 viole de Gambe & 1 Basse Continue, les deux suivants à 1 viole de Gambe & 1 Basse continue ad libitum & les deux derniers à 1 viole de Gambe Seule ... par Jean Schenck .... IXe Ouvrage A Amsterdam chez Estienne Roger.... [c. 1710] obl. fol.
> Pp. 46. In score. Includes Ded. to Baron Diamantstein. Music consists of 6 sonatas for 1 or 2 gambas and BC. in score, and 1 solo for gamba.

575. SCHICKHARD, JOHANN CHRISTIAN. *M143 (ii)-146 (ii), 148, 149. VI Concerts a Quatre Flutes & Basse Continue ... par Jean Chretien Schickhardt. XIX ouvrage. A Amsterdam Chez Estienne Roger. [*c.* 1716] fol.

In 6 pt-bks. Imp. Flauto Primo (*M143*), *pp. 16, but pp. 13–16 defective;* Flauto Secondo (*M145*), *pp. 14;* Flauto Terzo (*M144*), *pp. 12;* Flauto Quarto (*M146*), *pp. 10;* Basso Continuo (*M148*); *ibid.* (*M149*) (*both pp. 13*). *M143 includes Ded. to Mon. de Brandt.*

576. SCHOLL, D. *C71. Vrede-Triomph, of te Thalia's Lust-Hoff. Beplant met Verscheyde Geurige Allemanden, Couranten, Baletten, Sarabanden, en Gigen. A.3. Verstelde Fioolen met een dubbelde Basseo-Continuo dienende tot Vermllingh vande Party. Door D. Scholl. . . . Violino Primo. Opera Sexta. Tot Delff, Gedrukt (voor den Autheur) by Pieter Oosterhout. . . . 1678. 4°

In 4 pt-bks. Violino Primo; Violino Secondo; Violino Terso; Basso Continuo (*all pp. 14*). *Each pt. includes Ded. to Sr. Lambertus Cleffius. Music consists of 29 dance mvts.*

577. SCOTCH. C79. A Collection of Original Scotch-Tunes, (Full of the Highland Humours) for the Violin: Being the First of this Kind yet Printed: Most of them being in the Compass of the Flute. London: Printed by William Pearson . . . for Henry Playford. . . . 1700. obl. 4°

Pp. 16.

578. SELF-INSTRUCTOR. *C76. The First, Second and Third Books of the Self-Instructor on the Violin: Or the Art of Playing on that Instrument, improv'd & made easy . . . by Plain Rules and Directions: With A Choice Collection of the newest Aires & Song-Tunes compos'd by the most able Masters; to which is added another Collection of Country-Dances now in use, with Plain & familiar Instructions how to Dance them, the whole work containing above 120 lessons: Also an excellent Solo by Mr. Courtville; All fairly and exactly engraven on Copper-Plates. . . . London Printed for & Sould by I. Hare. . . . 1700. obl. 8°

In 3 Parts. Unpaginated. I, pp. (31); II, pp. (25); III, pp. (22); all printed one side only. Composers are: [Anon.], *Mr. Barrett, Mr. Clark, Mr. Courtiville, Mr. Eccles, Mr. Finger, Mr. Forster, Mr. Ia. Graves, Mr. Keen, Mr. Keller, Mr. Morgan,*

INSTRUMENTAL WORKS

Mr. Peasable, Mr. Purcell. *Strip of printed paper partially stuck on to t-p. includes* Sould by Iohn Walsh. . . . London 16

579. SHERARD, JAMES. M151. Sonate à Tré doi Violini, e Violone col Basso per l'Organo di Giacomo Sherard Filarmonico Opera prima A Amsterdam chez Estienne Roger. . . . [1701] 4°
In 4 pt-bks. Imp. Vl. 1; Vl. 2; Vc.; Organ (all pp. 25, but p. 2 of Vc. pt. defective). Each pt. includes Ded. to Wriothesly, Duke of Bedford.

580. SIPRUTINI, EMANUEL. M156 (iii). Six Solos for a Violoncello or a Violin with a Thoroughbass, for the Harpsichord. . . . Sigr. Emanuel Siprutini. Opera Prima. London Printed for the Author, by T. Bennett. . . . [*c.* 1764] fol.
Pp. 29. In score.

581. SNEP, JEAN. C91. Sonates Allemandes, Courantes, Chaconnes, Rondeaux, Gavottes, Sarabandes & gigues a i Viole de Gambe & i Basse Continue de Mr. Jean Snep. . . . Opera Prima A Amsterdam chez Estienne Roger. . . [*c.* 1698] fol.
In 2 pt-bks. Viola da Gamba, *pp. (1), 17;* Basso Continuo, *pp. (1), 12. Each pt. includes Ded. to Nicolaus Cau. Paper slip pasted over publisher on which is printed* London sold by Francis Vaillant. . . .

582. SOLNITZ, ANTON WILLEM. *M171. VI Sinfonie Con duoi Violini, Alto Viola e Violoncello o Basso Continuo. . . . Composte de Antonio Guglielmo Solnitz Opera Terza. Stampate a spese di Fred. Ern. Fischer. . . . Leyden. [*c.* 1750?] fol.
In 4 pt-bks. Imp. Violino Primo, *pp. 12, but lacking pp. 1, 2, 5, 6, 9, 10;* Violino Secondo, *all pp. missing;* Alto Viola, *pp. 11, but pp. 2. 3 defective;* Basso Continuo, *pp. 12, but only pp. 1, 2 remaining. T-p. includes Ded. to Lothario Francesco Marchese di Hoensbroech.*

583. —— M126 (vi)-128 (vi). Six Sonatas for two Violins with a Thorough Bass for the Harpsicord or Violoncello Compos'd by Antonio Guglielmo Solnitz. London, Printed for I. Walsh . . . [1750] fol.
In 3 pt-bks. M128 (*Vl. 1*), *pp. 12;* M126 (*Vl. 2*); M127 (*BC.*) (*both pp. 10*). *Op. 1. Each pt. includes List of Walsh's pubs.*

584. SOLOS. M152. XII Solos for the Violoncello, VI of Sigr. Caporale; & VI Compos'd by Mr. Galliard. . . . 1746. [Printed for John Johnson. . . . London.] obl. fol.

> Each set of 6 solos pp. 24 and different t-p., which includes the printer's name etc. In score with BC. Ded. on above t-p. to the Prince of Wales by Johnson.

585. SONATAS. C98. A Second Collection of sonatas for two Flutes and a Bass, by Signr. Christopher Pez, to which is added Some Excellent Solo's out of the First Part of Corelli's Fifth Opera . . . the whole fairly Engraven. London Printed for I. Walsh . . . I. Hare . . . and P. Randall. . . . [1707] obl. fol.

> In 3 pt-bks. Recorder 1, pp. 11; Recorder 2, pp. 5; BC., pp. 8.

586. —— C30 (i). Six Sonatas or Solos Three for a Violin and Three for the Flute with a Thorough Bass for ye Harpsichord Theorboe or Bass-Viol Compos'd by Mr. Wm. Crofts & an Italian Mr. London Printed for and sold by John Walsh . . . & John Hare. . . . 1700. fol.

> Pp. 10. In score.

587. —— B45 (iii). Six Sonattas for the Harpsichord Composed by Arnold Galuppi and Mazzinghi London Printed for C. and S. Thompson. . . . [c. 1770] obl. fol.

> Pp. 27.

588. —— *C30 (iii). December Two Sonatas for Violins in Parts one by Signr Caldara and the other by Signr Gabrielli of the Choisest of their Works also a Solo for a Violin and Bass by Signr Torelli the Solo Proper for the Harpsicord or Spinnett. . . . 1704. [London, Printed for Walsh and Hare.] fol.

> In 5 pt-bks. Violino Primo; Violino Secondo; Alto Viola; Tenor Viola; Organo e Violoncello (all pp. 2). Only Organo pt. has above t-p. Imp., lacking Torelli's piece, but see No. 597.

589. SUITTES. *C99. Suittes Faciles Pour 1 Flute ou 1 Violon & 1 Basse Continuë de la Composition de Messieurs Du Fau, L'Enclos, Pinel, Lully, Bruyninghs, Le Fevre & autres habiles Maistres Avec les agréements marquez en faveur de Ceux qui Commencent à aprendre A Amsterdam Chez Estienne Roger. . . . [c. 1710] obl. 4°

In 2 pt-bks. Dessus, *pp. 13;* Basse Continue, *pp. 11. Printed slip pasted on to t-p. includes* London. sold by Francis Vaillant. . . *Music consists of 34 dance mvts.*

590. TESSARINI, CARLO. M113 (iii), 115 (iii), 116 (iii). Il Piacer del Amator di Musica Facile Sonatine da Camera a due Violini e Basso . . . da Carlo Tessarini. . . . Opera Quinta. . . . Si Vendano in Parigi nel addresso ordinario . . . [*c.* 1740] fol.

In 3 pt-bks. M116 (Vl. 1); M115 (Vl. 2) (both pp. 7); M113 (BC.), pp. 6.

591. —— M104 (ii). Six Sonatas or Duets for Two Violins Compos'd by Sigr. Carlo Tessarini Opera Seconda. London Printed for John Johnson. . . . [*c.* 1745] fol.

Pp. 25. In score, for 2 solo Vls.

592. —— M104 (i). Easy and familiar Airs for the Violin or German Flute with a figur'd Bass compos'd by Sigr. Tessarini of Rimini. . . . London Printed for John Cox. . . . [1751] fol.

Pp. 11. In score.

593. THEATRE. *C78 (i). Theater Musick being a Collection of the newest Ayers for the Violin, with the French Dances perform'd at both Theaters, as also the new Dances at ye late Ball at Kensington on ye Kings Birthday, and those in the new Opera of Rinaldo & Armida, with a Through Bass to each Dance, Compos'd by Mr. Iohn Eccles. . . . London Sould by I. Walsh. . . . [1698] obl. 8º

Pp. 28. Pp. 1–14 contain pieces for Vl. solo (one side only), pp. 15–28 contain pieces for Vl. and unfig. bass on opposite pages. T-p. preceded by engraving of Theatre Royal. Composers: Mr Clark, Mr Morgan, Mr Powell. *The only dramatic work named is 'Armida'.*

594. —— *C78 (ii). The Second Book of Theatre Musick: Containing Plain & Easie Rules with ye Best Instructions for Learners on ye Violin. Likewise all the New French Dances now in use at Publick Balls & Dancing-Schools; with variety of ye Newest Ayers, Song-Tunes & Dances, Perform'd in ye late Operas at ye Theatres: All of them being proper to Play on ye Hautboy. . . .

Fairly Engraven on Copper Plates. London Printed for & sold by I. Walsh. . . . 1699. . . . obl. 8°

> Pp. (33), printed one side only. Instructions, pp. 7; pieces for Vl. solo, pp. 24; scales for Ob., pp. 2. T-p. preceded by same engraving as above. Composers: Dr. Blow, Mr. Clark, Mr Finger, Mr Orme, Mr. D. Purcell. Dramatic works: 'The Island Princess', 'The Consort'. Also 'The Princess Ball'. Mr. Prist is mentioned as a dancer.

595. THEATRE. *C78 (iii). The Third Book of Theater Musick: Being a Collection of the newest Aires for the Violin. with ye Trumpett-Tunes, Scotch-Tunes, & French-Dances, made for ye Playhouse-es Particularly those in ye new Opera, likewise in Ephigenia, & ye Trip to the Jubilee with several new Cibells in two parts Treble & Bass, to which is added an Excellent Introduction for Young Beginners on ye Violin. Fairly Engraven on Copper Plates London Printed for & sold by I. Walsh. . . . 1700. . . . obl. 8°

> Pp. 31, printed one side only. Instructions same as above, pp. 7; pieces for Vl. solo, pp. 18; for Vl. and un-fig. bass, pp. 6 on opposite pages. Composers: Mr. Barrett, Mr. Clark, Mr. Ja. Graves, Mr. King. Dramatic works: 'The Trip to the Jubilee', 'The Grove', 'The Way of the World', 'Iphigenia'.

596. THORNOWETS, HENRY. D56 (ii). Sonate da Camera per il Flauto col Basso del Segr. Thornowets Trez Exactement Corrigee in Londra a Spese di Giovanni Walsh . . . e Giovanni Hare. . . . [1722] fol.

> Pp. 24. Imp., lacking pp. 17–24, these being replaced by most of a mvt. in 12/8 in G minor, a Sonata V in B flat, an incomplete Sonata VI in A minor, and the last 3 mvts. of a sonata in G minor (all for Vl. ?).

597. TORELLI, GIUSEPPE. *C30 (v). A Solo in G♭ for a Violin and a Bass by Signr Torelli The Solo Proper for the Harpsicord or Spinnett. [London, printed for Walsh and Hare. 1704] fol.

> Pp. 8–10. In score. See SONATAS, No. 588.

598. TRIOS. *C53 (i). Trios de Different Autheurs Choisis & Mis en Ordre par Mr. Babel Ce Livre sera Suivé dans peu d'un

INSTRUMENTAL WORKS

Second qui contiendra la Suite de ces pieces icy jusques au Nombre de 130. Livre Premier A Amsterdam ches Estienne Roger. . . . [*c.* 1720] obl. 4°

In 3 pt-bks. Dessus, *pp. 39;* Second Dessus, *pp. 35;* Basse, *pp. 34. No composers are given. Music consists of 61 excerpts from instrumental and vocal numbers in stage works.*

599. —— *C53 (ii). Trios de Different Autheurs Choisis et mis en ordre par Mr. Babel Livre Second A Amsterdam chez Estienne Roger. . . . [*c.* 1720] obl. 4°

In 3 pt-bks. Premier Dessus, *pp. 33;* Second Dessus, *pp. 30;* Basse Continue, *pp. 27. No composers are given. Excerpts No. 62–129 as in No. 598.*

600. TRIPLA. *C69. Tripla Concordia: Or, A Choice Collection of New Airs, in Three Parts. For Treble and Basse-Violins: By several Authors; Never before Published. The First Treble. London, Printed by Tho. Ratcliffe and Nath. Thompson, and are to be sold by John Carr. . . . 1677. obl. 8°

In 3 pt-bks. The First Treble; The Second Treble; The Basse (all pp. (7), 84). Each pt. includes Ded. to Hon. Goodwin Wharton by Carr, Address by Carr, List of Carr's pubs. Composers are: Mr. John Banister, Mr. Francis Forcer, Mr. William Hall, Mr. Rob. King, Mr. Matthew Lock, Mr. Robert Smith.

601. UCCELLINI, MARCO. †*C47. Sonate Correnti, et Arie, da Farsi con diversi Stromenti si da Camera come da Chiesa, à Uno, à Due, & à Trè. Opera Quarta di d. Marco Uccellini Musico, e Capo degl' Instromentisti del Serenissimo Sig. Duca di Modana. Canto Primo. En Anversa Pressio i Heredi di Pietro Phalesio. . . . MDCLXIII. fol.

In 4 pt-bks. Canto Primo *(Vl., Vl. 1);* Canto Secondo *(Vc., Vl. 2) (both pp. 43, (1));* Terza Parte *(Vl. solo, Vc.), pp. 24;* Basso Continuo, *pp. 47, (1). Each pt. includes Index. Music consists of 6 sonatas for Vl., 8 for Vl. and Vc., 8 for 2 Vls. and Vc., 20 correnti for 2 Vls., 15 arias for 2 Vls.; all with BC.*

602. —— †*C48. Sonate sopra il Violino e Diversi Altri Strumenti a Uno, Due, Tre. E Correnti con Una Toccata a Due Violini da Sonarsi Tutte Due le Parti con Una Violino Solo. Di D. Marco Ucellini Capo [etc., as above] Libro Septimo. Prima

Parte. In Anversa, Pressio i Heredi di Pietro Phalesio. . . .
MDCLXVIII. fol.

> In 4 pt-bks. Prima Parte (*Vl.*, *Vl. 1*, *Vl. 2*), *pp. 39*, (*1*); Seconda Parte (*Vl. 2*, *Theorbo*, *Violone*, *Trombone*), *pp. 31*, (*1*); Terza Parte (*Vl. solo*, *Theorbo*, *Vc.*), *pp. 23*, (*1*); Basso Continuo *pp. 35*, (*1*). Each pt. includes Index. Music consists of 4 sonatas for Vl., 6 for 2 Vls., 1 for Vl. and Theorbo, 1 for Vl. and Violone, 1 for Vl. and Trombone, 3 for 2 Vls. and Vc., 1 for 2 Vls. and Theorbo, 6 corrente for 2 Vls., toccata for 2 Vls.; all with BC.

603. VALENTINE, ROBERT. C97. Six Setts of Aires and a Chacoon for two Flutes and a Bass Compos'd by Mr. Valentine at Rome. . . . London Printed for I. Walsh . . . and I. Hare. . . . [1718] fol.

> In 3 pt-bks. Recorder 1; Recorder 2; BC. (all pp. 8).

604. VERACINI, ANTONIO. *C34. Sonate da Camera a Due, Violino, e Violone, ò Arcileuto, col Basso per il cimbalo de Antonio Veracini Fiorentino opera Terza. a Amsterdam ches Estienne Roger. . . . [c. 1710] fol.

> In 3 pt-bks. Violino, pp. 19; Violoncello, pp. 17; Organo, pp. 14. Music consists of 10 sonatas. The Vc. and Organ pts. are virtually identical, both being figured.

605. VERACINI, FRANCESCO MARIA. M65. XII Solos for a Violin with a Thorough Bass for the Harpsicord or Bass Violin Compos'd by Francesco Maria Veracini Fiorentino. Opera Prima. London. Printed for and sold by I. Walsh. . . . [1733] fol.

> Pp. 81. Imp., lacking pp. 1–14, 69–81. In score.

606. VISCONTI, GASPARO. C26. Gasperini's Solos for a Violin with a through Bass for the Harpsicord or Bass Violin Containing Preludes . . . composed by Seignr. Gasparo Visconti Opera Prima London Printed for I. Walsh . . . and I. Hare. . . . [1703] obl. fol.

> Pp. 31. In score. Includes Ded. to William, Duke of Devonshire.

607. VITALI, GIOVANNI BATTISTA. †*C58. Violino Primo. Balletti Correnti, Gighe, Allemande, e Sarabande à Violino, e Violone, ò Spinetta con il Secondo Violino à beneplacito. Del

INSTRUMENTAL WORKS

Sig. Gig. Battista Vitali Opera Quarta. In Venetia 1677. Stampa Del Gardano. 4°
In 3 pt-bks. Violino Primo; Violino Secondo; Violone, o Spinetta *(all pp. 23, (1)). Each pt. includes Index. Music consists of 2 Allemandes, 5 Balletts, 5 Courants, 8 Gigs, 3 Sarabands, one Zoppa.*

608. —— *C60. Violino Primo. Sonate a due, trè, quattro, e cinque Stromenti di Gio. Battista Vitali Musico di Violone da Brazzo in S. Petronio di Bologna, & Academico Filaschise Opera Quinta. ... In Bologna, per Giacomo Monti. 1669. ... 4°
In 5 pt-bks. Violino Primo; Violino Secondo *(both pp. 36)*; Alto Viola, *pp. 13, (1)*; Violone, *pp. 19, (1)*; Organo, *pp. 36. T-p. has Ded. to Francesco Maria Desiderii. Each pt. includes Index. Music consists of 11 sonatas and a capriccio.*

609. —— †*C61. Violino Primo Sonate da Chiesa à Due Violini del Sig. Gio. Battista Vitali Bolognese Vice Maestro di Capella del Serenissimo Signor Duca di Modona, & Accademico Filaschise, a Filarmonico. Opera Nona. In Venetia 1684. Alla Stampa del Gardano. 4°
In 3 pt-bks. Violino Primo, *pp. 54, (1)*; Violino Secondo, *pp. 47, (1)*; Organo, *pp. 59, (1). Each pt. includes Index. Music consists of 12 sonatas.*

610. —— C59. Violino Primo. Varie Sonate alla Francese, & all' Itagliana à sei Stromenti. ... Da Gio. Battista Vitali. ... Opera Undecima. In Modona, Per Gio. Gaspara Ferri. 1684. ... 4°
In 6 pt-bks. Vl. 1; Vl. 2 (Vl. 2, Viola 2); Vl. 3 (Vl. 3, Viola 3); Alto Viola; Tenor Viola; Spinetta, o Violone *(all pp. 31, (1)). T-p. has Ded. to Ferdinando Carlo, Duke of Mantua. Each pt. includes Index.*

611. VIVALDI, ANTONIO. M131, 135–7, 140, 142. Vivaldi's most Celebrated Concertos in all their parts for Violins and other Instruments. ... Compos'd by Antonia Vivaldi Opera Terza. London. Printed for I. Walsh ... and I. Hare. ... [1715, 1717]. fol.
In 2 sets, each paginated separately. Imp., only the following pt-bks. remaining: M140 (Vl. 1), pp. 27, pp. 18; M131 (Vl. 3), pp. 17, pp. 12; M136 (Vl. 4), pp. 15, but t-p. and pp. 1–6 defective,

pp. 12, but pp. 8–12 missing; M142 (Viola 1), pp. 13, but p. 2 defective, pp. 11; M135 (Vc.), pp. 15, pp. 13, but pp. 9–10 defective; M137 (BC.), pp. 16, pp. 12.

612. VREDE, VREUGHT. *C70. Vrede Vreught, Violino I. Antwerpsche. Bestaende in Ballet Cour. Sarab. Gicq. Allemand. &c. Met Dry Instrumenten van 2. Experte Violisten Ghecomponeert. La Paysible Joye d'Anvers Consistan en Ballet, Cour. Sarab. Gicque Alemande &c. Composée de 2 Experts Maistres du Violon par Trois Instrumens. t'Antwerpen. By Lucas de Potter.... 1679. 4°

In 3 pt-bks. Violino I; Violino II (*both pp.* 54, (1)); Violino III & Bas Viol, *pp.* 46. (1). *Each pt. includes Ded. to H. P. Pasquali de Deckere and Anna Vander Rydt by Joannes Claessens, Index. Composer of each piece given. Composers are Carel Rosier and Pieter Picart. Music consists of 56 mvts., mostly dances, for 2 Vls. and bass Viol (unfigured) or 3 Vls.*

613. WALOND, WILLIAM. D51. Six Voluntaries for the Organ or Harpsichord Composed by William Walond.... London Printed for J. Johnson.... [c. 1755] obl. fol.

Pp. 2, 21. *Op.* 1. *Includes List of subscribers.*

614. WATER MUSIC. M83 (ii). Handel's Celebrated Water Musick Compleat. Set for the Harpsicord. To which is added, Two favourite Minuets, with Variations for the Harpsicord, by Geminiani. London. Printed for I. Walsh.... [1743] fol.

Pp. 27. *Includes List of Walsh's pubs.*

615. WERNER, GREGOR JOSEPH. *M113 (ii), 115 (ii), 116 (ii). sYMphonIae seX senaeqVe sonatae, qVae posterIores pro CapeLLIs VsVrpanDae anterIores Vero eX caMerIs VenIrent eXCIpIenDae. A GregorIo Werner, aLte tItVLatI prInCIpIs ESTARHASY CapeLLae MagIstro ConCInnatae, aC eXposItae. EX Vrbe EIsenstatt, proXIMe aD CoLLes LeYthae In HUngarIa. 1759. fol.

In 3 pt-bks. Violino Primo (M116), *pp.* (2), 24; Violino 2do. (M115), *pp.* 24; Cembalo (M113), *pp.* 20. *T-p. and 2 pp. of Ded. to Antonio Carolo Esterhazy in Vl. 1 pt. only. T-p. (except for imprint) and 2 dedicatory pp. are chronogrammatic, giving date (of composition?*) *1735 ten times. Chronogrammatic date of imprint is 16. xi. 1759. The 6 symphonies and 6 sonatas are arr. alternately.*

616. WICHEL, PHILIPPO VAN. *C46. Violino I. Fasciculus Dulcedinis Unius, Duorum, Trium, Quatuor et Quinque Instrumentorum. Auctore Philippe van Wichel Musurgo, Bruxellae quoque Regii Sacelli Symphoneta Exhibitus Reverendo. . . . Domino D. Antonio de Loose. . . . Opusculum Primum. Antuerpiae, apud Lucam de Potter, Typographum Musices. . . . MDCLXXVIII. 5 Partes. fol.

In 5 pt-bks. Violino I *(also Vl. solo), pp. 30, (1);* Violino II, *pp. 17, (1);* Alto e Tenor Viol *(also Vl. 1 and 3), pp. 11, (1);* Basso Viol, *pp. 10, (1);* Bassus Contin., *pp. 15. Each pt. includes Ded. to de Loose, Index. Music consists of 7 sonatas for Vl. solo, 3 for 2 Vls., 1 for Vl. and Bass Viol, 3 for 2 Vls. and Bass Viol, 1 for 3 Vls. and Bass Viol, and La Ciacogna for 2 Vls.; all with BC.*

617. YOUNG, ANTHONY. D52. Suits of Lessons for the Harpsicord or Spinnet in most of the Keyes. . . . Compos'd by Mr. Anthony Young. . . . London Printed for and Sold by I. Walsh . . . and I. Hare. . . . [1719] fol.

Pp. 30. Imp., lacking pp. 1–6 and t-p. defective.

618. ZIANI, PIETRO ANDREA. *C27 (ii). Ziani's Aires or Sonatas in 3 Parts for Two Violins and a Thorow Bass Containing the most refined Itallian Aire with Curious Passage's to Improve a Hand and Pleasant Harmony to Delight ye Ear Being Engraven from ye Authors Manuscript which was never before Printed ye whole Carefully Corected Opera Prima London Printed for I. Walsh . . . and I. Hare. . . . [1703] obl.

In 3 pt-bks. Violino Primo; Violino Secondo *(both pp. 8);* Basso Continuo, *pp. 6. Music consists of 22 dances arr. roughly in suites.*

III. THEORETICAL WORKS, ETC.

619. ABBOT, Henry. B18 (iii). The Use and Benefit of Church-Musick. . . . by Henry Abbot. . . . London: Printed for Jonah Bowyer. . . . 1724. 8°

> Pp. 23. *Anniversary Meeting of the Three Choirs, 1724. Ded. to Lord Bathurst.*

620. ANTIQUITIES. B18 (xii). Antiquities Sacred and Profane: Or, A Collection of Curious and Critical Dissertations on the Old and New Testament. . . . Done into English from the French, with Notes, by a Clergyman of the Church of England. . . . London; Printed for J. Roberts. . .; S. Wilmot, in Oxford; and C. Crownfield, in Cambridge. MDCCXXIV. 4°

> Pp. viii, 97, (2). *Deals with the poetry, music, and musical instruments of the Hebrews. The first dissertation is by Mr. Abbot Fleury; the second (also on poetry) is by the translator; the last two are designated from the French. Includes a page of engravings of Hebrew instruments. On p. 97 occur the words* The End of Book I. Vol. I. *Includes Ded. to Sir Charles Wager, Preface, Contents.*

621. BATTELL, Ralph. B18 (iv). The Lawfulness and Expediency of Church Musick. . . . By Ralph Battell. . . . London, Printed by J. Heptinstall, for John Carr. . . . 1694. 4°

> Pp. 25. *Anniversary Meeting of Gentlemen, Lovers of Music, 1693.*

622. BEDFORD, Arthur. A24. The Great Abuse of Musick. In Two Parts. . . . By Arthur Bedford, . . . London: Printed by J. H[eptinstall] for John Wyatt. . . . 1711. 8°

> Pp. (2), 276. *Includes Ded. to S.P.C.K., Contents.*

623. —— A25 (i). The Temple Musick: or, an Essay Concerning the Method of Singing the Psalms. . . . Before the Babylonish Captivity. . . . By Arthur Bedford. . . . London, Printed and Sold by H. Mortlock. . . . J. Walsh. . . . and Anth. Piesly . . . in Oxford. 1706. 8°

> Pp. (14), 253, (1). *Includes Preface, Contents, Index, Errata.*

624. BÉMETZRIEDER, ANTON. *D58. Music made Easy to every Capacity, in a Series of Dialogues; Being Practical Lessons for the Harpsichord, Laid Down in a New Method, so as to render that Instrument so little difficult that any Person, . . . may play well; become a thorough Proficient in the Principles of Harmony; and will compose Music, if they have a Genius for it, in less than a Twelvemonth. Written in French by Monsieur Bemetzrieder . . . And published at Paris . . . by . . . Monsieur Diderot, the Whole Translated, and adapted to the Use of the English Student, by Giffard Bernard. . . . Perused and Approved Of by Doctor Boyce and Doctor Howard. London: Printed by R. Ayre and G. Moore, . . . and Sold by W. Randall. . . . MDCCLXXVIII. . . . 4°

Pp. vi, iv, 87. Pt. I only. Includes an *Address to the* Music Masters and Organists of Great Britain *by Bernard, a translation of Diderot's Preface, and an Introduction in dialogue form between a Master and his Disciple. The dialogue of the main text is between a girl Disciple, the Master, and a Philosopher (the girl's father).*

625. BISSE, THOMAS. B18 (i). A Rationale on Cathedral Worship or Choir-Service. . . By Tho. Bisse. . . . The Second Edition. London: Printed for W. and J. Innys . . . 1721. 8°

Pp. 61, (1). Includes a list of Innys's pubs. Anniversary Meeting of the Three Choirs, 1720.

626. —— B18 (ii). Musick the Delight of the Sons of Men. . . . By Tho. Bisse. . . . London: Printed for William and John Innys. . . . MDCCXXVI. 8°

Pp. 52. Anniversary Meeting of the Three Choirs, 1726. Ded. to Dr. Croft.

627. BROSSARD, SÉBASTIEN DE. A2. Dictionnaire de Musique . . . Par M. Sebastien de Brossard. . . . Troisieme Edition. A Amsterdam. . . . Estienne Roger. . . . [1707?] 8°

Pp. 388. Includes Preface, Advice.

628. BURNEY, CHARLES. XXXVI. H 12. The Present State Of Music In France and Italy. . . . By Charles Burney. . . . The Second Edition, Corrected. London, Printed for T. Becket . . . J. Robson . . . and G. Robinson. . . . 1773. 4°

Pp. viii (wrongly arr., i.e. vii, viii, v, vi), 409, (10). Includes Glossary, Index.

629. —— XXXVI. H 13, 14. The Present State Of Music In Germany, The Netherlands, And United Provinces... By Charles Burney.... In Two Volumes: Vol. I.... London, Printed for T. Beckett... J. Robson... and G. Robinson.... 1773. 4°

> Vol. I—pp. viii, 376. Includes Introduction, Index. Vol. II—pp. (3), 352. Includes Advertisement, Errata and Index to both vols.

630. —— 780. 9. A General History of Music.... By Charles Burney.... Volume The First. London, Printed for the Author.... MDCCLXXVI. fol.

> In 4 vols., Vol. 2 dated MDCCLXXXII, Vols. 3 and 4 MDCCLXXXIX, Vol. I—pp. xx, (12), 522. Includes Ded. to Queen Charlotte Sophia, Preface, List of subscribers. Vol. II—pp. (2), 597, (1). Includes Errata. Vol. III—pp. xi, 622, (12). Includes Essay on Musical Criticism, Index, Errata. Vol. IV—pp. (2), 688, (13). Includes List of books on music, Index, Errata.

631. COMPLEAT. *M105 (i). [The Compleat Tutor For the Harpsichord or Spinnet... with Rules for tuneing the Harpsichord or Spinnet. Printed for... John Johnson.... London] [c. 1745?] 8°

> Pp. 36. Imp., lacking t-p., pp. 1, 2, 5, 6, and part of a folded diagram of the keyboard and notes inserted between pp. 2 and 3. (The t-p. has been mislaid since I first looked at this volume.) Much of the material is the same as in M105 (ii) but differently arranged. This is probably an earlier ed. because of the fingering instructions, viz. Note. Where this mark + is place (sic) over the Note you must play the Thumb; figure 1 is the first Finger; 2 the second; 3 the Third; and 4 the little Finger.

632. —— *M105 (ii). The Compleat Tutor [etc. as for M105 (i)].... [c. 1750?] 8°

> Pp. 36. Fingering instructions are: Note that in fingering your Thumb is ye First Finger, and so on to the little Finger which is the Fifth.

633. CORFE, JOSEPH. B15. Thorough Bass Simplified or the whole Theory & Practice of Thorough Bass.... by Joseph Corfe.... London, Printed and Published by Preston.... [1805?] obl. fol.

> Pp. (4), 56. Includes Preface, List of works published by Preston, Introduction, Index.

THEORETICAL WORKS

634. DESCARTES, RENÉ. A33. Renatus Des-Cartes Excellent Compendium of Musick: With ... Animadversions Thereupon. By a Person of Honour. London, Printed by Thomas Harper, for Humphrey Moseley.... sold at his Shop ... and by Thomas Heath.... 1653. 4°

> Pp. (13), 95. Includes To the Reader, Errata, and a second t-p. (p. 59):—Animadversions Upon The Musick-Compendium of Renat. Des-Cartes. London, Printed by Thomas Harper, for Humphrey Moseley... 1653. The Person of Honour was Lord William Brouncker.

635. DODWELL, HENRY (The Elder). A20. A Treatise Concerning the Lawfulness of Instrumental Musick in Holy Office. By Henry Dodwell, M.A. To which is prefixed, a Preface in Vindication of Mr. Newte's Sermon, concerning the Lawfulness and Use of Organs in the Christian Church, &c. ... The Second Edition, with large Additions. London; Printed for William Haws, MDCC. 8°

> Pp. (2), 143, (2). Includes a list of works published by Haws, Contents, Errata. The Vindication by Newte precedes the Treatise —pp. 84.

636. GEMINIANI, FRANCESCO. D65. Guida Armonica ... being a Sure Guide to Harmony and Modulation.... By F. Geminiani. Opera X. ... London Printed for the Author by John Johnson.... [1742] fol.

> Pp. (4), 34. Includes a Preface and Directions for using the book.

637. HAWKINS, JOHN. 780.9. A General History Of The Science and Practice Of Music, By Sir John Hawkins. In Five Volumes. Volume the First. London, Printed for T. Payne and Son. ... MDCCLXXVI. fol.

> Preceded by t-p.—A General History Of Music. Volume The First. Vol. I—pp. (7), lxxxiv, 465. Includes Ded. to George III, Preface, Preliminary Discourse. Vol. II—pp. 544. Vol. III—pp. 535. Vol. IV—pp. 548. Vol. V—pp. 482, (58). Includes Index and Errata to all vols.

638. HICKMAN, CHARLES. B18 (vi). A Sermon Preached at St. Bride's Church. ... By Charles Hickman. ... London: Printed for Walther Kettelby. ... 1696. 8°

Pp. (4), 22, (1). *Anniversary Feast of the Lovers of Music, St. Caecilia's Day,* 1695. Includes a list of sermons by Hickman published by Kettelby, Ded. to the Stewards of St. Caecilia's Feast.

639. HISTOIRE. A3, 4. *Histoire de la Musique, et de ses effets, Depuis son origine jusqu'a present.* . . . A Amsterdam, chez M. Charles le Cene. MDCCXXV. 12°

2 vols., each consisting of 2 books. Bk. I, pp. (4), 333, (1). Includes Preface and Errata. Bk. II, pp. 175. Includes Preface. Bk. III, pp. 322. Bk. IV, pp. 230. This work was begun by P. Bourdelot, continued by P. Bonnet-Bourdelot, and completed from their MSS. by J. Bonnet.

640. HOLDER, WILLIAM. A35. *A Treatise of the Natural Grounds, and Principles of Harmony.* By William Holder. . . . The Second Edition. London, Printed by J. Hepstinstall, for Philip Monckton. . . . MDCCI. 8°

Pp. (8), 204. Grove's Dictionary has 1731 as the date of the 2nd ed.; this is the date of the 3rd ed., printed by Pearson. Includes Index, Errata, Introduction.

641. KELLER, GOTTFRIED. B16. A Compleat Method for Attaining to Play a Thorough Bass. Upon Either Organ Harpsicord or Theorbo-Lute. by ye Late Famous Mr. Godfry Keller. . . . Note the many faults in ye late Edition of Mr. Keller's Rules are Corected in this. . . . London Printed for I. Walsh . . . I. Hare . . . and P. Randall. . . . [1707] fol.

Pp. 15, 1 side only. The 1st ed. was published by Cullen (1707?), and it was later reprinted as an Appendix to Holder's Treatise of the Natural Grounds . . . published by Pearson in 1731. This ed. uses the same plates as Cullen's.

642. KIRCHER, ATHANASIUS. B14(i). *Athanasii Kircheri Fuldensis e Soc. Iesu Presbyteri Musurgia Universalis.* . . . In X. Libros Digesta. . . . Tomus I. Romae, Ex Typographia Haeredum Francisci Corbelletti. . . . MDCL. . . . fol.

Pp. (18), 690. Includes Ded. to Leopold William, Archduke o Austria, etc., Verses, and Preface. Contains the first 7 of 10 bks.

643. —— B14 (ii). [As for B 14 (i)]. . . . Tomus II. . . . MDCL. fol.

Pp. 462, (36). Includes Indices and Errata. Contains the last 3 bks.

THEORETICAL WORKS

644. LAMPE, JOHANN FRIEDRICH. M123 (i). [A Plain and Compendious Method Of Teaching Thorough Bass. . . . By John Frederick Lampe. . . . London: Printed for J. Wilcox. . . . MDCCXXXVII.] 4°

> *Imp.*, *lacking t-p. and part of Plate I. Unpaginated, consisting of 22 Lessons printed on 93 Plates (one side of p. only). Lesson 19 is engraved by J. Legate, 21 by T. Atkins, remainder by B. Cole.*

646. —— M122. *Another copy. Imp.*, *lacking t-p. and with remaining pages defective.*

647. LOCKE, MATTHEW. A36. The Present Practice of Musick Vindicated Against the Exceptions and New Way of Attaining Musick Lately Publish'd by Thomas Salmon, . . . By Matthew Locke. . . . To which is added Duellum Musicum By John Phillips. . . . Together with A Letter from John Playford to Mr. T. Salmon . . . London, Printed for N. Brooke . . . and J. Playford. . . . 1673. 8°

> *Pp. (2), 96. Includes To the Reader, Verse.*

648. —— C19. Melothesia: or Certain General Rules for Playing Continued-Bass. With a choice Collection of Lessons. . . . Never before Published . . . by M. Locke. . . . The First Part. London, Printed for J. Carr. . . . 1673. obl. 8°

> *Pp. 9, (3), 84. The Lessons are by:* [Anon.], *John Banister, G. Diesner, Will. Gregory, M. Locke, J. Moss, Chr. Preston, John Roberts, Rob. Smith. An Advertisement to the Reader explains the signs for graces and fig. bass. Includes a list of Carr's pubs. Ded. to Roger L'Estrange.*

649. LORITUS, HENRICUS (GLAREANUS). B11(i). Glareani ΔΩΔΕΚΑΧΟΡΔΟΝ . . . Basiliae. [Basilcae per Henrichum Petri Mense Septembri Anno Post Virginis Partum. MDXLVII.] fol.

> *Pp. 470. The printer's colophon and date occur on the last page.*

650. LOULIÉ, ÉTIENNE. A37(i). Elements Ou Principes De Musique . . . en Trois Parties. . . . Par M. Loulie. A Amsterdam, Ches Estienne Roger. . . . 1698. 8°

> *Pp. 110, (2). Includes Preface and 2 pages of Roger's pubs.*

651. MACE, THOMAS. B9. Musick's Monument. . . . By Tho. Mace. . . . London, Printed by T. Ratcliffe, and N. Thompson, for the Author, and are to be Sold by Himself. . . . and by John Carr. . . . 1676. fol.
Pp. (*18*), *272*. T-p. preceded by engraved portrait of Mace. Includes Ded. to God, To the Reader (*2*), Preface, Verses to subscribers, List of subscribers, Advertisement.

652. MALCOLM, ALEXANDER. A21. A Treatise of Musick, Speculative, Practical, and Historical. By Alexander Malcolm . . . Edinburgh, Printed for the Author. MDCCXXI. 8°
Pp. *xxiii*, *608*. Includes a List of corrigenda, 2 folding diagrams, and 6 folding pages of music exx. at end.

653. —— A22. Another copy but in an inferior condition.

654. MASSON, CHARLES. A32. Nouveau Traité des Règles pour las Composition de la Musique. . . . Par C. Masson. . . . Quatriéme Édition, revûë & corrigée. A Amsterdam, aux depens d'Estienne Roger. . . . [1738?] 8°
Pp. (*2*), *148*. Includes Index.

655. MEIBOMIUS, MARCUS. A28, 29. Antiquae Musicae Auctores Septem. Graece et Latine. Marcus Meibomius. . . . Volumen I. Amstelodami, Apud Ludovicum Elzevirium, CIƆIƆCLII. 4°
Pp. (*46*), *followed by separate t-ps. and paginations:* Aristoxeni Harmonicorum Elementorum Libri III . . . *pp.* (*3*), *132*. Euclidis Introductio Harmonica . . . *pp.* (*2*), *68*. Nichomachi Geraseni Pythagorici Harmonices Manuale . . . *pp.* (*2*), *60*. Alypii Introductio Musica . . . *pp.* *80;* includes Boethii Musicae Libri IV Caput III *as p. heading prior to main text*, *pp.* *8*. Gaudentii, Philosophi Harmonica Introductio . . . *pp.* (*2*), *40*. Bacchii Senioris Introductio Artis Musicae . . . *pp.* (*2*), *36*. *A29 has t-p.* Aristides Quintiliani de Musica Libri III. . . . Volumen II [etc. as A28]. Pp. (*6*), *363*. Includes Notae In Martiani Capellae Librum IX De Musica *pp.* *339–63*. Both initial t-ps. have 'Ex dono Auctoris' in ink.

656. —— B11a. Another copy of A28, 29 bound in one vol. but in a different order, viz.: Aristoxenos, Aristeides and Martianus (same t-p. as A29) Gaudentios, Euclid, Alypios, Bakcheios, Nicomachos.

THEORETICAL WORKS

657. MORLEY, THOMAS. B11 (ii). A Plaine and Easie Introduction to Practicall Musicke.... By Thomas Morley.... Imprinted at London by Peter Short.... 1597. fol.

>Pp. (4), 183, (35). One page of the motet 'Eheu sustulerunt Dominum meum' is placed in the 2nd part of 'O amica mea', and vice versa.

658. NAISH, THOMAS. *B18 (vii). A Sermon Preach'd at the Cathedral Church of Sarum.... By Thomas Naish, ... London: Printed for James Lacy. ... John Cooke. ... and Edward Easton.... 1726. 8°

>Pp. vi, 23. Anniversary of the Society of Lovers of Music, 1726. Ded. to the Society in the City of New Sarum.

659. NIVERS, GUILLAUME GABRIEL. *A37 (ii). Traité de la Composition de Musique. Par le Sr. de Nivers, Compositeur en Musique & Organiste de l'Eglise St. Sulpice de Paris; Et traduit en Flamand par E. Roger. A Amsterdam, Chez J. L. de Lorme & E. Roger.... MDCLXXXXVII. 8°

>Pp. 112. Text in parallel columns, French and Flemish. Includes Ded. to Abraham Maubach, a merchant of Amsterdam, translator's Preface, author's Preface, and a poem by A. M. (Maubach?) to Roger. In three pts., with 10 pages of fugue exx. at the end.

660. PARALELE. *B18 (xiii). Paralele des Italiens et des François, en ce qui Regarde la Musique et les Opera. A Amsterdam, aux dépens d'Estienne Roger.... [c. 1702] 12°

>Pp. 40, (8). Includes Index, an Approbation by Fontenelle dated 25. i. 1702, and Addition qui n'est pas de l'Autheur.

661. PASQUALI, NICCOLÒ. M109 (x). Thorough-Bass Made Easy: Or Practical Rules for finding and applying its various Chords with little Trouble ... by Nicolo Pasquali. Edinburgh: MDCCLVII. Printed, and sold by the Author, and by R. Bremner ... also at ... J. Walsh's, and J. Johnson's in London: and W. Manwaring's in Dublin.... obl. fol.

>Pp. (2), 48. Text on 8° sheets inserted among 29 obl. fol. Plates of music exx. Imp., lacking last 6 pages and Plates 22-25. Last Plate has A. Bell Sculpt. Edinri. T-p. lists 3 other published works by Pasquali.

THEORETICAL WORKS

662. PLAYFORD, JOHN. A38. An Introduction to the Skill of Musick: In Three Books: By John Playford. Containing I. The Grounds and Principles of Musick. . . . II. Instructions and Lessons for the Treble, Tenor and Bass-Viols. . . . III. The Art of Descant, or Composing Musick in Parts; Made very Plain and Easie by the late Mr. Henry Purcell. The Fourteenth Edition. Corrected and Enlarged. London: printed by William Pearson . . . for Henry Playford. . . . 1700. 8°

>Pp. (16), 180, (2). Bks. II and III have their own t-ps., viz.: An Introduction To the Playing on the Bass, Tenor, and Treble-Viols; And also on the Treble-Violin, Book II. . . . MDCC., and An Introduction to the Art of Descant. . . . Book III. With the Additions of the Late Mr. Henry Purcell. . . . MDCC. Includes 2 pages of recent pubs. by H. Playford.

663. ROGER, ESTIENNE. ★A1. Catalogue des livres de Musique, Imprimée à Amsterdam, chez Etienne Roger & continuée d'Imprimer par Michel Charles le Cene. . . . A Amsterdam. Chez Michel Charles le Cene, Libraire. [n.d.] 12°

>Pp. 72. Includes additional items in MS. and advertisement.

664. ROUSSEAU, JEAN. A31. Traité de la Viole. . . . Par Iean Rousseau. . . . A Paris, Par Christophe Ballard. . . . MDCLXXXVII. . . . 8°

>Pp. (13), 151. Includes Ded. to Monsieur de St. Colombe, Preface, Contents, Privilege, Errata.

665. ——— ★B46. Méthode Claire, Certaine Et Facile, Pour apprendre à chanter la Musique. Sur les Tons naturels & sur les Tons transposez. . . . Avec les Régles du Port de Voix, & de la Cadence . . . Et un Eclaircissement sur plusieurs difficultez nécessaires à sçavoir pour la perfection de l'Art. . . . Par Jean Rousseau. . . . Quatrieme Edition. . . . A Paris, chez l'Autheur. . . . Et chez Christophe Ballard. . . . MDCXCI. . . . obl. sm. 8°

>Méthode, pp. (6), 64; Eclaircissement, pp. 38. Includes Ded. to Lambert, Maistre de la Musique de la Chambre du Roy, and Preface. The Méthode is in 3 pts.

666. ——— ★B47. Methode Facile pour Apprendre a Chanter en Musique. Par un celebre Maistre de Paris. A Paris, par Christophe Ballard. . . . MDCXCVI. obl. sm. 8°

>Pp. 27, (1). A condensed version of Rousseau's Méthode but without the Eclaircissement. Includes Privilege.

667. SALINAS, FRANCISCUS. B7. Francisci Salinae ... de Musica libri Septem, . . . Salmanticae Excudebat Mathias Gastius. MDLXXVII. ... fol.

> *Pp. (14), 438, (18).* Many marginal notes, underscorings, and loose inserted diagrams. Includes Ded. to Roderico de Castro, Licence, Verses, Preface, Indices. No errata slip.

668. SALMON, THOMAS. B18 (ix). A Proposal to Perform Musick, in Perfect and Mathematical Proportions. . . . By Thomas Salmon. . . . With Large Remarks upon this whole Treatise, By . . . John Wallis. . . . London: Printed for John Laurence, . . . 1688. 4°

> *Pp. 41.* Wallis's remarks are dated 17. xii. 1687, pp. 29–41. Includes Ded. to John Cutts, and letter from E. Bernard. Includes 2 pages of Laurence's pubs.

669. SHERLOCK, WILLIAM. B18 (v). A Sermon Preach'd at St. Paul's Cathedral. . . . By W. Sherlock. . . . Dean of St. Paul's . . . London: Printed for W Rogers. . . . MDCXCIX. 8°

> *Pp. 27, (1).* Anniversary Meeting of the Lovers of Music, 1699. Includes list of bks. by Sherlock published by Rogers.

670. SIMPSON, CHRISTOPHER. A34. A Compendium of Practical Musick in Five Parts. . . . By Christopher Simpson. . . . London, Printed by William Godbid for Henry Brome. . . . MDCLXVII. 8°

> *Pp. (14), 176.* Includes To the Reader, letters from Locke and Jenkins, Contents, Ded. to William Cavendish, Duke, etc., of Newcastle, and an Advertisement for Chelys, Minuritionum. Portrait of Simpson lacking.

671. —— B12. Chelys, Minuritionum Artificio Exornata. . . . Authore Christophoro Simpson. Editio Secunda. London, Printed by W. Godbid for Henry Brome. . . . MDCLXVII. fol.

> *Pp. (10), 67.* Text in Latin and English in parallel columns. Includes portrait of Simpson, Ded. to Sir John Bolles, Bart., verse to Bolles by J. A. Ghibbesi (pub. Rome 1661 by F. Moneta), To the Reader, To the music lover, Contents.

672. SISTRUM. B18 (x). D. Benedicti Bacchini De Sistris. . . . Jacobus Tollius Dissertatiunculam & notulas adjecit. . . . Trajecti

ad Rhenum, Ex Officina Francisci Halma, Academiae Typographi, CIƆIƆCXCVI. 4°

> *Pp. 42. Includes Ded. to D. D. Theodoro à Velthuysen by Tollius, and an engraving of a sistrum.*

673. SPECIMENS. M71. Specimens of Various Styles of Music referred to in A Course of Lectures read at Oxford & London, and Adapted to Keyed Instruments, by Wm. Crotch.... [Vol. I] London, Printed for the Author, by Rt. Birchall.... [1807] fol.

> *Pp. 21, 165, (1). Includes list of Crotch's pubs., and 6 pp. of MS. at the end containing chants by various composers.*

674. —— M72. Specimens [etc., as M71].... [Vol. II].... [1807] fol.

> *Pp. viii, 153, (1). Includes the same list of publications as in M71.*

675. —— M73. Specimens [etc., as M71]. ... by Wm. Crotch. A New Edition with corrections & Additions.... [Vol. III].... London, Published By the Royal Harmonic Institution. ... [1822?] fol.

> *Pp. (2), 164. Vol. no. added in MS. T-p. is in a different typography from Vols. I and II.*

676. TURNER, WILLIAM. B18 (viii). Sound Anatomiz'd, In A Philosophical Essay on Musick.... To which is added, A Discourse, concerning the Abuse of Musick. By William Turner. London, Printed by William Pearson, for the Author, and sold by M. Turner.... 1724. 4°

> *Pp. (4), 80, 7, the latter being On the Abuse of Musick. Includes Preface.*

677. VOSSIUS, ISAAC. A27. De Poematum Cantu et Viribus Rhythmi. Oxonii e Theatro Sheldoniano. An. Dom. MDCLXXIII. Prostant Londini apud Rob. Scot, Bibliog. 8°

> *Pp. 136. Ded. to Arlington, First Secretary of State.*

678. WALLIS, JOHN. A30. Claudii Ptolemaei Harmonicorum Libri Tres.... Johannes Wallis.... Oxonii, E Theatro Sheldoniano.... 1682. 4°

> *Pp. (18), 328. The t-p. is in Greek and Latin. Includes Ded. to Charles II, Preface, Contents.*

THEORETICAL WORKS

679. WARREN, AMBROSE. B18 (xi). The Tonometer: Explaining and Demonstrating ... all the 32 ... different Notes. ... Contained in Each of Four Octaves inclusive, of the ... Common Scale. ... With their exact Difference and Distance. ... Never before published. By Ambrose Warren. ... Printed by J. Cluer and Alex. Campbell; and sold by B. Creake. ... 1725. ... 4°

> *Pp. 24. Includes 3 folding pages of diagrams, Ded. to James Hamilton, Lord Paisley, Verse.*

680. WETENHALL, EDWARD. A26. Of Gifts and Offices in the publick worship of God. A Treatise in Three Parts. ... Prayer, Singing, Preaching. ... By Edward Wetenhall. ... Dublin, Printed by Benjamin Tooke. ... MDCLXXIX. 8°

> *Pp. 805. The 3 pts. were published separately in 1678, and each has its own t-p., e.g. Of the Gift and Duty of Singing to God. ... pp. 207–576. This part has 2 t-ps. mostly stuck together, the lower one dated MDCLXXVI. Ded. to Dr. Richard Busby.*

681. ZACCONI, LODOVICO. B17. Prattica di Musica Seconda Parte. ... Compostae fatto dal M.R.P. Fra Lodovico Zacconi. ... In Venetia, MDCXXII Appresso Alessandro Vincenti. fol.

> *Pp. 283. Includes Ded. to Madalena Archduchess of Austria, To the Reader.*

682. ZARLINO, GIOSEFFO. B13. De Tutte l'Opere del R. M. Gioseffo Zarlino da Chioggia. ... Il Primo Volume. Contenente L'Istitutioni Harmoniche. ... In Venetia, MDLXXXIX. Appresso Francesco de' Franceschi Senese. fol.

> *Pp. 30, 448. In 4 vols., each with t-p. similar to above, viz.: Il Secondo Volume. Continente Le Dimostratione Harmoniche. ... pp. 14, 287. Sopplimenti Musicali. ... Terzo Volume. ... pp. 14, 330, 20. Il Quarto & Ultimo Volume. Continente Il Trattata Della Patientia, ... pp. 2, 132.*

INDEX I

Including composers, authors, editors, arrangers, performers, dedicators, dedicatees

Performers' names in italics
Items the composer of which is known but who is not specifically mentioned are enclosed in square brackets

Abbatini, Antonio Maria, 324.
Abbot, Henry, 619.
Abell, John, 1.
Accorona, Padre Fr. Ant., 80.
Ackroyd, Samuel, 110, 272.
Addison, Joseph, 3.
Agrell, Johann Joachim, 525.
Agus, Giuseppe, 380.
Alberti, Domenico, 382, 504.
Albinoni, Tommaso, 384, 504.
Alcock, John, 4.
Aldrich, Henry, 50, 51, 54, 207.
Allevi, Giuseppe, 80.
Aloysius, Joannes Baptista, 6.
Alypios, 655, 656.
Amadori, Giuseppe, 516.
Anders, Hendrik, 385.
Ann, Princess of Denmark, 20.
Anne, Queen of England, 208, 421.
Annibali, Domenico, 163, 174.
Aragoni, Sigr., 174.
Aristeides Quintilianos, 655, 656.
Aristoxenos, 655, 656.
Arlington, 677.
Arne, Cecilia, 196, 205, 316, 372.
Arne, Thomas Augustine, 8, 9, 31, 49, 298, 387, 429, 519.
Arnold, Samuel, pp. ix, x, 54, 92, 587.
Attwood, Thomas, 11.
Auletta, Pietro, 352.
Auraniae, Philippo Gulielmo, 412a.
Auretti, Sigra., 431–4.
Avison, Charles, 295, 388–95, 569.
Avoglio, Sigra., 192–3, 197.
Ayrton, Edmund, 54.

B., Le Chevalier, 533a.
Bacchini, D. Benedict, 672.
Bach, Carl Philipp Emmanuel, 298.
Bach, Johann Christian, 396, 553.
Bach, Johann Sebastian, 397–406.
Baildon, Joseph, 12, 49.

Bakcheos (the Elder), 655, 656.
Ball, William, 454.
Baltzar, Thomas, 459–60.
Banister, John, 430, 459, 548, 600, 648.
Bannister, Mr., 97, 106, 109.
Barbandt, Carl, 407.
Barbella, Francesca, p. xii.
Barberini, Sigra., 435.
Barbier, Mrs., 33, 151, 260.
Barrett, John, 14–16, 255, 515, 578, 595.
Barrington, John, 13.
Barroness, The (see Lindelheim).
Barsanti, Francesco, 408.
Bassani, Giovanni Battista, 17.
Bates, William, 409.
Bathurst, Lord, 619.
Battell, Ralph, 621.
Batten, Adrian, 51.
Beard, John, 162–3, 174–9, 185, 193, 197, 203.
Becker, Diedrich, 410.
Becket, 459.
Bedford, Arthur, 622–3.
Beilby, Thomas, 411.
Bémetzrieder, Anton, 624.
Benevoli, Horatio, 324.
Bennegar (Antonio Benegger?), p. xii.
Berenclow, Bernard Martin, 207, 255.
Berenstadt, Gaetano, 164.
Berg, George, 49, 412.
Bernard, Gifford, 624.
Bernardi, Francesco (see *Senesino*).
Bertolli, Francesca, 163, 169.
Besardus, Joannes Baptista, 412a.
Betti, Martino, 413–14.
Bevin, Elway, 50.
Biber, Heinrich Johann Franz von, 415.
Bickerstaffe, Isaac, 82.
Billington, Thomas, 19.
Binder, Christlieb Sigismund, 528.
Birckenstock, Johann Adam, 416.
Bisse, Thomas, 625–6.
Blackett, Lady, 390.

INDEX

Blackmore, Sir Richard, 290.
Blackwell, Isaac, 46.
Blagrave, Thomas, 327.
Blathwayte, Colonel, 388.
Blow, John, 20–21, 50–51, 53, 79, 110, 206–8, 272, 303, 417, 594.
Boden, 319–20.
Boethius, 655–6.
Bolles, Sir John, 671.
Bonnet, J., 639.
Bonnet-Bourdelot, P., 639.
Bononcini, Giovanni Maria, 333, 418.
Bononcini, Marco Antonio, 34–45.
Boonen, Jakob, 511.
Borosini, Francesco, 167.
Borunlaski, Joseph, 419.
Boschi, Francesca Vanini, 169a, 170.
Boschi, Giuseppe, 167, 171.
Bourdelot, P., 639.
Bowes, Miss, 393.
Bowes, Mrs., 569.
Bowman, Thomas, 22.
Boy, The (see *Holcombe*).
Boyce, William, 23–31, 50, 54, 420, 464.
Bracegirdle, Anne, 79, 130, 255.
Brady, Nicholas, 285–6.
Brandt, Mon. de, 575.
Brentbank, 298.
Brewer, Thomas, 326.
Brivio, Giuseppe Ferdinando, 224.
Broennemuller, Elias, 421.
Bronorio, Sigr., 432–4.
Brossard, Sebastien de, 627.
Brouncker, Lord William, 634.
Brown, Richard, 272.
Brünnings (Bruyninghs), 589.
Bryan, Joseph, 54.
Buchanan, Mrs., 419.
Bull, John, 53.
Bullimore, 460.
Burgess, Henry (the Younger), 422.
Burney, Charles, 298, 316, 628–30.
Burton, John, 423.
Busby, Richard, 680.
Byrd, William, 51–53.

Caesar, William (alias Smegergill), 326.
Cailo, Carlo, p. xii.
Caldara, Antonio, 588.
Campanini, Barberini, 31.
Campion, Mary, 124, 255, 360, 364–5.
Campioni, Sigr., 432–3.
Campioni, Sigra., 431–4.
Cannabich, Christian, 553.
Carestini, Giovanni, 162, 178, 180.
Carey, Henry, 31, 171, 298.
Carissimi, Giacomo, 207, 324.
Carr, John, 600.
Cartocci, Catarina Francesca, 273.

Carwarden, John, 454.
Casarini, Sigra., 172–3, 188.
Casati, Gasparo, 47, 145.
Caselli, Sigra., 235.
Cassani, Sigr., 5, 223.
Casson, Margaret, 48.
Castello, Dario, 426.
Castro, Roderico de, 667.
Cau, Nicolas, 581.
Cavendish, William Duke of Newcastle, 670.
Cazzati, Mauritio, 56, 427.
Cesarini, Carlo Francesco, 244–7.
Champness, Samuel, 316.
Charles II, 46, 51, 53, 678.
Charles, Lord Halifax, 304.
Charles, Duke of Somerset, 309, 559.
Charlotte Sophia, Queen, 630.
Chilcot, Thomas, 58.
Child, William, 50–51, 53–54, 454.
Christ Church, Dean of, 207.
Christiana, Queen, 436.
Church, John, 110, 208.
Cibber, Susanna, 185, 192–3.
Coleman, Charles, 326–7, 454, 548.
Coleman, Edward, 326–7.
Clark, Thomas, 110.
Clarke, Jeremiah, 51, 53–54, 110, 207, 298, 351, 386–7, 429, 515, 519, 527, 578, 593–5.
Clarke, John, 59, 60.
Clayton, Thomas, 61–64.
Cleffius, Lambertus, 576.
Clive, Catherine, 192–3.
Cobb, John, 326.
Cobb, Richard, 454.
Cobbold, Mrs., 48.
Cocchi, Gioacchino, 49, 92.
Collasse, Pierre, 2.
Colrane, Lord, 236.
Conti, Francesco, 65–66.
Conti (see *Gizziello*).
Cook, Mr., 255, 265.
Cook, Richard, 454.
Cooke, Benjamin, 257, 450.
Corbet, Sir Richard, 437–8.
Corbett, William, 436.
Corelli, Arcangelo, 437–53, 460, 485.
Corfe, James, 81–82.
Corfe, Joseph, 83–84, 231, 633.
Cornaro, Marc' Antonio, 157.
Cornetti, Paulo, 145.
Corri, Domenico, 85.
Courteville, Raphael, 86–87, 255, 386, 515, 578.
Cowley, Abraham, 133.
Creyghton, Robert, 51.
Crispi, Pietro, 553.
Croft, William, 51, 54, 88–91, 110, 255, 298, 351, 502, 515, 586, 626.

INDEX

Cross, Mrs., 5, 61.
Crotch, William, 673–5.
Crouch, Anna Maria, 103–4.
Cumberland, H.R.H. the Duke of, 140.
Cutler, James, 288.
Cutts, John, 668.
Cuzzoni, Francesca, 164, 167.

Davis, Mr., 255, 379.
Dean, Thomas, 455.
Deckere, H. P. Pasquali de, 612.
Deerings, Lady, 326.
Defesch, Willem, 93–94.
Demoivre, Daniel, 456.
Denby, 298.
Dering, Richard, 46, 95.
Descartes, René, 634.
Desiderii, Francesco Maria, 608.
Desnoyer, M. G., 435.
Diamantstein, Baron, 574.
Dibdin, Charles, 96–109, 298.
Dibdin, Charles, 97, 99, 103–4.
Diderot, Denis, 624.
Diesineer, Gerhard, 457, 648.
Dieupart, Charles, 458.
Dignum, Charles, 109.
Dodwell, Henry (the Elder), 635.
Doggett, Thomas, 5, 79.
Dotti, Sigra., 167.
Draghi, Giovanni Battista, 242, 461, 548.
Dryden, John, 21, 174, 203, 303.
Du Bellamy, Mr., 85.
Du Faux, 589.
Duni, Egidio Romualdo, 113.
Dunstall, Mary, 82.
Duparc, Elisabeth (see Francesina).
Dupuis, Thomas Sanders, 54, 114.
Durans, Caspar Chrysostomus, 117.
Durante, Silvestro, 324.
D'Urfey, Thomas, 259.
Durham, Dean of, 121, 313.
Dyer, Mrs., 311.

Eaglesfield, Mr., 386.
Ebdon, Thomas, 118–23.
Eccles, John, 79, 124–33, 255, 272, 386, 460, 503, 526–7, 578, 593.
Eccles, Salamon, 386, 459–60.
Edwards, Miss, 192–3.
Edwin, Catherine, 113.
Elford, Richard, 255.
Eminent Master, 134–5.
Épine, Francesca Margarita de l', 5, 32, 44, 151, 213, 223, 260, 265, 268–9, 333, 335.
Erard, Mr., 174.
Essex, Count of, 168.
Esterhazy, Antonio Carolo, 615.
Esto, John, 548.

Euclid, 655–6.
Evans, Mrs., 527.

Fabri, Stefano, 324.
Falle, Philip, pp. ix–xiii.
Farinelli (Carlo Broschi), 113.
Farmer, Thomas, 460, 548.
Farquhar, George, 301.
Farrant, Richard, 50–51.
Farrinelli, Michel, 459.
Faulkner, Miss, 12, 93–94, 332.
Fausan, Sigr. and Sigra., 435.
Felton, William, 462.
Ferdinand Carlo, Duke of Mantua, 610.
Festing, Michael Christian, 136–40.
Filtz, Anton, 553.
Finch, Edward, 460.
Finger, Gottfried, 141, 386, 430, 463, 502–3, 527, 578, 594.
Fiore, Angelo Maria, 464.
Fiorenza, Nicolà, p. xii.
Firmin (Henry Fireman?), p. xi.
Fischer, Johann Christian, 142, 465–6.
Fischer, Johann Christian, 465.
Fisher, F. E., 467.
Fisher, William, 143.
Flackton, William, p. xi.
Fleury, Abbot, 620.
Foggia, Francesco, 146, 324.
Fontana, Fabrizio, 517.
Forcer, Francis, 600.
Forster, Georg, 578.
Francesco, Lothario, 582.
Francesina, La (Elisabeth Duparc), 175–6, 179, 185, 195–7, 203.
Frasi, Giulia, 191, 193, 224, 233.
Frecknold, 459.
Freddi, Amadio, 148.
Frederick, Archbishop of Canterbury, 4.
Frederick, Elector of Hanover, 274.
Frederick, Emperor, 276.
Frederick Augustus, King of Saxony, 325.
Freeman, Mr., 301.
French, Richard, 149–50.
Froude, 31.

Gabrielli, Domenico, 469, 588.
Galli, Caterina, 172–3, 188, 191, 224, 350.
Gallia, Maria, 64.
Galliard, Johann Ernst, 32–34, 151, 257, 470, 584.
Galuppi, Baldassare, 92, 152, 528, 587.
Gandolphi, Maximilian, 415.
Garth, John, 295, 471–6.
Gasparini, Francesco, 7, 244–7.
Gasperini (see Gasparo Visconti).
Gaudentios, 655–6.
Geertsom, Jan van, 324.
Geminiani, Francesco, 477–9, 614, 636.

INDEX

Gentleman of Oxford, 153–4.
Gentleman of Wigan, 155.
George I, 90, 290.
George III, 54, 637.
George, Prince of Wales, 91.
George (Gouge), Mr., 127.
Giardani, Felice, 480.
Gibbons, Christopher, 46.
Gibbons, Orlando, 50–51.
Gibbs, Joseph, 481.
Gilbert, John, 272.
Gillier, Jean Claude, 255, 272.
Giordani, Tommaso, 85.
Giovanni del Violone, 244–7.
Girardeau, Isabella, 5, 223.
Giustiniani, Girolamo Ascanio, 291.
Gizziello, Francisco, p. xi.
Gizziello (Giacchino Conti), 163.
Gladwin, Thomas, 31.
Glareanus (see Henricus Loritus).
Gluck, Christoph Willibald von, 482.
Godeau, Antoine, 284.
Godefrido, F., 156.
Golding, Sir Edward, 454.
Goldwin, John, 51, 54.
Good, Mr., 61.
Goodgroome, John, 326–7.
Gorton, William, 483.
Gouge (see *George*).
Gouy, Jacques de, 284.
Grandi, Alessandro, 95, 157.
Granom, Lewis Christian Austin, p. xi.
Gratiani, Bonifazio, 207, 283, 324.
Graves, James, 578, 595.
Gravina, p. xii.
Green, G., 298.
Greene, Maurice, 54, 158–60, 296, 484.
Gregory, William, 327, 454, 648.
Grimaldi, Nicolino, 5, 7, 223, 265–7.
Guglielmo, Prince Giovanni, 449, 571, 573.

Hacquart, Carolus, 485–7.
Hall, Henry, 54, 209, 517.
Hall, William, 600.
Handel, George Frideric, pp. ix, x, 31, 70, 161–204, 221, 298, 488–501.
Hankey, Sir Joseph, 481.
Hart, Philip, 255, 505.
Hasse, Johann Adolph, 350, 352–4, 431–5.
Hawkins, Sir John, 637.
Haydn, Franz Joseph, 210.
Hayes, Philip, 49, 506.
Haym, Niccolò Francesco, 168, 211–13, 265.
Heighington, Musgrave, 214–15, 296, 298.
Hely, Benjamin, 507.
Hennio, Aegidio, 216.
Henrietta Maria, Dowager Queen, 95.
Herschel, Friedrich Wilhelm, 508.

Heudeline, 509.
Hickman, Charles, 638.
Hicks, 255.
Hill, 370.
Hill, Roger, 327.
Hilton, John, 327.
Hine, William, 54, 209.
Hobein, Johann Friedrich, 510.
Hodgson (Hudson), Mrs., 89, 125–6, 226, 255, 362.
Holcombe, Henry, 31.
Holcombe, Henry (The Boy), 37–39, 43, 64, 162, 178.
Holder, William, 640–1.
Holles, Thomas, 27.
Hoogendorp, Gulielmo, 485.
Hopkins, John, 278, (?) 287.
Hoppe, Johann Gottlieb, 525.
Howard, Lady, 303.
Howard, Robert, 129.
Howard, Samuel, 31, 49, 217–19, 298, 624.
Hud, Joannes, 554.
Hudson (see *Hodgson*).
Hudson, George, 454, (?) 548.
Hudson, Robert, 220.
Hughes, Mr., 15, 41–42, 45, 61–64, 87, 151, 255, 302, 333.
Humphrey, Pelham, 51, 53, 206, 208.

Incledon, Charles Benjamin, 100–1.
Isaac, Bartholomew, (?) 226, 272.
Ives, Simon, 327, 454, 548.

Jackson, John, 46, 272.
Jackson, William (of Exeter), 227–8.
James I, 278.
James, Duke of Chandos, 262.
James, Bishop of Lichfield and Coventry, 313.
James Hamilton, Lord Paisley, 679.
Jefferies, George, 46.
Jeffreys, John, 505.
Jenison, Ralph, 450.
Jenkins, John, 282, 326–7, 454, 548, 670.
Jermyn, Lord, p. ix.
Johnson, Robert, 326.

Keen, Edward, 386, 527, 578.
Keller, Gottfried, 578, 641.
Kelleri, Fortunato, 525.
Kempis, Nicolaus à, 511.
Kent, James, 54, 230–1.
Kent, Marchioness of, 261.
King, Robert, 54, 110, 207, 386, 515, 595, 600.
Kircher, Athanasius, 642–3.
Konink, Servaas van, 512–13.
Kunzen, Adolph Carl, 525.
Kvysten, Petro, 486.

INDEX

La Barre, Michel de, 514.
Lambert, Michel, 665.
Lampe, Johann Friedrich, 31, 232, 387, 429, 518-19, 644-6.
Lampugnani, Giovanni Battista, 233, 235, 352.
Lanaye, Guillaume de, 512.
Lanier, Nicholas, 326-7.
Lanzetti, Salvatore, 520-1.
Laroon, 255.
La Tour, Philibert de, 533a.
Lawes, Henry, 46, 236, 326-7.
Lawes, William, 51, 326-7, 454.
Lawrence, Mr., 64-66, 333, 338, 348.
Le Camus, Sebastian, 237.
Leclair, Jean Marie, 522.
LeClerc, Jean, 49.
Le Fevre, 589.
Legne, Coslo, 528.
Legrenzi, Giovanni, 238, 523-4.
L'Enclos, Fau, 589.
Lenton, John, 272, 386, 502, 527.
Leopold I, Emperor, 281.
Leopold William, Archduke of Austria, 642.
L'Estrange, Roger, 648.
Leveridge, Richard, 31, 239-41.
Leveridge, Richard, 34, 61, 64, 151, 240-1, 247, 255, 333, 337, 341.
Lidarti, Christiano Giuseppe, 49.
Lincoln, Dean of, 358.
Lindelheim, Johanno Maria (The Baroness), 35, 212, 265.
Lindsey, Mrs., 5, 36, 61, 64, 245, 333-4, 336, 342-4, 346.
Lobwasser, Ambrosius, 276.
Locke, Matthew, 46, 51, 206, 208, 242, 529, 600, 647-8, 670.
Loeillet, Jean Baptiste, 530-1.
Lonati, Carlo Ambrogio, 532.
Loritus, Henricus (Glareanus), 649.
Louis XIV, 2.
Loulié, Étienne, 650.
Lowe, Thomas, 10, 12, 27, 172-3, 188, 191-3, 205, 372-3.
Lucio Francesco, 80, 248.
Lully, Jean Baptiste, 2, 79, 249, 459, 533a, 533b, 534.
Luther, Martin, 298.

Mace, Thomas, 651.
Madalena, Archduchess of Austria, 681.
Malcolm, Alexander, 652.
Mancini, Francesco, 223, [381].
Mancini, Sigra., 151.
Manina, Sigra., 151.
Mantua, Duke of, 254.
Marais, Marin, 534-8.
Marcello, Benedetto, 291, 295, 320.

Marchitelli, Pietro, p. xii.
Marcorelli, Giovanni Francesco, 324.
Marella, Giovanni Battista, 49.
Marenzio, Luca, 253.
Marlborough, Duchess of, 3.
Marsh, Alphonso, 327.
Martianus Capella, 655-6.
Masson, Charles, 654.
Matteis, Nicolà, 540-1, 561.
Mattheson, Johann, 291.
Maubach, Abraham, 659.
Maurice, Landgrave of Hasse, 276.
Mazzaferrata, Giovanni Battista, 542.
Mazzinghi, Joseph, 528, 587.
Meibomius, Marcus, 655-6.
Mell, Davis, 459.
Menervetti, Angelo, 355.
Merula, Tarquinio, 543-4.
Miller, Edward, 298, 319-20.
Milton, John (the Elder), 298.
Milton, John (the Younger), 136, 175, 192-3, 257.
Minozzi, Marcello, 280.
Mondonville, Jean Joseph Cassanea de, 545.
Monsigny, Pierre Alexandre, 92.
Montagnana, Antonio, 169, 171.
Monteverdi, Claudio, 254.
Montford, 386.
Monticelli, Sigr., 233, 235.
Morgan, George, 256, 386, 578, 593.
Morley, Thomas, 50, 657.
Moss, John, 327, 648.
Motley, Richard, 386.
Mudge, 546.
Munninckx, P. F., 547.

Naish, Thomas, 658.
Nardi, Sigr., 431-4.
Nares, James, 54.
Nathaniel, Bishop of Durham, p. x, 312.
Negri, Sigra., 163.
Newcastle, Duke of, 27.
Newte, 635.
Nicomachos, 655-6.
Nivers, Guillaume Gabriel, 659.

Oldis, Valentine, 454.
Ord, Mrs., 389.
Orme, Robert, 594.
Oswald, James, 258.

Paccini, Sigr., 167.
Paisible, James, 386, 502, 578.
Pasquali, Niccolò, 661.
Patrick, John, 54.
Paulwheel, 459.
Pearson, Mrs., 151.
Pellegrini, Ferdinando, 549.

INDEX

Pepusch, Johann Christoph, 260–4, [333–48], 349, 437–8, 450, 452, 550–2, 555.
Pergolesi, Giovanni Battista, 352.
Pescatore, Leonardo, p. xi.
Petersen, David, 554.
Petrobellus, Francesco, 281.
Pez, Johann Christoph, 555, 585.
Phillips, John, 647.
Picart, Pieter, 612.
Piccini, Nicolò, 92, 556.
Pinel, (?) Julie, 589.
Pittenio, Petro, 486.
Playford, Henry, 110, 206–8, 303–4, 386.
Playford, John, 46, 95, 282, 287–8, 326–7, 647, 662.
Polidori, Ortensio, 273.
Ponzoni, Count Nicolò, 544.
Pool, Anthony, 459.
Pope, Alexander, 356.
Porpora, Nicolò Antonio, 274.
Porta, Francesco della, 275.
Porter, Walter, 548.
Porto, Rev. D. Victoria, 148.
Powell, 593.
Prelleur, Pierre, 557–8.
Preston, Chr., 648.
Priest, (?) Josia, 594.
Prince, Mrs., 252.
Ptolemy, Klaudios, 678.
Purcell, Daniel, 207, 255, 301–2, 502, 517, 526, 594–[5].
Purcell, Frances, 312.
Purcell, Henry, 20, 49, 51, 53–54, 79, 206–8, 272, 298, 303–12, 386, 559–61, 578, 662.

Radcliffe, James, 313.
Rameau, Jean-Philippe, 562.
Ramondon, Lewis, 314, 516–17.
Ramondon, Lewis, 61, 265, 270.
Randall, John, 31.
Rathiel, 298.
Ravenscroft, Thomas, 277, 298.
Reading, John, 272, 459.
Real, Joseph, 563–4.
Redding, Miss (Mrs.), 64.
Reinhold, Frederick Charles, 163, 171–3, 175–6, 179, 185, 188, 191–3, 197, 202.
Ricci, Francesco Pasquale, 553.
Richard, Lord Bishop of Durham, 295.
Richardson of Winton, 517.
Richelieu, Duc de, 237.
Riemschneider, Sigr., 171.
Riley, William, 315.
Ritschel, Giovanni, 528.
Robert, Mr., 255.
Roberts, John, 648.
Robinson, Anastasia, 164, 179, 185.
Roffee, J., 272.

Roger, Estienne, 659, 663.
Rogers, Benjamin, 46, 50–51, 454.
Roieri, Claudio, p. xii.
Roland, Madame, 536.
Romanzini, Miss, 99, 108.
Roseingrave, Thomas, 565.
Rosiers, Charles, 612.
Rousseau, Jean, 664–6.
Rousseau, Jean-Jacques, 316.
Rovetta, Giovanni, 317.
Rozelli, 566.
Rush, George, 567.
Russell, 31.
Russell, Mr., 196.
Rydt, Anna Vander, 612.

S., S., 287.
Sabbatini, Galeazzo, 280, 318.
Sackville, Count Charles of Middlesex, 352.
St. Colombe, Mons. de, 664.
Saint Germain, Conte de, 224, 321–3, 568.
Salinas, Franciscus de, 667.
Salisbury, Bishop of, 83.
Salmon, Thomas, 647, 668.
Sancroft, William, 282.
Sandley, Benjamin, 454.
Sartori, Claudio, p. xiv.
Savage, William, 162, 171, 176, 192–3, 202.
Savile, Jeremiah, 326.
Scarlatti, Alessandro, [265–71], 333–48.
Scarlatti, Domenico, 569.
Schenck, Jean, 570–4.
Schickhard, Johann Christian, 575.
Schneider, Johann Christian Frederick, 325.
Scholl, D., 576.
Scola, Adam, 352.
Scott, 296.
Senesino (Francesco Bernardi), 164, 167.
Serlupi, Marc' Antonio, 253.
Shakespeare, William, 58.
Shalon, 92.
Sharp, John, I, p. x, 110.
Sharp, John, III, pp. x–xiii.
Sharp, Thomas, II, pp. x, xii, xiii.
Shaw, Mrs., 255.
Sherard, James, 579.
Sherlock, William, 669.
Shmelt, Col. van, 459.
Sibilla, Mrs., 172–3, 191.
Simonelli, 516.
Simpson, Christopher, 454, 459, 670.
Simpson, John, p. xi.
Siprutini, Emanuel, 580.
Slicher, Pietro, 469.
Smegergill (*see* Caesar).
Smith, John Christopher, 296.
Smith, Robert, 459, 600, 648.
Snep, Jean, 581.

INDEX

Sodi, Sigra., 431–4.
Solnitz, Anton Willem, 582–3.
Spencer, John, 114.
Spethe, Andreas, 276.
Stamitz, Karl, 553.
Stanley, John, 31, 328–30.
Stephenson, Miss, 14, 229.
Sternhold, Thomas, 279.
Strada del Po, Anna, 162–3, 169, 174, 178, 180, 184.
Strode, Samuel, 58.
Subligny, Madam, 331, 515.
Suett, Mr., 85.
Sullivan, Mr., 197.

Tallis, Thomas, 50–51, 54.
Tarditi, Paolo, 324.
Tate, Nahum, 285–6.
Taylor, James, 332.
Taylor, John, 454.
Taylor, Capt. Silas, 454.
Teenoe, 386.
Telemann, Georg Philipp, 291.
Tessarini, Carlo, 504, 590–2.
Thomas, Bishop of Bath and Wells, 206.
Thornowets, Henry, 596.
Tofts, Catherine, 40, 61, 64, 211, 244, 246, 265, 271, 333, 339–40, 347.
Tollett, Thomas, 386, 459.
Tollius, Jacob, 672.
Tompkins, William, 326.
Torelli, Giuseppe, 588, 597.
Traetta, Tommaso, 49.
Trapp, Joseph, 88.
Travers, John, 31, 54, 79, 293–4, 349.
Tricario, Giuseppe, 324.
Tudway, Thomas, 54, 272.
Turner, Robert, 230.
Turner, William, 53, 110, 206, 208, 676.
Turpin, Count of, 480.
Tye, Christopher, 51.

Uccellini, Marco, 601–2.
Urbani, Valentino, 5, 223, 265, 333, 345.

Valentine, Robert, 603.
Van De Cruyce, D. Paschasio Francisco, 156.
Vaux, 454.
Velthuysen, Theodoro a, 672.
Vento, Mattia, 92.
Venturi, Stefano, 355.
Veracini, Antonio, 604.
Veracini, Francesco Maria, 605.
Vernon, Joseph, 92, 316.
Vincent, Thomas, 31.

Vinci, Leonardo, 491.
Visconti, Gasparo, 606.
Visconti, Gasparo, 414.
Visconti, Sigr., 233, 235.
Vitali, Giovanni Battista, 607–10.
Vivaldi, Antonio, 504, 611.
Vossius, Isaac, 677.

Wager, Sir Charles, 620.
Wainwright, 298.
Wales, Prince of, 584.
Wallis, John, 668, 678.
Walond, William, 356, 613.
Waltz, Gustavus, 171, 178.
Wanless, Thomas, 289.
Warner, 326.
Warren, Ambrose, 679.
Warren, Edmund Thomas, 49.
Watts, Isaac, 292, 319–20, 357.
Webb, William, 326.
Webbe, Samuel (the Elder), 358.
Weldon, John, 51, 54, 110, 208, 255, 359–69, 515.
Werner, Gregor Joseph, 615.
Wetenhall, Edward, 680.
Wharton, Goodwin, 600.
Wheall, William, 298.
Wheeler, Miss, 85.
Whitton, 298.
Wichel, Philippo van, 616.
William III, pp. ix, x.
William, Duke of Devonshire, 606.
William, Marquis of Hartington, 255.
Williams, Thomas, 319–20.
Wilson, John, 272, 326–7.
Wiltshire, John, 128.
Winchester College, Warden of, 230.
Winchester, Dean of, 230.
Wise, Michael, 46, 51, 53, 272.
Witsen, Nicolaas, 570, 572.
Worgan, James (the Elder), 371.
Worgan, John, 296, 372–5.
Wright, Miss, 92.
Wriothesley, Duke of Bedford, 579.
Wroth, 386.
Wynne, John, 376–8.

York, H.R.H. Duke of, 471.
Young, Anthony, 379, 617.
Young, Cecilia, 92, 162, 174, 178, 197.
Young, William, 548.

Zacconi, Lodovico, 681.
Zamperelli, Dionisio, 528.
Zarlino, Gioseffo, 682.
Ziani, Pietro Andrea, 618.

INDEX II

Publishers, music-sellers, engravers

Aertssens, Hendrik, 439, 441, 445.
Amadino, Ricciardo, 254.
Atkins, Thomas, 644.
Aylmer, Brabazon (the Elder), 559.
Ayre, R., 624.
Baker, Thomas, 4.
Ballard, Christophe, 2, 237, 249, 664-6.
Barber, Joseph, 388, 395, 569.
Becket, T., 628-9.
Bell, A., 661.
Bennett, Thomas, 580.
Birchall, Robert, 673-5.
Blaeu, P. & J., 533a, 533b.
Boivin, François, 522.
Bonneuil, Hi., 536.
Bowyer, Jonah, 619.
Bremner, Robert, 92, 316, 392-3, 471, 473, 549, 661.
Broderip & Wilkinson, 59-60, 319-20.
Brome, Henry, 670-1.
Brooke, N., 647.
Brown, Daniel, 286.

Cambridge University, 279.
Campbell, Alexander, 679.
Carr, John, 242, 309, 430, 600, 621, 648, 651.
Churchill, Awnsham & John, 289.
Clark, John, 292.
Cluer, John, 167, 498, 679.
Cole, Benjamin, 644.
Cole, J., 438.
Cooke, Benjamin, 257, 388, 437, 450.
Cooke, John, 658.
Corbelletti, Francesco, 642-3.
Corrie & Sutherland, 85.
Cox, John, 480, 592.
Creake, Bezaleel, 679.
Cross, Thomas, 86, 129, 271, 301, 369, 437, 505.
Cross, William, 153.
Crownfield, C., 620.
Cullen, John, 211, 266-8, 271, 306, 339-41, 345, 347-8, 641.

Dale, Joseph, 227.
De' Franceschi, Francesco (Senese), 682.
Delorme, J. L., 512, 514, 659.
Denson, R., 569.

Easton, Edward, 658.
Elzevir, Ludwig, 655-6.
Endter, Wolfgang Moritz, 415.
Eynden, Arnold, 485.

Ferri, Giovanni Gasparo, 610.
Fischer, Frederick Ernst, 582.
Ford, Richard, 292, 357.
Foucault, Henri, 536.

Gardano, 6, 148, 157, 607, 609.
Gardano, Angelo, 253.
Gastius, Matthias, 667.
Geertsom, Jan van, 248, 324.
Godbid, William, 46, 95, 236, 282, 326-7, 529, 548, 670-1.
Gosset, R., 300.
Goulding, D'Almaine, Potter & Co., 121.
Goulding, George, 19, 123.
Greuenbruch, Gerhard, 412a.

Halma, Franciscus, 421, 672.
Hare, Elizabeth, 219.
Hare, Joseph, p. x, 5, 32-34, 41-45, 61, 90-91, 151, 223, 244-7, 260-2, 265, 269-70, 381, 408, 413-14, 416, 418, 451, 453, 455-6, 461, 490-1, 502-4, 507, 515-17, 526-7, 530-2, 540-1, 550-1, 555, 561, 565, 578, 585-6, 588, 596-7, 603, 606, 611, 617-18, 641.
Harper, Thomas, 634.
Haws, William, 635.
Haxby, Thomas, 473.
Hazard, Joseph, 112.
Heath, Thomas, 634.
Henchman, William, 559.
Heptinstall, John, 21, 286, 288-9, 303, 309, 312, 430, 559, 621-2, 640.
Hett, Richard, 292.
Heus, Jean Philippe, 469.
Hill, Joseph, 528.
Hodgkin, T., 285.
Hoffmeister & Co., 397-400, 403-4, 406.
Hoffmeister & Kühnel, 401-2, 405.
Hummell, A., 396.
Hurel, Jean, 534-6.

Innys, William & John, 425, 626.

Johnson, James, 419.

INDEX

ohnson, John, 58, 81-82, 253, 293-5, 380, 389-90, 412, 438, 448, 452, 462, 467, 471, 478-9, 584, 591, 613, 631-2, 636, 661.
Johnson, R. (Mrs.), 393-4, 473.
Jones, Edward, 206-7.

Keble, S., 112.
Kettelby, 638.
King, Charles, 112.
Knol, Klaas Klaase, 385.

Lacy, James, 658.
Lane, Isaac, 67-69.
Laurence, John, 668.
Le Cene, Michel Charles, 639, 663.
Leclerc, Jean, 522.
Legate, J., 644.
Linley, Francis, 358.
Longman, Lukey & Co., 553.
Lovisa, Domenico, 291.

Magni, Bartolomeo, 6, 148, 157, 273.
Magni, Francesco, 281.
Mainwaring, William, 661.
March, John, 290.
Mascardi, 283.
Mears, Richard, 88, 164-6, 498.
Miller, William, 298, 319-20.
Monckton, Philip, 640.
Monti, Giacomo, 608.
Moore, G., 624.
Mortlock, H., 623.
Moseley, Humphrey, 634.

Norman, Barak, 507.

Oosterhout, Pieter, 576.

Palthenius, Hartmann, 276.
Payne, Thomas & Son, 637.
Pearson, William, 1, 20, 110, 208, 272, 287, 304, 306, 351, 386, 577, 641, 662, 676.
Pennington, L., 70-71, 73-74, 313.
Peters, Carl Friedrich, 325.
Petri, Henrico, 649.
Phalèse, Magdalena, 511.
Phalèse, Pierre, p. x, 47, 56, 80, 145-6, 156, 216, 238, 275, 317-18, 426-7, 547, 601-2.
Piesly, Anthony, 623.
Playford, Henry, p. x, 21, 110, 206-8, 272, 287-8, 303-4, 312, 351, 386, 417, 430, 459-60, 559, 577.
Playford, John, 46, 95, 236, 282, 326-7, 454, 529, 548, 647.
Playford, John (the Younger), 548.
Potter al Giglio Bianco, Luca di, 612, 616.

Preston, Thomas (& Son), 11, 83, 96-109, 118, 633.
Purcell, Frances, 312, 559-60.

Randall, Peter, p. x, 5, 61, 64, 212, 223, 265, 333-8, 342-4, 346, 461, 516-17, 585, 641.
Randall, William, 203, 230, 624.
Ratcliff, Thomas, 242, 600, 651.
Rebenlein, Georg, 410.
Richardson, John, 287.
Riley, Edward, 313.
Roberts, James, 620.
Robinson, George, 628-9.
Robson, James, 628-9.
Roeless, Jonge, 533.
Roger, Estienne, p. x, 17, 284, 442, 449, 458, 463-4, 487, 509, 512-14, 538, 570-5, 579, 581, 589, 598-9, 604, 627, 650, 654, 659-60.
Rogers, William, 669.
Rutherford, John, 510.

Sala, Giuseppe, 523-4.
Scot, Robert, 677.
Scotto, Gerolamo, 355.
Seiller, Georg, 486.
Senese (see De' Franceschi).
Seyffert, Stanno, 117.
Sheardown, William, 319-20.
Short, Peter, 657.
Silvani, Marino, 17.
Simpson, John, p. xi, 28, 30, 134, 136, 140, 217, 349, 376, 480, 482.
Smart, George, 114-16.
Smith, Christopher, 165-6, 498.
Smith, Thomas, 473.
Smith, William, 138, 558.
Sowler, George, 190.
Stationers, Company of, 319-20.

Thompson, Charles & Samuel, 566, 587.
Thompson, Nathaniel, 242, 600, 651.
Thompson, Peter, 481.
Thompson & Sons, 428, 501, 525, 563-4.
Thorowgood, Henry, 423.
Tonson, Jacob, 3.
Tooke, Benjamin, 680.
Turner, Mrs., 88.
Turner, M., 676.
Turner, William, 278.
Tyther, John, 22.

Vaillant, Francis, 581, 589.
Vincenti, Alessandro, 280, 543-4, 681.

Walsh, John, pp. x, xi, 5, 8-9, 12, 23-26, 32-45, 61, 64-66, 90-91, 151-2, 162-3, 169, 171-6, 178-89, 191-204, 211-13,

INDEX

223–4, 233, 235, 244–7, 255, 260–2, 265, 269–70, 307–8, 333–8, 342–4, 346, 350, 352–4, 381–4, 387, 393, 408, 413–14, 416, 418, 420, 422, 424–5, 429, 431–5, 437, 440, 443–4, 446–7, 451, 453, 455–6, 461, 470–1, 477, 484, 488–96, 499–500, 502–4, 515–17, 519–21, 526–7, 530–2, 539–41, 545–6, 550–2, 555, 561–2, 565, 568, 578, 583, 585–6, 588, 593–7, 603, 605–6, 611, 614, 617–18, 623, 641, 661.

Welcker, Peter, 49, 247, 407, 409, 411, 474–5, 567.
Wilcox, John, 518, 644.
Wild, Joseph, 286.
Williams, Thomas, 319–20.
Wilmot, S., 620.
Wright, Hermond (or Harman), 184, 189.
Wyatt, John, 622.

Young, John, 483.

INDEX III

Works for the stage

(excluding those in Arnold's edition of Handel)

Abdelazer (Purcell), 559.
Achille et Polixene (Collasse and Lully), 2.
Admeto (Handel), 490.
Agreeable Disappointment, The (see Love Betrayed).
Agrippina (Handel), 490.
Alceste (Lampugnani), 233.
Alcina (Handel), 162, 493.
Alessandro (Handel), 490.
Alexander the Great (Finger), 503.
Alfonso (Lampugnani), 235.
Almahide, 5, 381.
Ambitious Stepmother, The (Lenton), 502.
Amphitryon (Purcell), 559.
Antioco (Gasparini), 7.
Arianna (Handel), 492.
Ariodante (Handel), 171, 493.
Arminio (Handel), 163, 493.
Arsinoe, Queen of Cyprus (Clayton), 61–63.
As You Find It (Eccles), 255.
Atalanta (Handel), 171, 493.

Berenice (Handel), 171.
Bonduca (Purcell), 559.
British Enchanters, The, 131–2, 226.

Calypso and Telemachus (Galliard), 32–34, 151.
Camilla, 35–45, 381, 517.
Chances, The, 128.
Chemical Counterfeits, The, or Harlequin Turned Worm Doctor (Prelleur), 557.
Clotilda, 65–66, 381.
Consort, The, 594.
Constant Couple, The, or A Trip to the Jubilee, 301, 595.
Courtship a la Mode (Croft), 502.
Cunning Man, The (see Devin du Village).

Daphne and Amintor, 92.
Deidamia (Handel), 171.
Demofoonte (Duni), 113.
Devin du Village (The Cunning Man) (Rousseau), 316.
Diocletian, The History of (see Prophetess).

Distressed Innocency, or The Princess of Persia (Purcell), 559.
Double Dealer, The (Purcell), 559.
Double Disappointment, The, 13.

Elpidia (Vinci), 491.
Enrico (Galuppi), 152.
Ezio (Handel), 171, 492.

Fair Penitent, The (Eccles), 125.
Fairey Queen, The (Purcell), 559.
Faramondo (Handel), 171.
Farewell Folly (see Quacks).
Fate of Troy (see Virgin Prophetess).
Flavio (Handel), 164.
Fops Fortune (see Love Makes a Man).

Giustino (Handel), 493.
Gordian Knot Untied, The (Purcell), 559.
Graces, The, 108.
Grove, The (D. Purcell), 595.

Harlequin Turned Worm Doctor (see Chemical Counterfeits).
Henry the Second, King of England, 311.
Humours of the Age (Finger), 503.

Idaspe (F. Mancini), 223, 381.
Incostanza, Delusa, L', 224.
Indian Queen, The (Purcell), 559.
Iphigenia, 595.
Island Princess, The, 594.

King Arthur (Purcell), 559.

Land of Enchantment, The, 99.
Love at a Loss (Finger), 502.
Love Betrayed, or The Agreeable Disappointment, 255, 362.
Love Makes a Man, or Fops Fortune (Finger), 503.
Love's Triumph, 244–7, 381.
Lovers Stratagem (Paisible), 502.

Mad Lover, The (Eccles), 130, 503.
Maid in the Mill, 252.
Maid of the Mill, The, 92.
Married Beau, The (Purcell), 559.

INDEX

Old Bachelor, The (Purcell), 559.
Orlando (Handel), 171, 492.
Ottone (Handel), 171.

Partenope (Handel), 171, 491.
Pastor Fido, Il (Handel), 493.
Persée (Lully), 249.
Pirro e Demetrio, 169a, 170, 211-13, 265-71, 381.
Poro (Handel), 492.
Princess of Persia (*see* Distressed Innocency).
Prophetess, The, or The History of Diocletian (Purcell), 309, 559.
Psyche (Locke), 242.

Quacks, The, or Farewell Folly, 241.

Radamisto (Handel), 165-6.
Rinaldo (Handel), 491.
Rinaldo and Armida (J. Eccles), 593.
Rodelinda (Handel), 167-8, 490.
Rosamond (Clayton), 3, 64.

Schiava, La (Piccini), 556.
Scipione (Handel), 490.

She Would and She Would Not (Weldon), 255, 365.
Sir Harry Wildair (Finger), 503.
Siroe (Handel), 171.
Sosarme (Handel), 169, 171, 492.

Tamerlano (Handel), 490.
Tempest, The (Locke), 242.
Tender Husband, The, 302.
Thomyris, 333-48.
Tolomeo (Handel), 171.
Triomphe de l'Amour, Le (Lully), 533.
Trip to the Jubilee (*see* Constant Couple).

Unburied Dead, The, 82.
Unhappy Penitent, The (D. Purcell), 502.

Venus and Adonis (Pepusch), 260.
Villain, The, 126.
Virgin Prophetess, The, or The Fate of Troy (Finger), 503.
Virtuous Wife, The (Purcell), 559.

Way of the World, The, 595.
Women Will Have Their Wills, 127.

INDEX IV

Song titles (in italics) and first lines

Collections are not itemized unless asterisked, but single sheets from collections of arias are included. The original spelling has been retained. '(*ibid.*)' indicates that title and first line are identical.

A Round her see Cupid flying, 41.
Albacinda Drew the Dart, 239.
As May in all her youthful Dress, 82.
Ask me not how calmly I, 10.
At noon in a Sultry Summers day, 314, 369.
At St. Osyth by the Mill, 219.
At the sound of the horn, 101.
Attend ye fair ye rural Train, 82.
Autumn, 220.
Away to the Woodlands away, 123.
Away you Rover for shame give over, 344.

Bacchus he it is who fires me, 225.
Balin a mone, 13.
Belinda's pretty, pretty pleasing Form, 127.
Blushing Violets sweetly smelling, 268.
Bonny Lad there was, A, 252.
Bright Gems that twinkle from afar (*ibid.*), 99.
Bright Wonder of Nature, 345.
Brightest Sylvia lovely Creature, 82.
British Phaenix, The, 82.
By shady Woods and purling streams, 256.
By those Pigs neyes, 79.

Can you leave ranging, 336.
Caution, The, 79.
Cease cruell tyrannising, 42.
Celia, 361.
Celia my heart has often Rang'd, 365.
Celia you in Vain deceive me, 361.
Charming Creature, every Feature, 63.
Charming fair for thee I languish, 44.
Charms of Belinda, The, 82.
Charms which blooming Beauty shows, The, 134.
Come all ye young Lovers, 28.
Come dissolving Softness come, 150.
Come fill up the Bowl, 331.
Come O Sleep, 266.
Constant Lover, The, 29.
Content, 123.
Coquet, The, or Complaining Shepherd, 82.
Cupid instruct an am'rous Swain, 364.
Cupid O at lenght (*sic*) reward me, 43.

Damon Restrain your Wand'ring Eyes, 379.
Dream on Anacreon, The, 214.
Du pupille che sono due stelle, 267.

Enchantress, The, 82.
Ere raging Seas between us roll (*ibid.*), 100.
Ever Merry gay and Airy, 342.

Fair Cloe my Breast so alarms, 79.
Fair Dorinda happy may'st thou Ever be, 35.
Fair Sylvia, cease to blame my Youth, 82.
Fair Thief, The, 373.
Fairest work of Happy Nature, 82.
Fancy, 123.
Fancy leads the fetter'd senses, 123.
Farewell Love and all soft Pleasure, 337.
Fast by the Margin of the Sea, 215.
Female Rake, The, 82.
Fill the Glass, 240.
Find me a lonely Cave, 126.
Flood shall quit ye Ocean, The, 45.
Fly, fly ye winged Cupids, 86.
Fond Reason, ah! where art thou fled, 378.
Forgive thou fairest of thy kind, 147.
Fortune Ever known to vary, 40.
Fox Chase, The, 101.
From grave Lessons and Restraint, 366.

Gay kind and airy, 245.
Generous Confession, The, 217.
Generous Protestation, The, 82.
Gentle Love this Hour befriend me, 321–2.
Gentle Sighs, a while releive (*sic*) us, 211.
Go, Perjur'd Maid, 79.
Go Shepherd you're a Rover, 246.
Good folks come here, 170.

Had I but the Wings of a Dove, 332.
Hark, hark, o'er the Plains, 205.
Help th' unpractis'd Conqu'ror, 132.
Her bright Eyes are Stars that charm us, 267.
Honey-Moon, The, 82.
Houn non so che nel cor, 169a, 170.

INDEX

How happy is the Maid, 217.
How wellcome my Shepherd, 142.
Hunting Song, A, 155.
hunting Song for two Voices, A, 221–2.

I gently touch'd her Hand (*ibid.*), 124.
I Love a plain lass, 247.
I revive now you're turning, 340.
I tell with equal Truth and Grief, 373.
If you my wandring Heart wou'd find, 29.
I'll sing of my Lover all Night and all Day, 229.
Impertinent Poet, The, 82.
In Cloes sparkling, sparkling Eyes, 89.
In Praise of Wine, 225.
In softest Musick, 368.
In vain gainst Love, in vain I strove, 311.
In vain I Fly from sorrow, 39.
In vain is Complaining, 338.
I'o Victoria, 141.
I'o Victoria round my Temples bind, 141.

Jack Ratlin, 106.
Jack Ratlin was the ablest Seaman, 106.
Jockey, 229.
Jockey and Jenny, 372.

Kindly thus my Treasure, 244.

Lady of the May, The, 82.
Lapland Song, 123.
Lass of St. Osyth, The, 219.
Lawyers Pay You With Words (*ibid.*), 107.
Let all your boast of wealth and Love, 123.
Let Ambition fire thy mind, 359.
Let me wander not unseen, 177.
Liberia, 16.
Liberia's all my Thought, 16.
Listning she turns, 226.
Love and Folly, 14.
Love and Folly were at Play, 14, 15.
Love and Wine, 243.
Love in her bosome, 362.
Love thou airy vain Illusion, 270.
Love Triumphant over Reason, 378.

Maid that's made for Love & me, The, 323.
Marriage Song, The, 362.
May I tell you that I'me dyeing, 269.
Meads and the Groves, The, 375.
Morning is charming All Nature is gay, The, 155.
Mountebank, The, 241.
Mourn Hapless Caledonia Mourn, 258.
Must then a faithful Lover go, 130.
My delight, my Dear, my Princess, 341.
My sheep I've forsaken, 123.

Night and Day let's Drink and Kiss, 243.
Night expecting the dread morrow, 19.
Noon, 48.
Nothing like Grog, 105.
Nymph that seems to Love inclin'd, The, 82.

O Cupid, gentle Boy, 33.
O Nymph of Race divine, 37.
O what had my Youth with Ambition to do, 123.
O wouldst thou know what Sacred Charms, 323.
O'er Moorlands and Mountains, 123.
Oh I must fly, cease to try, 347.
Oh Men what silly things you are (*ibid.*), 108.
One Long Whitson Holliday, 259.

Panthea, 360.
Panthea all the Senses Treats, 360.
Parent Bird whose little Nest, The, 232.
Parson among the Pease, The, 259.
Pastora's come with Myrtle Crown'd, 374.
Paternal Love, 232.
Plague of these musty old lubbers, A, 105.
Plague us not with Idle storys, 131.
Pleasing visions shall attend thee, 32.
Pleasure calls fond hearts recover, 335.
Polly, 94.
Power of Music, The, 82.
Pray now John let Jug prevail, 79.
PrettyWanton come away, 82.
Pritty warbler cease to hover, 339.
Pursue ye flying Fair, 34.

Queen of Darkness Sable night, 62.
Questo conforto, 7.

Race Horse, The, 109.
Ravish'd Lover, The, 30.
Reconciliation, The, 149.
Reflections of Marie Antoinette, 11.
Retirement, The, 150.
Rise, O Sunn, 271.
Roger of the Dale, 315.
Rural Life, 218.

Sappho's Hymn to Venus, 371.
See Sirs, see here a Doctor rare, 241.
See the Course throng'd with gazers, 109.
Serenading Song, The, 301.
Shepherd's Wedding, The, 374.
Shoud ere the fair disdain you, 346.
Shy Decoyer, The, 82.
Since in vain I strive to gain you, 348.
Snow Drop, The, 160.
Snows are dissolving on Torne's rude side, 123.

INDEX

Soft Ioys young loves gay pleasure, 212.
Soldier's Farewell On the Eve of a Battle, 19.
Soldiers Life, The, 96.
Spring renewing all things gay, 94.
Stay, ah stay, ah turn, 125.
Still I follow, still she Fly's me, 65.
Swain in Extacy, The, 82.
Sympathizing Tear, The, 123.

Tears of Scotland, The, 258.
These Eyes are made so killing, 36.
This this my lad's a Soldiers life, 96.
Thus Damon knock'd, 301.
Time has not thin'd my flowing Hair (ibid.), 227.
Tinker, The, 98.
Tinker I am, my name's natty Sam, A, 98.
'Tis fervid Noon, 48.
To bid the World along Farewell, 11.
To touch your Heart, 87.
Too lovely Cruel Fair, 213.
Too plain dear youth, 217.

Ungrateful you Fly me, 38.
Upon a Lady being drown'd, 215.

Venus beauty of the Skies, 371.

Wakefull Nightingale, The, 363.
Wakefull Nightingale that takes no Rest, The, 363.
Wasted with Sighs, 128.
Were Celia kind as she is Fair, 135.
What argufies Pride and Ambition (ibid.), 102.
What Lover ever can hope for Favour, 334.

When faintly gleams the doubtful Day (ibid.), 97.
When Fairies are lighted by Nights Silver Queen (ibid.), 103.
When Fanny Blooming fair, 30.
When first I fair Caelinda knew, 82.
When gentle Sleep had charm'd my Breast, 214.
When India's waves are known to freeze, 79.
When Jockey was blest with your love, 372.
When Loves inciting and Pow'r inviteing, 66.
When Lucinda's blooming Beauty, 82.
When one's gone ner'e Keep a pother, 343.
When Orpheus sweetly did complain, 82.
When Phebus begins Just to peep o'er the Hills, 123.
When Phoebus the tops of the Hills, 221-2.
When your Angellick Face I'd Seen, 367.
Where e'er I turn my eyes around, 220.
Where ever I'm going and all the Day long, 13.
Whilst Joyless light conveying, 370.
Who to my wounds a balm advises (ibid.), 104.
Why Belvidera tell me why, 302.
Why has not love reflections Eyes?, 143-4.
With Head reclin'd, 160.
With scorn repuls'd, poor Damon sought, 149.

Ye gentle gales that from the Air, 129.
Ye gentle winds that from the Sea, 315.
Your musty old Rules, 82.

INDEX V

Subjects, occasions, instruments, performing media

Excluding Arnold's edition of Handel's works

Anglican Service (excluding anthems and psalms), 50–55, 59, 83–84, 114–16, 118–22, 209, 231, 312–13.
Anthems, 4, 27, 46, 50–55, 60, 67–78, 90–91, 110, 112, 118–22, 208–9, 230–1, 296, 313, 358.
Archlute, 604.

Bassoon, 145, 156, 426, 470, 487, 490–3, 511.

Canon, 49, 464.
Cantata, 8–9, 22, 24, 57, 133, 138, 158–9, 174, 261–4, 274, 328–30.
Canzona, 543–4.
Capriccio, 608.
Catalogue, 663.
Catch, 49, 272.
Cembalo, see Harpsichord.
Chamber ensemble (i.e. 3 or more instruments with bass), 415, 463, 484, 524, 575–6, 582, 588, 608, 610, 612, 616.
Church music (writings on), 619, 621, 625, 635, 680.
Clavéçin, see Harpsichord.
Composition, 654, 659, 662.
Concerto grosso, 388–9, 394–5, 436, 449–52, 477–8, 488, 504, 518, 546, 569, 611.
Cornett, 156.

Dictionary, 627.
Divisions, 430.
Divisions on a ground, 459–60.
Duet (instrumental), 412, 483, 563–4, 566, 591.
Duet (secular vocal), 20, 24, 79, 81, 203, 221, 225, 236–7, 243, 256, 349–50, 372.

Fantasia, 405–6, 514.
Flute (arr. of song), 10–11, 13–14, 19, 29–30, 35–45, 62–63, 65–66, 79, 82, 85, 87, 93, 96–109, 123–5, 127–8, 130–1, 134–5, 141, 143, 147, 149, 153–5, 160, 170, 177, 211–13, 217–19, 226–7, 240–1, 242, 245, 247, 252, 259, 266–71, 301, 314–15, 331–2, 335–6, 338–41, 350, 353–4, 360–6, 368–9, 373.

Flute concerto, 477, 518.
Flute(s) (with BC.), 424–5, 431–5, 458, 465, 495–6, 520–1, 531, 545, 592.
Flutes (unaccompanied), 412, 563–4.
Fortepiano, 313, 411, 506, 553.
France, music in, 628, 660.
Fugue, 399–400, 505, 514, 565.

Gentlemen, Lovers of music, Anniversary, 621.
Germany, music in, 629.
Glee, 49.
Greek music, 655–6.
Guitar, 48, 98, 101, 106–7, 227, 563–4, 566.

Harmony, 636, 640.
Harp, 516–17.
Harpsichord concerto, 395, 422, 462, 489, 506, 567.
Harpsichord solo (including cembalo, clavéçin, spinnet), 382, 397–407, 409, 417, 419, 461, 466, 474–6, 484, 498–500, 505–6, 510, 515–17, 525–6, 528, 545, 549, 560, 562, 565, 587, 613–14, 617.
Harpsichord (with string acc.), 411, 473, 508, 545.
Hebrew music, 620.
History of music, 630, 637, 639, 652.
Horn, 412, 493, 563–4, 566–7.
Hymn, 46, 110, 206–8, 228, 282, 296, 319–20, 351, 357, 547.

Instructions: Keyboard, 560, 624, 631–2.
Instructions: Lute, 412a.
Instructions: Performance (including fig. bass), 389–90, 526, 560, 562, 633, 641, 644, 646, 648, 661, 668.
Instructions: Psalm-singing, 285, 287–9, 623.
Instructions: Singing, 665–6.
Instructions: Viol, 507, 534, 537–8, 548, 662, 664, 671.
Instructions: Violin, 386, 578, 594–5.
Italy, music in, 628, 660.

Jewish music, 623.

INDEX

Jubilate (see Anglican Service).

Keyboard (unspecified), 396, 421, 423, 479, 501, 556.

Lovers of Music, Anniversary, 638, 658, 669.

Lute, 412a, 516–17.

Madrigal, 253–4, 355.
Magnificat and Nunc dimittis (see Anglican Service).
Mass, 17, 325.
Motet, 6, 46–47, 56, 80, 95, 117, 145–6, 148, 156–7, 216, 238, 248, 273, 275, 317–18, 324, 546.

Netherlands, music in, 629.

Oboe, 421–2, 424–5, 465, 490–3, 495, 512–14, 531, 594.
Ode, 21, 27, 88, 140, 204, 214, 356.
Opera (account of), 660.
Opera (instrumental music), 381, 431–5, 502–3, 516–17, 533, 533a, 533b, 593–5, 598–9.
Oratorio, 70, 172–202, 210.
Orchestral music, 502–3, 511, 559, 615.
Organ concerto, 395, 422, 464, 489, 506.
Organ solo, 409, 473–6, 505, 516–17, 565, 613.
Overture, 387, 429, 490–4, 519, 533, 553, 556–8.

Pianoforte, 419, 466, 473–6, 510, 553.
Psalms (excluding those in main entry), 319–20, 507.

Quartet (secular vocal), 20, 359.

Recorder, 155, 386, 408, 421, 426, 430, 456, 458, 512–14, 530–1, 536, 575, 589, 596, 603, 685–6.
Rondeau, 465.

Scottish music, 424–5, 428, 460, 577, 595.
Sistrum, 672.
Song (for solo voice excluding opera and oratorio arias), 1, 8–16, 19–20, 22, 24, 28–31, 48, 58, 82, 85–87, 89, 93–94, 96–109, 123–39, 141–3, 147, 149–50, 153–5, 159–60, 205, 215, 217–20, 226–7, 229, 232, 236–7, 239–41, 252, 255, 258–9, 301–8, 311, 314–15, 321–3, 326–7, 331–2, 352–4, 360–71, 373–9, 421.
Strings (with voices), 17, 56, 80, 93, 123, 143, 145, 156, 216, 280–1, 328–30, 353–4.
Suite (including collections of dances), 385–6, 397, 401, 410, 417–18, 421, 424–5, 430–5, 437–48, 454, 456, 458, 461, 469, 486, 498–500, 509, 512–14, 523, 527, 536–8, 540, 547, 571–2, 576, 578, 581, 589, 601–2, 606, 608, 612, 614.
Symphony, 511, 582, 615.

Te Deum (see Anglican Service).
Theatre music (instrumental), 386, 502–3, 559, 593–5, 598–9.
Theorbo, 426, 511, 602.
Three Choirs Festival, Anniversary, 619, 625–6.
Toccata, 516–17.
Trattenimento, 464.
Trio sonata, 390–3, 410, 420, 426–7, 430, 437–46, 463, 467, 482, 487, 495–6, 511–14, 522–4, 531, 542, 555, 561, 568, 579, 583, 585, 590, 601–3, 608–9, 616.
Trio (excluding trio sonata), 457, 459, 529, 533, 533a, 533b, 566, 598–600.
Trio (secular vocal), 20, 81, 236–7, 349.
Trombone, 426, 511, 602.
Trumpet, 412, 493.
Tuning (harpsichord), 526.

Viol (bass), 156.
Viol (tenor), 156.
Viol(s) (with BC.), 454, 463, 487, 534–5, 537–8, 554, 570–1, 574, 581.
Viol(s) (unaccompanied), 381, 483, 486, 507, 509, 548, 573–4.
Violetta, 426.
Violin (with BC.), 380, 413–14, 416, 421, 424–5, 428, 430–5, 447–8, 453–5, 458, 460, 464, 480–1, 509, 511, 524, 532, 541, 550–1, 572, 580, 589, 592–3, 595, 597, 601–2, 604–6, 608, 616.
Violin(s) (unaccompanied), 386, 430, 527, 577–8, 591, 593–5.
Violoncello concerto, 471.
Violoncello(s) (with BC.), 428, 464, 470, 487, 520–1, 539, 580, 584.
Violoncello(s) (unaccompanied), 464.
Voluntary, 474, 565, 613.